To understand why most Christian churc [barcode] to flood their world with spiritual life, ca ~~book. You~~ will also come away with knowledge of what you can do to change this situation, starting right where you are.

DALLAS WILLARD
Professor of Philosophy, University of Southern California
Author, *Renovation of the Heart* and *The Divine Conspiracy*

Don't be misled! This book is not a tirade against the Pharisees. That would be pharisaism of the worst kind! Rather, with meticulous scholarship and penetrating insight, Gary Tyra provides both a historical basis for the development of the Pharisaic tradition confronted by Jesus as well as an analysis of the psychological/ social emergence of the Pharisaic temperament among contemporary evangelical churches. As I read this book, and the fascinating exploration of Matthew's gospel with a focus on the Sermon on the Mount, I envisioned Jesus nodding as if to say, "You've got it right. This is what I meant by becoming an authentic Kingdom-disciple!" Those who read this book will find a fresh and invigorating approach to discipleship-making that exposes and avoids the anxiety and fear-driven impulse toward legalistic perfectionism. They will also discover a practical and biblically-based curriculum for teaching and preaching a gospel of discipleship that is pleasing to God and graceful to behold.

RAY S. ANDERSON
Senior Professor of Theology and Ministry
Fuller Theological Seminary, Pasadena, CA
Author, *An Emergent Theology for Emerging Churches*

Defeating Pharisaism: Recovering Jesus' Disciple-Making Method will make an important contribution to the evangelical movement. The issues faced by Jesus in his encounters with the Pharisees are still faced today—whether we will conform to an outward show of religion or be truly transformed from within.

DR. GEORGE O. WOOD
General Superintendent, The General Council of the Assemblies of God

Gary Tyra has seen the Pharisees and they are us. With clarity and insight, Dr. Tyra examines who the Pharisees were and how today's Evangelical church is riddled with the very attitudes and beliefs that Jesus warned against. Readers of this book will see how Matthew's gospel, and the Sermon on the Mount in particular, was used as a polemic against the teaching and behavior of the Pharisees at the time. They'll also see how the Sermon on the Mount can be used today as a starting point for addressing the spirit of pharisaism in the church today in order to truly follow Christ's command to make disciples.

DAN STANLEY
Discipleship Ministries Training Coordinator
General Council of the Assemblies of God

Riveting, scholarly! Gary Tyra has done a wonderful job presenting fresh insights into the disciple-making method of Christ. This is a must read for anyone who is serious about Jesus' approach to making disciples that can and will change the world.

PHIL HOTSENPILLER
Teaching Pastor, Yorba Linda Friends Church

Gary Tyra offers us a gift from his considerable pastoral and scholarly experience. This book is a fascinating look at a surprisingly overlooked subject. For all of Jesus' commentary on the Pharisees, the church has neglected to learn from their mistakes. Dr. Tyra corrects this oversight and offers us an even clearer lens on the discipleship alternative offered by Jesus himself.

TOD BOLSINGER, PHD
Pastor, San Clemente Presbyterian Church
Author, *ShowTime: Living Down Hypocrisy by Living Out the Faith*

The local church always lives in a set of tensions between the culture, the way of Jesus Christ and the temptations of religion. Tyra unveils a deep and often hidden agenda of the people of God—to replace the goodness and grace of God with a set pattern of belief and practice that is more about control than it is about faith, more about certainty than it is about mystery. But this book is not just a critique, it is, more importantly, a solution. Tyra calls the Church back to the primary agenda of Jesus in Matthew's Gospel, to call disciples to follow him—not to become contemporary Pharisees, but to be maturing and mission-tuned adult learners who are transformed by the Word of God, in the model of Jesus, and the ever-present community of the Holy Spirit. This is a primary agenda for every pastor and church leader.

GARETH ICENOGLE
Senior Pastor, Westside Presbyterian Church, Ridgewood, New Jersey

Much of the unbelieving world keeps an arm's length from anything called Christian. Why? Because the world experiences the hot breath of Christian judgment rather than embracing grace. In *Defeating Pharisaism* Gary Tyra unmasks the root of the problem and then shows us the way of life in the Kingdom of God. If the Christian church wants to put on the face of Jesus, rather than the face of those who opposed him, the Pharisees, this book is a vital contribution to that end. I know I will refer to it often.

GREG OGDEN
Pastor, Christ Church of Oak Brook, IL
Author, *Transforming Discipleship: Making Disciples a Few at a Time*

DEFEATING PHARISAISM

Recovering Jesus'
Disciple-Making Method

GARY TYRA

Authentic

COLORADO SPRINGS · MILTON KEYNES · HYDERABAD

Authentic Publishing
A Ministry of Biblica
We welcome your questions and comments.

USA   1820 Jet Stream Drive, Colorado Springs, CO 80921 www.authenticbooks.com
UK   9 Holdom Avenue, Bletchley, Milton Keynes, Bucks, MK1 1QR
         www.authenticmedia.co.uk
India   Logos Bhavan, Medchal Road, Jeedimetla Village, Secunderabad 500 055, A.P.

Defeating Pharisaism
ISBN-13: 978-1-60657-016-6

11 10 09 / 6 5 4 3 2 1

Published in 2009 by Authentic

A catalog record for this book is available through the Library of Congress.

Cover and interior design: projectluz.com
Editorial team: Andy Sloan, Kay Larson, Erika Bremer

Printed in the United States of America

To my family—Patti, Brandon, and Megan—whose love,
support, and patience made this book possible.
I love each of you more than words can express.

Contents

Part 3

Using The Sermon on the Mount to Defeat Pharisaism

ACKNOWLEDGMENTS

Writing and then seeing a first book published is both a painful and joyful experience, perhaps similar to that of giving birth to a firstborn child. This book would not have been possible without the help of some wonderful people whom God used in some remarkable ways during the course of its conception, gestation, delivery, and presentation to the world.

First and foremost, I want to express gratitude to my family: my beautiful wife Patti, a remarkably talented writer herself, who never gave up on me even when I was tempted to give up on myself; and my kids, Brandon and Megan, whose consistent expressions of affirmation and encouragement served to energize me spiritually and psychologically time and again.

Secondly, a special word of thanks is due to Mike and Midge Sands, dear friends, who, like my wife and kids, have inspired me by their unconditional love and support over a period of many years.

Thirdly, I wish to acknowledge how indebted I am to my theological and ministry mentors: the late Ray Anderson who modeled for me a grace-oriented approach to other human beings; Dallas Willard whose lectures and books inspire me to never give up the "hot pursuit of Christ"; and Greg Ogden and Gareth Icenogle whose Doctor of Ministry seminar at Fuller Seminary encouraged me to want to do something about the discipleship deficit presently at work within most evangelical churches.

Fourthly, this book would still be a manuscript sitting on a shelf if it were not for the support and assistance provided by my publisher, Volney James, and the book's editor, Andy Sloan. Thanks, Volney, for believing in this project. Thanks, Andy, for your partnership in making this book as readable as it is!

Fifthly, I am grateful to my students at Vanguard University, especially those who have provided consistent expressions of enthusiastic support for this project. I am gratified at their keen interest in the topic, and humbled by their apparent fondness for me, their professor.

Finally, I simply must communicate my deepest gratitude to the many people I have pastored over the years: members of Faith Chapel, West Covina, California; Christian Life Center, Fullerton, California; and Yorba Linda Community Church, Yorba Linda, California. The fact that there are too many of you to name individually does not diminish in the least my profound gratitude for the time we spent together doing our best to function as Pharisaism-defeating, disciple-making communities of faith. I hope that reading this book provides all of you with a proud sense of ownership.

INTRODUCTION

I love the church—the community of disciples Christ came to the world to create. It has been my privilege to spend over three decades in professional ministry: pastoring three churches, serving my denomination as a pastor to pastors, and functioning as a professor of biblical and practical theology in a Christian university and helping form and mentor future ministry leaders.[1] I can attest to the fact that the typical evangelical church is filled with good people, many of whom are sincere Christ-followers whose heartfelt aim is to keep growing in their ability to imitate Jesus' remarkable capacity to love God with all his heart, mind, soul, and strength and to love his neighbor as himself. At the same time, to be honest, I have to acknowledge my concern that the ethos of too many evangelical churches is earmarked by certain actions and attitudes of which Jesus himself was highly critical.

Some writers are fond of making the assertion that if Jesus were to walk the earth today he would not choose to attend the typical evangelical church—nor would most evangelical churches want him to![2] If there is any truth to this statement it is because the lives of too many evangelical Christians are more reminiscent of Jesus' enemies, the Pharisees, than of

Jesus himself. As much as I love the church, I have to say that I believe Jesus *would* have a problem with some things that go on each week in churches that purport to represent him to the world.

Not very long after arriving at my second pastorate a parishioner invited me out to lunch so that we could become better acquainted. After chatting a while about various issues, my new friend came to the point. He wanted to know where I stood on the issue of race relations. He told me the story of what had caused him to leave a previous church. The pastor had offended him greatly when he dared to conduct a dedication ceremony for an infant born of parents who were of different races, African-American and Caucasian. With tremendous passion in his voice, my parishioner/interrogator inquired, "Pastor, what could I count on you doing in such a situation? Would you conduct such an indecent ceremony, or would you have the courage to refuse to do so?"

When I unflinchingly indicated that I would behave in the same way as his previous pastor, this man's face became beet red. The veins in his neck and forehead bulged. The adrenalin racing through his body literally caused him to bounce up and down in his chair as he expressed his consternation at my position. He then launched into a tirade about the radical importance of racial segregation.

Eventually the man began to calm down and breathe a bit more deeply. Calling him by name, I gently asked him this question: "Should you find yourself in heaven, only to have Jesus introduce you to a black man, obviously expecting you to shake his hand, what would you do?"

The response of this longtime evangelical church member stunned me. He said, "My Jesus would never ask me to do that!"

When I asked this parishioner if his response to my question meant that he did not believe there will be people of color in heaven, he went on to say, "Oh, there'll be colored people in heaven all right. It's just that they will have their area and we'll have ours!" I think Jesus would have a problem with this.

Not long after this incident I was made aware that another member of this church was concerned that visitors and new adherents would sometimes indulge their smoking habit just outside the church's front entrance. This veteran church member had determined that part of his ministry responsibility was to safeguard the image of the church. So whenever necessary he would confront such a visitor, lecturing him or her about how cigarette smoking was a sinful activity and that doing so on the front steps of the church was sending a wrong message to those driving by. In his attempt to protect his church's image this man was chasing away the kind of people our congregation was trying to reach. I think Jesus would have a problem with this.

One of the most pious, well-respected members of this church was a godly woman who firmly believed that God spoke to her in her dreams. One weekday morning she made a special trip to the church office to speak with me about a very serious issue. The church had slowed in terms of numerical growth. The worship services were not as spiritually vibrant as she thought they ought to be. What was the cause? She was certain that there must be "sin in the camp." Her dream the night before had confirmed her suspicion. In this dream she had caught me red-handed enjoying a cocktail. Convinced that I had a secret drinking problem, she had come, like the prophet Nathan to King David, to call me to account. She was tactful but persuaded. When I assured her that I did not have a drinking problem, she looked at me skeptically, saying, "But my dream was so real!" Despite my best effort to assure her that, while I am not perfect, alcohol is not one of my vices, she left my office shaking her head. I am fairly sure that to this day she remains convinced that I am a secret alcoholic. I think Jesus would have a problem with this.

In 1996 my wife, Patti, and I made the decision to plant a new church in Southern California. Our aspiration was to preside over a ministry that would make it easy rather than hard for unchurched people to consider the claims of Christ and, hopefully, to yield their lives to his loving lordship. While remaining committed to the goal of not compromising the gospel message, our aim was to do a good job of contextualizing it for the particular culture we felt called to reach.

Over the years, many veteran churchgoers would hook up with us, at least for a while. It saddens me to say that more than a few times we had to say goodbye to good, talented folks who simply could not become comfortable with the nontraditional manner in which we engaged in worship, nurture, community, and mission and the way we embraced obviously imperfect people whose lives were often earmarked by a lack of both piety and prudence. I still love the veteran churchgoers who eventually made the decision to move on to affiliate with more traditional evangelical churches, but it is also true that every time this would happen the momentum of our ministry would take a hit.

Someone once made the observation that many evangelical church members find it easier to accept a new, heretical teaching than a new, nontraditional philosophy of ministry. To the degree this is true, I think Jesus would have a problem with this.

One person our church plant reached came to us with multiple tattoos forming colorful "sleeves" on both arms and a "collar" around his neck. He would often tell me and others that ours was the only church he had ever been to where he had not felt judged and marginalized by congregational members and leaders. I don't know how overstated this man's testimony was; but to the degree that it was true with regard to any other evangelical church, I think Jesus would have a problem with this.

Here is a final story. A few years back I was teaching a ministry-related course for older, nonresidential students who were returning to college to earn a degree. One evening a student who was a member of his denomination's board of directors related the story of a leadership crisis that had recently occurred in one of their churches. The pastor of this church had come under ecclesiastical discipline. Not responding appropriately to the denomination's prescribed process toward rehabilitation, he had been suspended from his ministerial duties.

When the official board convened a special congregational meeting to explain this disciplinary action, they were greeted by a group of hostile church members who "wanted their pastor back." As the denominational official sent to preside over the meeting attempted to address the congregation, a female church member grabbed a microphone near the piano and began to sing a worship chorus that contains the prayer "Lord, bring us back to your holy place." Not able to be heard over the singing, the denominational official addressed the young woman directly, politely asking her to refrain from singing so he could speak to the congregation. She responded by screaming into the microphone, "We don't have to listen to any of your bulls—t!" Then, without a pause of any kind, she returned to her singing: "Lord, bring us back to your holy place." I think Jesus would have a problem with this!

Legalism is the idea that our righteousness before God is earned rather than received as a gift. *Dogmatism* refers to an arrogant, stubborn assertion of opinion or belief. *Sociological pugilism* is a tendency toward being confrontational, combative, adversarial, and hostile in the way one relates to those not a part of the in-group or clique. *Judgmentalism* is a willingness to criticize and condemn those who approach the religious life differently than we do. *Separatism* is the felt need to separate ourselves from anyone who does not practice a piety similar to our own (out of either personal disdain or the fear that associating too closely with impious people will result in our spiritual defilement before God). *Trivialism* is the tendency to focus on minor, relatively unimportant issues while ignoring the truly consequential ones. *Hypocrisy* is saying one thing while consciously doing another, pretending to be more spiritually mature than we really are.

I doubt there are very many evangelical pastors who can honestly say they have not encountered such attitudes and actions in the course of their ministries. An increasing number of books, magazine articles, and blogs express concern over the negative image conservative Christians project to the world. It has become more and more apparent that *the Pharisaism we find Jesus wrestling with in the Gospels is alive and well in our evangelical churches.*[3]

This is a crucial issue. Perhaps more than any other factor, the presence of this Pharisaism in the lives of evangelical church members, along with the corresponding lack of genuine Christian discipleship, accounts for the lack of growth experienced by many of our churches, the burnout experienced by many of our pastors, and the mass migration of tens of thousands of young people from evangelical churches either to no church affiliation at all or to churches that, in their attempt to be culturally relevant, may be guilty of altering and compromising the gospel.[4]

That is the bad news. The good news is that I firmly believe there is something church leaders and workers can do to defeat the presence of Pharisaism in their churches. In this book I will argue that Jesus proactively used the Pharisees as an anti-model (negative example) of what an authentic Christ-follower should be like. In other words, while teaching his disciples how to live their lives in the power and purpose of God's kingdom he kept pointing to the Pharisees and saying, in essence, "Unfortunately, these people don't get it. You must not be like them."

Furthermore, my contention is that while this proactive, anti-Pharisee approach to making disciples is discernable in all the Gospels, it is especially evident in the Gospel of Matthew and its presentation of Jesus' Sermon on the Mount. Nearly all scholars agree that the Sermon on the Mount has what it takes to function as a discipleship curriculum. Add to this scholarly consensus my thesis that throughout the Sermon on the Mount we find Jesus using the Pharisees as anti-models of authentic kingdom living, and the result is a breakthrough understanding of the Sermon on the Mount and Jesus' disciple-making method. By the time you have finished reading this book I believe you will agree with me that, properly understood, the Sermon on the Mount can be incredibly useful to us evangelicals in our goal of building disciple-making congregations that succeed at forming Christian disciples who are all but impervious to the spiritual and ecclesiastical poison that is Pharisaism. Honestly, I cannot think of a more important development at this crucial time in the history of the evangelical movement.

I have deliberately written this book in a manner that strives to be accessible to church leaders and workers while also including some technical details important to the most critical of readers. Given the fact that the book's foundational premise might be considered somewhat provocative (i.e., that Jesus' disciple-making method has largely been lost and now needs to be recovered, and that keeping the polemic between Jesus and the Pharisees in view is key to properly interpreting the Sermon on the Mount), I want to do my best to demonstrate that each component of my overall argument possesses scholarly support.

Divided into three main sections, part one of the book will focus on the goal of trying to help us better understand what Pharisaism is and how it negatively impacts evangelical churches. In chapters one through three we will treat such topics as the origin, history, main tenets, and life-practices of the Pharisees; the movement's "essence" and popularity in first-century Jewish society; the possible discontinuity that exists between the historical Pharisees and those we read of in the Gospels; the specific critiques that Jesus leveled at this group; the fact that a Christian form of Pharisaism (the worst aspects of religious fundamentalism: legalism, dogmatism, separatism, pugilism, trivialism, etc.) is indeed present in too many contemporary evangelical churches; some of the specific problems this form of Pharisaism creates within the churches it infects; and, finally, some possible root causes of Christian Pharisaism.

The goal of part two of this book is to help us increase our understanding of Jesus' Sermon on the Mount and the role the Pharisees played in Jesus' approach to making disciples. In chapters four through eight we will examine the Sermon on the Mount's literary and historical context, including such issues as how, when, where, by whom, and why the Gospel of Matthew was written; the emphasis upon discipleship found in this Gospel; the especially harsh treatment this Gospel provides the Jewish religious leaders in general and the Pharisees in particular; how the Sermon on the Mount fits into Matthew's narrative; the importance of the Sermon to Matthew's spiritual and ministry formation goals; the degree to which Matthew's especially harsh rhetoric against the Pharisees shows up in Jesus' most famous sermon; and why Matthew makes such great use of literary irony in the chapters leading up to the Sermon.

In these chapters we will also observe the fact that many scholars are convinced that the Sermon on the Mount has what it takes to function as a discipleship curriculum; what Jesus actually had to say in the Sermon on the Mount about life in God's kingdom; and how he used the Pharisees as negative role models in the process of training his disciples.

In part three of this book I will propose a disciple-making strategy that will serve to defeat the phenomenon of Pharisaism present in too many contemporary evangelical churches. In chapters nine and ten we will explore what it means to make disciples; how important it is to make disciples; some basic prerequisites for an effective disciple-making ministry; the one ministry dynamic all successful contemporary disciple-making churches seem to employ; some encouraging statistics which seem to indicate that church members are willing to do what is necessary to experience genuine spiritual transformation; the distinction between a disciple-making experience and a disciple-making environment; how churches can make disciples using the Sermon on the Mount as a basic curriculum and John Wesley's system of interlocking groups as the delivery system; and, finally, a model of what an actual Pharisee-busting curriculum based on the Sermon on the Mount might look like.

Obviously, I believe this is important stuff. It is a shame for any Bible-believing church to be filled with legalistic, ritualistic, super-spiritual members (and leaders) whose lack of theological acuity and psychological security not only causes them much misery but also motivates them to behave in a judgmental, hardhearted, and separatist manner toward others. The presence of Pharisaism in our contemporary evangelical churches is hindering church effectiveness, hastening pastoral burnout, chasing away a generation of young believers, and contributing to a new form of Christianity that runs the risk of giving away too much in order to create a church experience that strives to be culturally relevant. This need not be. Pharisaism can be defeated. If we care to listen, Jesus can show us the way.

I hope you will read what I have to say in this book about recovering Jesus' disciple-making method and then discuss it with other concerned workers and leaders in your church. I have seen it work.[5] You can use the Sermon on the Mount to defeat Pharisaism in your church. As the saying goes, "Let the healing begin!"

Notes

1. I am speaking here of Vanguard University of Southern California, located in Costa Mesa, California.
2. See, for example, Brian McLaren, *A Generous Orthodoxy* (Grand Rapids: Zondervan, 2004), 79–80.
3. Actually, it is not just in the Gospels that we find passages that address the problematic attitudes and actions described above. Though the apostles did not feel the need to use the Jewish terms "Pharisee" and "Pharisaism" when writing to a Gentile audience, and after the controversy recorded in Acts 15 Pharisaical Jews and Christians are routinely referred to loosely as "Judaizers," the apostolic writings contain many warnings against Judaizing the faith and manifesting such Pharisaical attributes as *ritualism* (e.g., Romans 2, 4, 14; Galatians 5; Philippians 3; Hebrews 13:9–16); *legalism* (e.g., Acts 15; Romans 5–8; Galatians 3–5; Ephesians 2; Colossians 2–3; 1 Timothy 4); *separatism* (Ephesians 2; 1 Corinthians 1–4, 12; James 2); *judgmentalism* (e.g., Romans 12, 14–15; 1 Corinthians 13; 2 Corinthians 10–13; Ephesians 4; Philippians 1–4; Titus 3; James 2–3); *spiritual pride* (e.g., Romans 11:19; 1 Corinthians 4:6–7; 2 Corinthians 12:20; Galatians 6:3–5; Philippians 2:3; Colossians 3:12; Titus 3:2; James 3:13; 1 Peter 5:5); and *hypocrisy*

(e.g., Romans 2; 1 Corinthians 5; Hebrews 10; 2 Peter 2; Jude; Revelation 3:1–3. Furthermore, the writings of the early church fathers also contain many passages that warn against the very same Pharisaical attributes listed above (e.g., *The Epistle of Clement to the Corinthians* 2, 9, 13–16, 21, 30–32, 35, 38; *The Epistles of St. Ignatius* 2:8, 10, 5:6; *The Teaching of the Twelve Apostles* 3–5, 8). These historical writings also contain passages that exhort believers to avoid Judaizing the faith (e.g., *The Epistle of Barnabas* 4, 19, 20). It is no wonder that Jesus used the Pharisees as an anti-model for Christian discipleship: the tendency toward Pharisaism is indeed pervasive!

4. I make an important distinction between *emerging* churches that merely seek to contextualize the gospel for the emerging generations and the so-called *Emergent* movement, which, I fear, may at times be guilty of theological accommodation to a post-Christian culture that has embraced a thoroughgoing moral relativism and religious pluralism. Accommodating churches can be post-evangelical or liberal in affiliation.

Support for the idea that many young adults have been hurt by and disenchanted with the Pharisaism they have experienced in fundamentalist evangelical churches can be found in various sources. For example, see chapter 12 of Robert Webber, *The Younger Evangelicals: Facing the Challenges of the New World* (Grand Rapids: Baker, 2002), 174–79; Appendix A of Eddie Gibbs and Ryan K. Bolger, *Emerging Churches: Creating Christian Community in Postmodern Cultures* (Grand Rapids: Baker Academic, 2005), 239–328; Dan Kimball, *They Like Jesus But Not the Church: Insights from Emerging Generations* (Grand Rapids: Zondervan, 2007); and David Kinnaman, *unChristian: What a New Generation Really Thinks about Christianity . . . and Why It Matters* (Grand Rapids: Baker, 2007).

5. I will elaborate a bit on the effect that a modified, gradually implemented version of this disciple-making strategy had in my own pastoral ministry in chapter ten and in the book's conclusion.

Part 1

UNDERSTANDING PHARISAISM

1

WHO WERE THOSE GUYS?

A recurring line in the classic film *Butch Cassidy and the Sundance Kid* ran, "Who are those guys?" Butch and Sundance are running for their lives, being followed by a tenacious group of antagonists. With a growing sense of weary exasperation, the two outlaws repeatedly look over their shoulders, spy their relentless pursuers, and then pose the question, "Who are those guys?" I think of this famous line as I begin this chapter, the purpose of which is to answer questions such as Who were the original Pharisees? How did the group emerge? What did they believe, teach, and practice? What was their goal, their main motivation? How well received were they at the time of Jesus?

These are some of the preliminary issues that must be addressed before we can give serious consideration to the theory that Jesus deliberately used the Pharisees as a whole as an anti-model in his disciple-making ministry. In order for us to deal effectively with the problem of Pharisaism in our contemporary evangelical churches, we simply must possess a basic understanding of the historical Pharisees. Who were those guys?

A Brief History of the Pharisees

We should probably begin this attempt to improve our understanding of the ancient Pharisees by seeking to discern the when, how, and why of this Jewish sect's entrance onto the stage of human history. The following historical analysis will strive to identify the historical antecedents to the movement known as Pharisaism in a way that will yield insights into what this group was about.

The term "Pharisee" seems to have first come into usage about a hundred years prior to the birth of Christ.[1] Many scholars see the word "Pharisee" as a derivation of the Hebrew word *Parush*, or the Aramaic *Perishaya*, which means "separated" and "isolated."[2] This would suggest that at the heart of what it means to be a Pharisee is the idea of *separation*. Thus, one way to analyze the historical emergence of Pharisaism as a religious movement is to trace the theme of separatism from the time of Ezekiel the prophet to the Pharisees of Jesus' day.[3]

The Ministry of Ezekiel

The prophet Ezekiel ministered to the Jews living in Babylon during the period of Judah's exile there. The message of the preexilic prophets had been that this season of divine discipline would surely arrive because of the Israelites' failure to fully obey the law of the Lord delivered to them by Moses (e.g., Jeremiah 32:17–24). During this period of displacement and captivity, and due in no small part to Ezekiel's ministry, three important developments took place that would dramatically impact the history of Israel: (1) the attention of the Jewish people became fixed once again on the law (it was hoped that a renewed devotion to the law would result in their liberation); (2) the first synagogues were formed (these were places of worship other than the temple in Jerusalem where prayers were offered and the law was expounded upon); and (3) the office of the scribe took on special prominence (the scribes functioned as primary teachers of the law).

W. D. Davies, an expert on the Pharisees, asserts that a renewed devotion to keeping the law of Moses not only helped the people of Israel survive the exile, but afterward became the reason for their very existence as a people distinguished from all others. This explains why, in the wake of the exile, the Jews became a "people of the Book" (the law), why the synagogue became such a prominent feature of Jewish life, and why the scribe, as an instructor of the law, became such an important person in the Jewish community.[4]

Law, synagogue, scribes: the New Testament indicates that all three of these institutions were very important to the Pharisees of Jesus' day. While no direct connection can be made between Ezekiel's ministry and Pharisaism per se, at the very least these historical developments would prove crucial to the eventual emergence of the Pharisees.

The Ministry of Ezra

With the eventual return of a remnant of Jews to their homeland, the people of Israel once again encountered the threat of compromise and assimilation. As Ezra 6:21 points out, these repatriated exiles understood the need to *separate* themselves "from the unclean practices of their Gentile neighbors." It was at this point in Israel's history that a pious Jew named Ezra stepped forward and set in motion further developments that some scholars believe eventually led to the emergence of the Pharisees. Indeed, Pharisee scholar Robert Herford goes so far as to suggest that "the starting point of any history of Pharisaism must of necessity be the work of Ezra," due to the fact that "Ezra stood forth at a most critical period to save the Jewish religion, and with it the national life, from relapsing into decay through contact with Gentile ideas and practices."[5]

15

If there is any truth to the idea that Ezra "saved" the Jewish religion, even a cursory reading of the book that bears his name will demonstrate that he did so by accomplishing two things: first, he set up a barrier between Jew and Gentile (see Ezra 9–10); and second, he hammered away at the idea that the Torah (the first five books of the Bible) is the revelation of the divine will given to Israel and therefore every faithful Jew had a duty to conform to it.

In Ezra 7:10 we read, "Ezra had devoted himself to the study and observance of the Law of the LORD, and to teaching its decrees and laws in Israel." It is therefore quite conceivable that the earliest roots of the separatist sect that would become Pharisaism are to be found in Ezra's ministry of forcing the postexilic Jews to begin taking the Law of Moses (the Torah) seriously and separating themselves from the nations round about. Advancing this view, Herford boldly observes, "The Jew had a religious life to live, else he would not be a Jew. The Torah was to be his guide in living that life; but he could not follow its guidance unless he were shielded to some extent from contact with the Gentile world, with its many temptations to apostasy. There, in fewest words, is the explanation of the work of Ezra. . . . I have secured what is needed as the starting point for the process which in course of time produced Pharisaism."[6]

The Sopherim and the Great Synagogue

If Ezra's ministry was the "starting point," then the next step in the historical process that eventually gave rise to the movement known as Pharisaism was taken by his successors. Verses 1, 4, 9, and 13 of Nehemiah 8 all contain references to Ezra as the *sōphēr*, the scribe. The period of time that occurred during and after Ezra's era was known as the period of the *Sōphĕrīm*, the scribes who inherited Ezra's teaching ministry.[7]

Though Ezra himself was also a priest (see Ezra 7:11), not all of the Sopherim were (though it is likely that many Levites might have pursued an Ezra-like teaching ministry).[8] While these teaching scribes certainly had an opinion about the way the temple ceremonies should be conducted, it was the priests who maintained actual control of matters relating to the temple cultus.[9] The Sopherim exercised their influence not through the temple but through the synagogue, as they endeavored to teach the common people how to apply the Torah to everyday aspects of life. Thus it was through the synagogue that "the Sopherim came into close contact with the individual Jew in his private capacity, and acquired there an influence which was never afterwards shaken."[10] (We need to keep this in mind when, later in this chapter, we take note of the popularity of the Pharisees of Jesus' day.) As time passed, the local synagogues and the scribes associated with them became increasingly important to Israel's social fabric and spiritual consciousness.

Some scholars see a connection between the Sopherim and a teaching authority known as "the Great Synagogue."[11] This term referred to a body of especially well-respected scribes whose commentary (*midrash*) on the Torah came to be viewed as authoritative for many in the Jewish community. Herford writes, "From the time of Ezra, then, down to the year 270 BC or thereabouts, the work of interpreting and teaching the Torah was carried on by those who, as individuals, were called Sopherim, and collectively were styled the Great Synagogue. Their teaching was necessarily based on the Torah; and their interpretation, Midrash, was presumably a simple explanation and application of the text to the case before them, whatever that might be."[12]

According to Herford, we find in the Sopherim and the Great Synagogue a prototype of what would later become the Pharisees—and after them the founders of rabbinic Judaism. But this does not mean that we have thereby discovered the immediate impetus for the emergence of the Pharisee sect, which would not occur until several centuries later.

The Hasidim

It appears that the Great Synagogue mysteriously receded into insignificance in or about 270 BC,[13] making it impossible to establish a direct causal connection between the Sopherim and the Pharisees. This body of teachers likely began to disappear when the Persian rule of Judea was displaced by the Greek. The Persians had allowed the inhabitants of Judea a measure of cultural and religious freedom. But with the advent of Greek rule under Alexander the Great and his successors, the Jews began their long struggle with the formidable cultural force known as Hellenism, the spread of Greek culture. Hellenization was the method by which Alexander sought to unify his empire: everyone in the empire would be required to embrace Greek language, culture, and religion. When aggressively promoted, Hellenism made it very difficult for pious Jews to practice the faith of their fathers as dictated by the Torah.[14]

Despite this attempt to force Greek culture on the Jews, the ancient concern to maintain a distinction (a separation) between Israel and all other nations remained very much alive. This ancient concern manifested itself in a dramatic manner with the Maccabean revolt in 167 BC, in which Jewish zealots, led by Judas Maccabeus and his brothers, rebelled against the oppressive and especially offensive Syrian rule. Taking part in the revolt were some religious extremists known as the *Hasidim* ("pious, or righteous, ones"). The strict and ascetic manner in which the Hasidim sought to stay true to the religious customs passed down to them from the time of Moses has caused some scholars to see them as forerunners of the Pharisees.

This general conclusion, correct though it may be, requires some nuance. The Hasidim were Jews who simply wanted the freedom to exercise the religion of Moses in an unencumbered manner. They lacked any political motivation whatsoever.[15] But after the victory of the revolt, the Maccabean family heads, the original military leaders of the uprising, began to consolidate political power. The goal of the Maccabeans was not just religious freedom but political autonomy—and after that was achieved, hegemony as well. These differing goals meant that, even though the enemy of Hellenization had been thwarted by the revolt, a divergence began to appear between moderate and extremist defenders of the Torah.[16] A two-party system was beginning to take shape, and an adequate understanding of how the Pharisees emerged as a separatist sect requires that we dig a little deeper—doing our best to understand what lay behind this bifurcation of Jewish society.

The era in Jewish history that immediately followed the Maccabean revolt is known as the time of the Hasmonean princes. During this relatively brief era of political independence, Simeon, the brother of Judas Maccabeus, became the virtual king of the region. Rather than take the title of king, however, he chose to wield his political authority as Israel's high priest, as did his son and successor, John Hyrcanus ("John the High Priest").[17] History tells us that a great deal of tension existed between the supporters of Hyrcanus and those members of the Hasidim who were not at all concerned about the consolidation of political power. The sources behind this tension were multiple: sociological, religious, and political.

The supporters of John Hyrcanus tended to be the aristocratic priestly families who were quite comfortable with the mingling of religion with politics and who "were not inclined to let their devotion to the Torah restrict their freedom to work for the political interests of what was now the kingdom."[18] These priestly families were adamant that the authoritative text of their religion was only the five books of the Pentateuch (the Torah). This meant the complete rejection of the oral tradition (as developed by the Sopherim of the Great Synagogue), which sought to extend the authority of the Torah into every area of life.[19]

Opposing the priestly families were the more conservative members of the Hasidim: those who were in close touch with the common folk, those whose chief concern was that the Torah be upheld and protected from worldly compromise. For this faction, the Torah was divine revelation given to provide guidance for every facet of life and was to be obeyed by every Israelite. Further, the Hasidim asserted that since the Torah had been given to all Israel it should be interpreted not just by the priestly caste but by anyone who possessed the necessary knowledge to do so (i.e., by educated laymen). Finally, the conservative Hasidim held that the Torah was not limited to the Pentateuch but also included the divine teaching passed on in the oral tradition, which constituted the Torah's true interpretation.[20]

You may have already surmised that we are witnessing here the genesis of the tension and rivalry between the two groups that would become known as the Sadducees and Pharisees. After contrasting the main differences between the supporters of the politically motivated Maccabean rulers and the spiritually motivated members of the Hasidim, Herford notes, "These two extremes had names by which they were distinguished. Those who formed the governing class, the great families and the chief priests, were the Sadducees. Those who maintained the full strictness of the religion of Torah were the Pharisees."[21]

According to this view, further steps toward the emergence of the Pharisees were taken by the ultraconservative members of the Hasidim, who not only rebelled against the Hellenistic program that came from *without* the Jewish nation but also from a religious and political program that emanated from *within* the Jewish community itself (i.e., the religion and politics of the Sadducees). As the tension between the Hasidim and the rest of Jewish society increased, the idea of separation changed dramatically.

Though we are ever closer, we have yet to unearth the main (immediate) historical root of the Jewish party that served as Jesus' antagonists, however.

The Haberim

As I have already indicated, it was not until about 135 to 105 BC, strictly speaking, that the designation "Pharisee" actually made its first appearance.[22] John Hyrcanus, high priest and virtual king at the time, became concerned that certain practices required by the law of Moses were not being properly observed, especially the "separation" of the tithes.[23] Hyrcanus appointed inspectors to see to it that the tithes were properly separated. In support of this initiative, a group of Jews formed a voluntary association of "those who definitely pledged themselves to separate their tithes in accordance with the Torah."[24] The members of this association referred to themselves as *Haberim,* "companions." Furthermore, their pledge went beyond the separation of the tithes to the other matters of the law. The Haberim committed themselves to practice "all the laws of clean and unclean laid down in the Torah."[25]

The Talmud (a collection of ancient rabbinic writings considered authoritative by Orthodox Jews) indicates that there were four grades of Haberim, reflecting slightly different levels of strictness in their observance of the laws of ritual purity. But each of these grades of Haberim felt the need to separate themselves from the common folk—the *am-ha-aretz,* or "people of the land"—who made no attempt at all to maintain ceremonial purity before God. The members of the first grade of Haberim were called *Pherushim,* i.e., "Pharisees."[26] This seems to be the first appearance of the term "Pharisee" in the history of the Jewish people. Again, Herford writes, "The particular reason why they were called Pharisees (Pherushim, separated), was that they formed themselves into separate societies pledged to observe certain rules in the matter of meat, drink, clothing, etc., according as these were clean or unclean, allowed or forbidden. They thereby 'separated' themselves from such as were less strict, or who at least did not take their pledge as a guarantee of strictness."[27]

Here, at last, we have what appear to be the direct forebears of the Pharisees of Jesus' day.

To summarize, while the word "Pharisee" ("separatist") may have emerged only a century or so before the time of Christ, the members of the sect known as the Pharisees were heirs of a separatist tradition that reaches all the way back to the postexilic ministry of Ezra. This "father of all scribes" had called for the postexilic Jews to *separate* themselves "from the unclean practices of their Gentile neighbors." His spiritual descendants, the Sopherim and members of the Great Synagogue, continued this theme in their teaching of the Torah and the development of the oral tradition that sought to apply the "principles of separation" (clean versus unclean) to every aspect of everyday life. (We know that the Pharisees of Jesus' day were greatly enamored with this oral tradition.)

Furthermore, this separatist impulse seems to have survived the demise of the Great Synagogue and manifested itself in the Hasidim during the Maccabean revolt, and afterward during the era of the Hasmonean princes. Initially it was the desire to properly observe the Torah's teaching regarding the "separation" of the tithes that caused some very pious Jews to take the pledge that included them in the Haberim. Eventually their concern for ritual purity caused them to separate themselves from anyone, Jew or Gentile, who was unwilling to take the pledge along with them. The members of the first level of the Haberim, and therefore the most numerous, were referred to as "Pharisees." But because the upper levels of the Haberim were even stricter in their attention to the teachings of the Torah, there is a sense in which all the Haberim were considered Pharisees. This was the first official use of the term "Pharisee" to describe a separatist sect that functioned in opposition to the Sadducees and the common people of the land.

Our historical analysis would seem to indicate, then, that the separation referred to in the name "Pharisee," *parush,* may be thought to refer not only to a separation from the Gentiles and their unclean practices but also to fellow Jews (both aristocrats and common folk) who did not, in the minds of the Pharisees, take the teachings of the Torah seriously enough.[28] The fact is that both types of separation seem to be present in the Pharisees of Jesus' day.

The Main Tenets and Lifestyle Practices of the Pharisees

Now that we have improved our understanding of when, how, and why the Pharisees emerged as a distinct group within the nation of Israel and precisely from whom and what they felt the need to separate themselves, we must press on to identify their basic beliefs and how these beliefs were lived out in the world.

Biblical scholar A. T. Robertson suggests that this endeavor to understand the basic teachings of the Pharisees is of the utmost importance. "It is impossible to understand the atmosphere of Christ's earthly life without an adequate knowledge of the Pharisees. They largely created the atmosphere which the people breathed, and into which Jesus came. Our Lord had to relate His message and mission at once to this dominant theology of His time in Palestine."[29]

There is a problem, however, in that the New Testament authors evidently assumed that their readers already possessed a basic knowledge of the Pharisees' theology. As a result, they failed to provide a full description of it.[30] Further, when we consult the Talmudic literature we are not completely certain whether the theology we find there reflects the thinking of the rabbis in first-century Palestine or those of a later era.[31] Still, between the New Testament, the writings of Josephus, the Psalms of Solomon, the Testaments of the Twelve Patriarchs, 2 Esdras, the Talmud, and the Midrash we are able to piece together at least a broad understanding of the theology of the Pharisees.[32]

In general, the Pharisees believed: (a) in both divine sovereignty and human free agency; (b) in the oral law, which was held to be equal in authority with the Old Testament Scriptures; (c) in the resurrection and a future life; (d) in the idea of a Messiah who would someday come to overthrow the yoke of the Romans and reestablish political sovereignty in Israel;[33] and (e) in the reality of angels, demons, and other spirits.[34]

An examination of Jesus' interaction with the Pharisees indicates that the main disagreement between them arose from the fact that Jesus did not share the Pharisees' belief that the oral law was equal in authority with the Old Testament Scriptures. This was not a minor doctrinal disagreement. A case can be made for the idea that the Pharisees ended up rejecting Jesus because he seemed, in their view, to undermine the authority of the Torah. On the other hand, the lifestyle of the Pharisees was earmarked by a fastidious observance of not just the teachings of the Torah but also of the teachings of the rabbis as presented in the oral tradition. This was a commitment that Jesus simply did not share. In fact, Jesus was convinced that many of the life practices dictated by the oral law contravened the clear teachings of the written law (see Mark 7:1–13). In other words, *while Jesus did not necessarily disagree with every tenet held by the Pharisees, he did have a big problem with the set of life practices to which their dogged devotion to the oral tradition committed them.*

One of the main lifestyle issues especially important to the Pharisees was Sabbath-keeping. While it is true that the Law of Moses does indeed contain a very clear command to observe the Sabbath and keep it holy (Exodus 20:8), the Pharisees could not help but wonder how this was to be accomplished with precision. They wanted to be absolutely *certain* they did not inadvertently engage in an activity that constituted a technical violation of the Sabbath.

For this reason the rabbis were prompted to expand on the basic command found in Scripture, indicating what specific everyday actions were prohibited by it. The goal was to build a fence or hedge around the law so as to guard against a careless, unintended violation of it. For instance, A. T. Robertson cites a passage from the Book of Jubilees that spells out the Pharisees' radical commitment to observe the Sabbath: "Everyone who desecrates the Sabbath, or declares that he intends to make a journey on it, or speaks of either buying or selling, or he who draws water and has not provided it upon the sixth day, and he who lifts a burden in order to take it out of his dwelling-place, or out of his house shall die. And every one who makes a journey, or attends to his cattle, and he who kindles a fire, or rides upon any beast, or sails upon a ship or the sea upon a Sabbath day, shall die."[35]

Robertson goes on to cite other Sabbath restrictions presented in the Talmud: lifestyle prohibitions that serve to demonstrate how the super-scrupulous Pharisees approached the practice of their religion. For example, if a person broke a bone on the Sabbath it could not be set. Cold water could not be poured on a sprained hand or foot. It was impermissible to write on the Sabbath unless one was writing on something dark or with the hand upside down. It was unlawful to read by lamplight or clean one's clothes. Women were forbidden to look in the mirror on the Sabbath lest they succumb to the temptation to pull out gray hairs. Some knots could be untied on the Sabbath; others had to be left alone. Vinegar could be used for a sore throat as long as it was swallowed, but gargling was a Sabbath violation. An egg laid on the Sabbath could be eaten only if one intended to kill the hen responsible for it.[36]

The Pharisees' view of the Sabbath is especially important because of the tension it created between some members of this sect and Jesus. In addition to their commitment to keep the Sabbath, the Pharisees were equally concerned, however, to observe the distinction between the clean and the unclean as called for in the Torah (Leviticus 10:10). Many of the rules the Pharisees chose to live by rested on the Levitical laws that were originally intended to promote good hygiene and keep the people of Israel separate from the idolatrous behaviors of their Canaanite neighbors. But it seems that the rabbis felt the need to radically fine-tune their understanding of what the law of Moses required so as to eliminate any possibility of a mistake. Therefore the rabbis made careful distinctions between various kinds of utensils and vessels, indicating how they should be approached and for what purpose.[37]

Further, with regard to the necessary purification of people and things, distinctions were made between various types of water (pond water, spring water, running water in streams, collected water from the pond or spring or stream or rain water, clean and unclean water); what kind of water was to be used for this or that function; and precisely how the water was to be used to accomplish these various functions. For instance, with regard to the matter of ritual hand washing, simply pouring water on the hands was considered sufficient before eating ordinary food, but before eating holy things the hands had to be completely dipped in water. Similar scruples applied to the cleansing of various cups, platters, and pots (see Mark 7:3–4).[38]

The Pharisees also maintained that important distinctions needed to be made between themselves and various kinds of people (unclean Jews, Samaritans, Gentiles, and women). According to the Pharisees, "A rabbi must not talk with a woman in public and not too much with his wife, else he will go to Gehenna."[39] The Jewish prayer book contains this liturgical prayer: "Blessed art thou, O Lord God, King of the universe, who hast not made me a heathen. Blessed art thou . . . who hast not made me a bondman. Blessed art thou . . . who hast not made me a woman."[40]

Robertson summarizes his discussion of the separatist, distinction-maintaining life practices of the Pharisees by saying, "The Pharisee thus has pride of race, of position, of sex, and of laborious personal purity by attention to the formulae for righteousness, by doing which he gained salvation."[41] In other words, the Pharisee firmly believed that his very salvation depended on his maintaining a ritual purity as well as a moral purity before God. This ritual and moral purity before God mandated his separation from everyone else who did not share his worldview. This is perhaps the most important tenet in the belief system operative among the Pharisees. Ironically, this strong conviction tended to produce a lifestyle that reflected a significant amount of pride and arrogance on the one hand and a certain amount of spiritual insecurity on the other.

The Essence of Jewish Pharisaism

The above discussion leads us to a consideration of primary motivations. How might the essence of Pharisaism be defined? What was the goal of their religious lives? What motivated the Pharisees to practice their religion the way they did?

Positive Assessments

Some scholars tend to view the Pharisees only in a positive light and therefore describe their motivations only in glowing terms. Indeed, it seems that many scholars feel the need to function essentially as apologists for the Pharisees. As such, they express frustration when anyone attempts to portray the Pharisees in anything but a positive manner.[42]

While not exactly an apologist for the Pharisees himself, W. D. Davies presents the argument that the essence of Pharisaism was a sincere commitment to apply the entire law to the entirety of life. According to Davies, the Pharisees were convinced that the Sadducees were living in an unholy manner. This was due primarily to the fact that the Sadducees focused all their attention on the literal or written law and completely ignored the oral tradition. Against this, the Pharisees insisted that in order to really serve God one must also embrace the oral tradition so that all of life would be brought under the influence of the law.[43]

The idea was that since circumstances change over time the application of the written law will change also. Davies writes: "By thus accepting both the oral tradition as well as the written Law, Pharisaism made possible the application of the Mosaic Law to ever-changing conditions. It made the Law the mint of prophetic truth. Strange as it may seem, the acceptance of tradition was the condition of adaptability. This was the aim of the Pharisees, and herein many have found the essence of Pharisaism. It was essentially an attempt by certain people within Israel to bring the whole of human life under the control of Law."[44]

According to this view, the essence of Pharisaism was an unflinching pursuit of spiritual integrity. The primary motivation of the Pharisees was simply the concern to be extremely thoroughgoing in their observance of the Torah. How could such a motivation possibly be criticized?

A similar perspective is put forward by Rabbi Samuel Umen, who argues that Pharisaism is simply the natural result of taking the Jewish religion seriously. As such, says Umen, far from being something to be critiqued or lamented, Pharisaism is a spiritual condition to be applauded. Umen writes, "Pharisaism is an attempt to make religion the dominant factor in the daily life of a human being and in society as a whole. It represents spiritual growth; it symbolizes ethical and moral progress; it defines Judaism; it is the key to the Jewish soul."[45]

Negative Assessments

On the other hand, one of the definitions for the word "Pharisee" offered by the *Oxford English Dictionary* is "a self-righteous person; a formalist, a hypocrite."[46] To whatever degree such a definition is indicative of popular sentiment, it would be easy to conclude that such a perspective is entirely owing to Christian bias. However, this tendency to associate Pharisaism with formalism, self-righteousness, and hypocrisy is not limited to the Christian community. The truth is that some of the most fierce criticisms of the Pharisees come not from Gentiles but from fellow Jews, specifically the rabbis who contributed to the Talmud later on in the first to fifth centuries of the Common Era. Robertson writes:

The Pharisees were not at one with themselves save in opposition to everybody else. There is no logical place to stop in the business of Pharisaic seclusiveness when once it is started. The line was drawn against the Gentiles, against the 'am-ha-'arets [*sic*] among the Jews, against the publicans and sinners, against the Sadducees, and then against some of the Pharisees themselves. The Talmud itself gives the seven varieties of the Pharisees, and all but the last one are afflicted with hypocrisy, the sin that Jesus so vigorously denounces, and that stirs the modern apologists of Pharisaism to such rage.[47]

Robertson goes on to list the seven varieties of the Pharisees presented in the Talmud: (a) the "shoulder" Pharisee who wears his good deeds on his shoulder in order to gain a reputation for piety; (b) the "wait-a-little" Pharisee who always has an excuse for not doing the good deed now; (c) the "bruised" or "bleeding" Pharisee who keeps running into things because he literally shuts his eyes whenever a woman comes into his field of vision; (d) the "pestle" or "mortar" Pharisee who walks with his head down in mock humility like a pestle in a mortar; (e) the "ever-reckoning" or "compounding" Pharisee who is always on the lookout for something "extra" he can do to make up for something he might have neglected; (f) the "timid" or "fearing" Pharisee whose relationship with God is marked by fear of punishment; and (g) the "God-loving" or "born" Pharisee, the true Pharisee who was, like Abraham, a true friend of God.[48]

While the inclusion of the last type of Pharisee presented in the list (the "God-loving" or "born" Pharisee) makes it clear that the later rabbis did not view all of the Pharisees of the first century as self-righteous, formalistic hypocrites, it is also apparent that the later rabbis were not uncritical of their first-century forebears. This passage from the Talmud indicates very clearly that, from the perspective of other Pharisees (that is, the Talmud rabbis), at least some of the Pharisees of

Jesus' day possessed motives that were less than healthy and noble.[49] Some of these less-than-noble motives included an inordinate desire for peer approval and admiration, a loophole mentality that was oriented toward discovering and doing the least that was required in one's relationship with God and others, an essentially ascetic understanding of moral formation, an actual attitude of spiritual pride and arrogance, a neurotic need to make certain that all spiritual obligations had been met and exceeded in a superfluous manner, and a heart haunted by the fear of divine punishment.

So, according to the Talmud, there were some goodhearted, well-intentioned Pharisees. But if this list is any indication, there were also many Pharisees whose spiritual motivations were more lamentable than laudable.

Biblical scholar J. Alexander Findlay agrees with this negative assessment of the essence of Pharisaism. After acknowledging that we Christians owe a debt of profound gratitude to the historical Pharisees for many things—the preservation of the whole Old Testament, the idea of public worship not in a central temple but in a local meeting house, the first suggestion to the world of democracy, the idea of compulsory education free and open to everyone, the idea of preaching from a text, the idea of an ordered and organized exposition, and even the structure and arrangement of our church buildings[50]—Findlay goes on to offer a diagnosis of what went wrong with Pharisaism. He writes, "The essential weakness of Pharisee religion is to be found in the fact that devotion to a Person, God, had been submerged in devotion to a thing, the book."[51]

According to this view, it was the Pharisees' focus on the book, rather than the God who graciously inspired the book, that led them to separate themselves from all non-Jews and from the careless, uninstructed "people of the land."[52] The strict Pharisee would not have anything to do with anyone who was not a fellow Pharisee. The main motivation of the typical Pharisee was a sense of duty rather than love. His standing before God depended upon his strict observance of the law of Moses as amplified by the oral tradition. *It was only by this super-scrupulous observance of the law that the Pharisee could achieve any sort of certainty regarding his salvation.*

A Mediating Assessment

Which of these two assessments (positive or negative) is the more accurate one? Perhaps both assessments contain grains of truth. Surely there were historical Pharisees, even in Jesus' day, who wanted nothing more than to live their lives in a manner pleasing to God and to encourage their fellow countrymen to do the same. On the other hand, it is also easy to see how a fear-based pursuit of a psychological certainty concerning salvation could manifest itself in several religious developments (for example, the development of an authoritative oral tradition, a legalistic approach to salvation, a preoccupation with religious rituals and external acts of piety, a separatist mindset, etc.) that together served to eliminate for the Pharisees any vestige of spiritual ambiguity. Could it be that at the heart of historic Pharisaism there existed not simply a concern for integrity but also an inordinate need to be certain, to be in control, to be able to determine precisely who was pleasing to God and who was not? Could it be that at the heart of historic Pharisaism there existed a fundamental inability to live with spiritual uncertainty and to exercise simple trust in the goodness and mercy of God?

According to this mediating view, *in addition to a legitimate concern for spiritual integrity, the Pharisees as a whole were motivated by a prob-lematic, futile, fear-based quest for spiritual certainty.*[53] While many of the Pharisees no doubt meant well, this latter motivation led the group as a whole down a path that would earn them the disapproval they received from both Jesus and the later rabbis.

The Popularity of the Pharisees

If there is any truth to the view that many of the Pharisees in the first century were guilty of self-righteousness, formalism, and hypocrisy, we might expect to find that the group as a whole was hated by the common people of their day. Ironically, this was not the case.

We have already cited A. T. Robertson's assertion that it is impossible to understand the atmosphere of Christ's earthly life without an adequate knowledge of the Pharisees.[54] Marcel Simon, in his book *Jewish Sects at the Time of Jesus*, indicates that in the New Testament era the Pharisees had become the most powerful religious party and the spiritual leaders most admired by the people. He writes, "At the beginning of their history the Pharisees were a handful of dissidents, sectarians in the most precise meaning of the term. Indeed, their very name means 'separated,' those who constitute a group apart. But in the period with which we are concerned, the situation was completely reversed: not only had the Pharisees become the most powerful religious party, they were also the spiritual leaders most widely heeded by the people. Their criteria were, increasingly, the ones that defined the good Jew."[55]

Likewise, W. D. Davies reports that by the time of Jesus the Pharisees had become "the most influential section of the Jewish community." Davies writes:

> By the first century of our era we have seen that the people whom we are discussing, the Pharisees, formed a well-defined element in Judaism. In a community that was perhaps peculiarly rich in conflicting currents of thought and practice, the Pharisees almost certainly formed the most influential section of the Jewish community. So influential indeed were they that it has come to be recognized generally that it was their beliefs and practices that really constituted what has been called conveniently, although misleadingly, "normative Judaism." Apart especially from the

Sadducees and certain Hellenized elements in Palestine and in the Dispersion, their tenets in varying and modified degrees came to be accepted probably by the majority of the pious in Jewry.[56]

The ideas expressed by Simon and Davies may explain why the Pharisees were so popular with the common people of their day. The fact is that people need both hope and heroes. The tenets of the Pharisees—with their emphasis upon the sovereignty of God, the resurrection and future life, and the messianic expectation—must have contributed to a sense of hope that was both national and personal at the same time. This hope was rehearsed and reinforced each Sabbath day in the local synagogue. Despite any tendency toward self-righteousness and hypocrisy that the Pharisees might have manifested, at least they were taking the religious life seriously.

I have observed that when rank-and-file believers are not confident of their own progress toward spiritual maturity, they will often do the next best thing and claim association with those they perceive to be making such progress. We all want to believe that we are somehow connected with some spiritual leaders who are getting it right and that we will somehow benefit from our association with them. (I suspect this is one of the reasons why many church members will vigorously, though perhaps unconsciously, resist the attempt of their pastoral leaders to climb off the pedestals upon which they are placed by their congregation.)

Whatever the cause, it appears that Pharisaism was a formidable force when Jesus of Nazareth began his public ministry. On the one hand, the popularity of the Pharisees might explain, at least in part, why Jesus chose to use this particular group as an anti-model for authentic Christian discipleship. Their popularity meant that every allusion Jesus made to Pharisaical belief or practice would be readily understood by his hearers. On the other hand, the popularity of the Pharisees might also explain how Jesus' vociferous opposition to this influential group earned him an early demise and why, of all the major groups operative in first-century Palestine (the Pharisees, Sadducees, Essenes, Herodians, and Zealots), it is the Pharisees alone that have survived to our day. It is one of the ironies of history that the Orthodox Judaism we know today is essentially a version of historical Pharisaism. Robertson explains, "With the destruction of Jerusalem all vanish save the Pharisees, who become practically the nation. Pharisaism after AD 70 may be said to be the religion of official Judaism, and it has remained so ever since."[57]

Who were those guys? I hope that the ground we have covered in this chapter has helped us form a foundational understanding of who the ancient Pharisees were and what they were about. The provocative thesis I am putting forward in this book is that Jesus not only found fault with most of the Pharisees of his day but that he actually used them in a proactive manner as an anti-model when making disciples. Given the tremendous popularity of this particular Jewish sect at that time, this was a very dangerous thing for Jesus to do. We simply have to assume that Jesus knew what he was doing. We can also assume that there was something about the way the Pharisees approached the religious life that concerned Jesus very much. In the next chapter we will seek to identify what that something was.

Notes

1. Robert Herford, *The Pharisees* (London: Unwin Brothers, Limited, 1924), 29.
2. Leo Baeck, *The Pharisees and Other Essays* (New York: Schocken Books Inc., 1947), 3. See also W. D. Davies, *Introduction to Pharisaism* (Philadelphia: Fortress Press, 1967), 6.
3. See Davies, *Introduction to Pharisaism*, 4.
4. Ibid.
5. Herford, *The Pharisees*, 18.
6. Ibid., 19.

7. Ibid., 20. See also Robert Herford, *Pharisaism: Its Aim and Its Method* (New York: G. P. Putnam's Sons, 1912), 16.

8. Herford, *Pharisaism: Its Aim and Its Method*, 16–17.

9. Ibid., 29.

10. Ibid.

11. Ibid., 17–21. See also Herford, *The Pharisees*, 21–22.

12. Herford, *The Pharisees*, 22.

13. Ibid., 21.

14. Ibid., 23.

15. Ibid., 27.

16. Herford, *Pharisaism: Its Aim and Its Method*, 38–41.

17. Herford, *The Pharisees*, 27–28.

18. Ibid., 28.

19. Ibid., 28–29.

20. Ibid., 29.

21. Herford, *Pharisaism: Its Aim and Its Method*, 41.

22. Herford, *The Pharisees*, 29.

23. Ibid., 30. Herford refers to the practice of "separating" the tithes. I suspect that this designation is informed by the fact that in an agrarian society the tithes typically take the form of produce and livestock (see Leviticus 27:30–33) and that before tithes such as these could be presented to the Levites and priests as per Numbers 18:21–29 and Deuteronomy 26:12–15 they first would need to be *separated* from the rest of that year's "income."

24. Ibid., 31.

25. Ibid.

26. Ibid., 31–32.

27. Herford, *Pharisaism: Its Aim and Its Method*, 41–42.

28. Ibid., 42. See also Davies, *Introduction to Pharisaism*, 9.

29. A. T. Robertson, *The Pharisees and Jesus* (London: Duckworth and Company, 1920), 2–3.

30. Ibid., 11.

31. Ibid., 35–36.

32. Ibid., 36.

33. Ibid., 37–42.

34. Marcel Simon, *Jewish Sects at the Time of Jesus* (Philadelphia: Fortress Press, 1967), 39–41. We should note that both Simon and T. W. Manson attribute the Pharisees' well-developed angelology and demonology to a Persian influence. Indeed, Manson goes so far as to suggest that the Greek word *Pharisaios* is a Hellenized form of the Aramaic for "Persian," *Parsháah,* and that there were several religious concepts that the Pharisees imported into Judaism from Persian thought: the idea of a divine purpose in history; the idea of a future life with rewards and

punishments; a well-developed angelology and demonology; the supreme authority of Scripture plus tradition. See also Davies, *Introduction to Pharisaism*, 10.

35. "The Book of Jubilees," 50, cited in Robertson, *The Pharisees and Jesus*, 45.

36. Robertson, *The Pharisees and Jesus*, 45–46.

37. Ibid., 46.

38. Ibid., 46–47.

39. Ibid., 47.

40. Ibid.

41. Ibid.

42. See, for example, Baeck, *The Pharisees and Other Essays*, 12; Jacob Neusner, *From Politics to Piety* (Englewood Cliffs, NJ: Prentice-Hall, Inc., 1973), 68; Donald Riddle, *Jesus and the Pharisees* (Chicago: University of Chicago Press, 1928), 27–28; Ellis Rivkin, *A Hidden Revolution* (Nashville: Abingdon , 1978), 27–28; Anthony Saldarini, *Pharisees, Scribes and Sadducees in Palestinian Society* (Wilmington, DE: Michael Glazier, Inc., 1988), 3, 144.

43. Davies, *Introduction to Pharisaism,* 24.

44. Ibid., 24–25.

45. Samuel Umen, *Pharisaism and Jesus* (New York: Philosophical Library, Inc., 1963), 2.

46. *Oxford English Dictionary*, cited in Davies, *Introduction to Pharisaism*, 2.

47. Robertson, *The Pharisees and Jesus*, 23.

48. Ibid., 23–27.

49. Ibid., 25. Robertson indicates that the rabbinic authors of the Talmud felt the need to point out that the "pestle" Pharisee "was also called the 'hump-backed' Pharisee, who walked as though his shoulders bore the whole weight of the law, or the 'tumbling' Pharisee, who was so humble that he would not lift his feet from the ground, or the 'painted' Pharisee, who advertised his holiness by various poses, so that no one should touch and bring defilement to him."

50. J. Alexander Findlay, *The Realism of Jesus* (London: Hodder and Stoughton, n.d.), 44–46.

51. Ibid., 46.

52. Ibid., 61.

53. I will elaborate on the meaning of the phrase "spiritual certainty" in chapter three.

54. Robertson, *The Pharisees and Jesus*, 2–3.

55. Simon, *Jewish Sects at the Time of Jesus*, 10.

56. Davies, *Introduction to Pharisaism,* 17.

57. Robertson, *The Pharisees and Jesus*, 22.

2

BAD BLOOD

I t is reported that a sign on the wall of Mother Teresa's children's home
in Calcutta displayed the following words of exhortation:

ANYWAY

People are unreasonable, illogical, and self-centered,

LOVE THEM ANYWAY

If you do good, people will accuse you of

selfish, ulterior motives,

DO GOOD ANYWAY

If you are successful,

you win false friends and true enemies,

SUCCEED ANYWAY

The good you do will be forgotten tomorrow,

DO GOOD ANYWAY

Honesty and frankness make you vulnerable,

BE HONEST AND FRANK ANYWAY

What you spent years building may be

destroyed overnight,

BUILD ANYWAY

People really need help
but may attack you if you help them,
HELP PEOPLE ANYWAY
Give the world the best you have
And you'll get kicked in the teeth,
GIVE THE WORLD THE BEST YOU'VE GOT ANYWAY.[1]

Evidently, even Mother Teresa had her critics.[2] My theory is that every significant personality in history, even those to whom history ends up being kind, has had to deal with enemies who sought his or her undoing. This was certainly true of Jesus of Nazareth. Most New Testament scholars will readily admit that, as a group, the Pharisees are portrayed in the Gospels as the enemies, rather than the friends, of Jesus.[3]

Why was this? Why this bad blood between Jesus and the Pharisees? My ultimate goal in this chapter is to help us gain a clearer understanding not only of the problem Jesus had with the Jewish Pharisees of his day but also of the religious actions and attitudes that constitute an approach to the Christian life that I refer to as New Testament Pharisaism. But before we can reach this goal we must first deal with a question that nags at many biblical and historical scholars: Can we trust what the New Testament has to say about the ancient Pharisees?

The Debate concerning the Historical Pharisees versus "Pharisaism"

If we are to be thorough in our analysis, the first question we must consider is this: Did the conflict between Jesus and the Jewish Pharisees really happen, or did the authors of the New Testament Gospels simply make it up? At the risk of greatly oversimplifying things, let me just say that some Pharisee scholars eagerly insist that the New Testament Gospels cannot be relied upon to produce an accurate portrayal of the Pharisees of

Jesus' day[4] and that the tension between Jesus and the Pharisees presented to us in these documents is not rooted in historical fact.[5] Other scholars contend that while Jesus may or may not have actually tussled with the Pharisees of his day, the Gospels, written several decades after the resurrection of Jesus, are reflective of a tension that existed between the church and synagogue, between the followers of Jesus and those of the Pharisees.[6] Still other scholars point out that the Gospels do on occasion speak of the Pharisees in a positive light, and that this would suggest that the New Testament's portrayal of the Pharisees and their interactions with Jesus is rather objective and historically trustworthy.[7]

As it relates to the goal of this chapter, I consider the debate briefly summarized above to be ultimately inconsequential. For one thing, it cannot be proved that the Gospels' accounts of the tension that existed between Jesus and the Pharisees are without historical foundation. Indeed, it is arguable whether the biblical authors would have felt the freedom (as some scholars maintain) to attribute to Jesus words and actions that possessed absolutely no historical integrity. Furthermore, even if it is granted that the authors of the Gospels might have deliberately portrayed the Pharisees in an especially negative light, one has to wonder what their motivation would have been for doing so. The fact that the Gospels contain some fairly positive references to at least some Pharisees would seem to undercut the idea that the New Testament's essentially negative portrayal of the Pharisees was motivated by nothing more than some lingering feelings of resentment or competition between the respective followers of Jesus and the Pharisees. So, could there have been another reason why the Pharisees are portrayed in the New Testament in a uniformly negative manner? Could it be that the biblical authors were concerned to steer their intended readers away from some specific traits and tendencies they knew would prove problematic to an authentic experience of Christian discipleship?

Regardless of the historical circumstances, the fact is that the New Testament portrays Jesus as denouncing a certain set of actions and attitudes that are attributed to the sect we know as the Pharisees. I refer to this set of actions and attitudes as "New Testament Pharisaism." *All historical questions aside, to the degree these problematic actions and attitudes are capable of being experienced by Christ's followers today (hence the term "Christian Pharisaism"), the denunciations uttered by Jesus are of extreme importance.* This is why it is imperative that we Christians seek to understand the bad blood that existed between Jesus and the Pharisees as the Pharisees are portrayed in our New Testament.

The Problem the Pharisees Had with Jesus

The next step in our analysis calls for us to identify what the Gospels have to say about why the Pharisees seemed to have been so annoyed and alarmed by the teaching and activities of Jesus.

New Testament scholar A. T. Robertson provides us with a list of no less than eleven complaints that the Pharisees filed against Jesus: (1) His illegitimate assumption of messianic authority (John 2:13–22); (2) His blasphemous speech (Matthew 26:65; Mark 14:64; Luke 5:17–26; John 5:18; 10:22–42); (3) His intolerable association with tax collectors and sinners (Matthew 9:10ff.; Mark 2:15ff.; Luke 5:29ff.; 7:29–30; 15:1–32); (4) His irreligious neglect of fasting (Matthew 9:14–17; Mark 2:18–22; Luke 5:33–39); (5) His partnership with Beelzebub (Matthew 9:34; 12:22–37; Mark 3:20–30; Luke 11:14–36); (6) His habit of breaking the Sabbath (Matthew 12:1–14; Mark 2:23—3:6; Luke 6:1–11; 13:10–21; 14:1–24; John 5; 9); (7) His failure to perform adequate signs (Matthew 12:38–45; 16:1; Mark 8:11; Luke 11:16–32); (8) His insolent defiance of tradition (Matthew 15:1–20; Mark 7:1–23; Luke 11:37–54); (9) His behaving as an ignorant impostor (Matthew 27:63f.; John 7:14–30); (10) His plotting to destroy the temple (Matthew 26:61; 27:39f.; Mark 14:58;

15:29; John 2:19–22); (11) His high treason against Caesar (Matthew 27:17–25; Mark 15:9–14; Luke 23:2; John 18:8–30; 19:15).[8]

The many New Testament passages presented above make it clear that the Pharisees, as a group, did not think much of Jesus. Several theories have been advanced for why the Pharisees were so prone to demonize the hero of our New Testament Gospels.

Maybe This Was a Family Squabble

Jewish scholar Asher Finkel has put forward the interesting and highly ironic theory that the tension we pick up on as we read the Gospels is actually indicative of an interparty conflict that occurred between Jesus, himself a Pharisaic teacher, and other Pharisees of a more zealous stripe. More precisely, Finkel contends that Jesus was raised and nurtured in an Essenic (hyper-Pharisaical) environment and embraced an Essenic world-view. In support of this contention Finkel points out some similarities he sees in Jesus' modus operandi and some of the practices of the Essenes as evidenced by some of the Dead Sea Scrolls and the testimonies of the Jewish historian Josephus and the Jewish philosopher Philo. According to Finkel, what Jesus and the Essenes had in common were things such as his having spent some time in the desert prior to the onset of his public ministry, the age at which he began his ministry, his routine of prayer and meditation, his selection of twelve men to carry his message onward, and the way he pronounced blessings and curses.[9]

This interesting theory that Jesus was not only a Pharisee himself but actually emerged from a community of hyper-Pharisees begs two crucial questions, however. The first question is this: *If Jesus was influenced by the Essene worldview, a worldview that emphasized retreat, isolation, and exclusivity, then how are we to understand his urbanity and inclusivity?* Finkel's response is that while Jesus was essentially an Essenic Pharisee, his particular mission called for him to deviate somewhat from the path of his contemporaries. Jesus' mission, as outlined in Luke 4:14–22, called for him to minister in the towns and villages rather than in the desert. It also required of him a close contact with (rather than separation from) the sick, the poor, the unclean, and the untouchable.[10] Finkel writes, "This can be concluded: although Jesus showed tendencies both as a Pharisaic and Essene teacher, a deviation from their ways emerged to clear the obstacles on the road of his proposed mission."[11] I must confess that, in my opinion, this argument that Jesus was originally an Essene (hyper-Pharisee) whose ministry philosophy evolved in such a way that he eventually became known as "a friend of tax collectors and 'sinners'" (Luke 7:34) strains credulity.

The second question that begs for a response is this: *If Jesus was himself a Pharisee, then how do we explain the polemic we find in the Gospels between Jesus and the Pharisees?* In response to this question Finkel reminds us that the Pharisaic movement was not monolithic in the time of Jesus; there were two great academies that competed with one another for pride of place. The fact is that Jesus, the teacher of Nazareth, felt an affinity to one school over the other. This explains the harsh rhetoric we find on Jesus' lips in the Gospels. Finkel explains: "The polemics with the Pharisees, the harsh 'woes' addressed to their teachers were, in fact, directed at the zealous Pharisees, the disciples of Shammai's academy. On the other hand, the Pharisaic approach adopted by the disciples of Hillel's school—their humbleness, restraint, clear argumentative reasoning and liberal stand—was close in spirit to that of the teacher of Nazareth."[12]

So, according to Finkel, the tension we find in the Gospels did not occur between Jesus and the Pharisees as a whole, but between Jesus, the disciple of the liberal Rabbi Hillel, and the overzealous disciples of the more conservative Rabbi Shammai. Thus Finkel would have us accept the idea that a correspondence existed between Jesus' previous training in a hyper-conservative Pharisaic environment and his later embrace of the more liberal teachings of the Rabbi Hillel. This seems to me to be a case of wanting to have it both ways. Once again, I must admit that Finkel's argument, while interesting and provocative, seems to have within it some glaring weak spots.

Maybe the Pharisees Had Some Genuine Theological and Political Concerns

Another possible explanation for why the Pharisees were antagonistic to Jesus is the notion that the Pharisees were genuinely concerned that his ministry endeavors smacked of heresy, if not treason. The Gospels seem to indicate that the Pharisees were especially critical of Jesus' contact with tax collectors and "sinners" (see Matthew 9:9–11; Luke 15:1–2) and with the apparently cavalier manner in which he approached the Sabbath (see Matthew 12:1–2, 9–14; Luke 13:10–17; John 9:13–16).

A case can be made for the idea that the Pharisees believed that the promise of divine deliverance for the nation depended upon the holiness of the people and that this mandated holiness before God required not only a scrupulous observance of the law of Moses as interpreted by the rabbis but also a strict separation from sinners, whether Gentile or Jewish. Therefore Jesus' refusal to uphold and advance this call to holiness and separation struck the Pharisees as not only heretical but treasonous as well. This, say some scholars, is why the Pharisees were so willing to do whatever was necessary to silence Jesus. They considered him to be a genuine threat to the spiritual and material welfare of the nation.

The problem with this perspective is that it fails to adequately account for the fierce vitriol we find in Jesus' denunciations of the Pharisees and teachers of the law. If Jesus had known, or even suspected, that there existed a goodhearted motive behind the Pharisees' antagonism to his fellowship with sinners and healing on the Sabbath, surely we would read of him having expressed his disagreement with them in a much more conciliatory manner.

Maybe the Pharisees Were Simply Jealous of Jesus' Popularity

A. T. Robertson sees the tension between Jesus and the Pharisees arising out of concerns that were much less noble on the part of the Pharisees:

> The short earthly ministry of our Lord, at most only three and a half years in length (about the duration of an average city pastorate), fairly bristles with the struggle made by the Pharisees to break the power of Christ's popularity with the people. Jesus is challenged at the very start, and is thrown on the defensive by the rabbis, who are the established and accepted religious leaders of the Jewish people. They wish no revolutionary propaganda that will interfere with their hold on the masses. They are jealous of their prerogatives, these men who "sit on Moses' seat" (Matthew 23:2).[13]

Robertson gives the impression that the Pharisees were less concerned about the spiritual and political welfare of the nation than they were the continuance of their own popularity and positions of authority. If this was indeed the case it would explain the scalding manner in which Jesus denounced the Pharisees at various times during his public ministry.

The Problem Jesus Had with the Pharisees

Have you ever wondered what it must have been like to have been on the receiving end of one of those scalding rebukes uttered by Jesus toward the Pharisees? In his last book, *My God and I: A Spiritual Memoir*, the late Lewis Smedes talks a bit about some of the eccentric personalities he studied under at Oxford University. Speaking of how some of the Oxford dons could be less than loquacious, he writes: "But, for curtness, it was hard to beat C. S. Lewis when he was present at his legendary

Socratic Club. Forget about suffering fools gladly, he did not suffer very intelligent people gladly. If someone asked him a dumb question, Lewis would snap his head off. To call him churlish would, I think, exaggerate his impatience, but only slightly; anything less than quick brilliance got short shrift from the beloved author of all those wonderful children's books."[14]

It is hard for us to think of C. S. Lewis behaving impatiently toward conversation partners. Likewise, we might like to think that Jesus never had a cross word for anyone, or that if he ever did it was only for those who made up the economic and political domination systems at work in his world: the Romans, the Herodians (Jewish supporters of King Herod), the Sadducees (priestly aristocrats who controlled the temple cultus and collaborated with Rome). But as we read the New Testament we find that Jesus did utter some harsh denunciations from time to time and that these were invariably directed at those whom the common people of his day considered to be spiritual heroes: the Pharisees and teachers of the law! Why? What was it about the Pharisees that caused Jesus to snap at them the way he did?

Any attempt to identify the main criticisms Jesus had with the program of the Pharisees must include a careful consideration of two major passages in particular. The first major passage is the fierce diatribe directed at the Pharisees by Jesus in Matthew 23:1–36.

In her book *We Are the Pharisees* Kathleen Kern focuses her attention on this passage, analyzing what Jesus has to say about the Pharisees in it. She sees Jesus beginning his invective by accusing the Pharisees of being hypocritical (23:1–3), heartless (23:4) show-offs (23:5–7). Then, according to Kern, Jesus goes on to indict the Pharisees for (1) their exclusivity (23:13); (2) the negative effect they had on their converts (23:15); (3) their use of manipulative, slippery speech (23:16–22); (4) their gnat-picking (super-scrupulous legalistic ethics) that nevertheless missed the heart of God (23:23–24); (5) their focus on pious rituals while at the same time ignoring the attitudes of greed and indulgence at work within them (23:25–26); (6) their obsession with appearing pious toward others while secretly and hypocritically harboring lawless impulses and engaging in sinful behaviors (23:27–28); and (7) their penchant for persecuting anyone who dared to disagree with them (23:29–36).[15]

The second major passage that reflects Jesus' critique of the Pharisees is the parable of the Pharisee and the tax collector found in Luke 18:9–14. In this important parable Jesus pictures the Pharisee as a prideful, arrogant, self-righteous, and judgmental prig.

Based on her read of both Luke 18:9–14 and Matthew 23:1–36, Kern summarizes Jesus' criticisms of the Pharisees as follows: they were self-righteous; they were exclusive; they were show-offs who sought prestige; they were hypocrites; they were oppressive and hardhearted toward others; they were legalistic; they were nitpickers with "tunnel vision"; and they were those who thought nothing of persecuting truly righteous people.[16]

In his book *Extreme Righteousness* Tom Hovestol creates a similar list of vices attributed to the Pharisees by Jesus. Focusing on the entirety of Jesus' interactions with the Pharisees, Hovestol sees Jesus finding fault with the Pharisees for their self-righteousness, doctrinal dogmatism, hyper-piety, traditionalism, legalism/moralism, separatism, and hypocrisy.[17]

A. T. Robertson likewise provides his readers with a comprehensive treatment of the condemnation of the Pharisees by Jesus. He sees Jesus condemning the Pharisees for no less than seven reasons: spiritual blindness (Matthew 9:12–13; 13:13–17; 15:12–20; 16:1–4; Mark 3:5; 4:12; 8:11–12; Luke 5:39; 8:10; 11:37–54; John 3:1–15; 9:39–41); formalism (Matthew 5:17–6:18; Luke 11:37–54; 18:9–14); prejudice (Matthew 11:16–19; Luke 7:29–35; John 5:39–40); traditionalism (Matthew 15:1–20; Mark 7:1–23); hypocrisy (Matthew 5:15–23; 6:2–6; 15:7–9; 16:5–12; 23:13–39; Mark 7:6–7; 8:14–21; Luke 6:37–42; 12:1–2; 13:15–17); blasphemy against the Holy Spirit

(Matthew 12:31–33; Mark 3:28–30; Luke 12:10); and the rejection of God in their rejection of him (Matthew 17:12; John 5:42–47; 7:47–49; 8:21–59; 10:25–38).[18]

The Essence of New Testament Pharisaism

Everything presented in this chapter thus far is designed to help us arrive at a fairly clear understanding of New Testament Pharisaism: those actions and attitudes which Jesus condemned in the original Pharisees and which he encouraged his followers to earnestly avoid. According to the Gospels, Jesus addressed his first followers about this on several different occasions, explicitly warning them to steer clear of the beliefs and behaviors of the scribes (teachers of the law) and the Pharisees (e.g., Matthew 16:6; Luke 12:1; 20:46–47). Judging by the manner in which the Gospels portray Jesus confronting the Pharisees, the following list of attitudes and actions may be viewed as a set of symptoms of New Testament Pharisaism. The New Testament reveals Jesus confronting the tendency of some Pharisees toward

- **Egoism** (self-righteousness and spiritual arrogance) – Some Pharisees tended to be so "confident of their own righteousness" that they looked down on everybody else (Luke 18:9–14).
- **Dogmatism / Sectarianism** – Some Pharisees tended to assume without question that their doctrinal positions were the epitome of absolute truth and that their party alone enjoyed God's approval (Luke 7:29–35; John 9:24–34).
- **Super-Spirituality / Hyper-Piety** – Some Pharisees tended to parade their piety about publicly, drawing attention to their super-scrupulous observance of religious rituals and spiritual disciplines to gain the attention and admiration of their peers (Matthew 6:1–2,5,16; 23:5–7).

- **Traditionalism / Ritualism** – Some Pharisees tended to deify human traditions, with the result that they became so overly concerned with a proper engagement in religious customs that they ended up substituting a real relationship with God with a feverous devotion to various religious rituals (Mark 7:1–13).[19]

- **Legalism / Separatism** – Some Pharisees tended to believe that a right relationship with God could be achieved and maintained by mere human effort and by isolating themselves from everyone who did not share their commitment to ritual purity (Matthew 9:10–13; Luke 15:1–32; John 5:39–40).[20]

- **Judgmentalism** – Some Pharisees tended to behave in harsh, unloving, ungracious, judgmental ways toward anyone who did not belong to their group or whose piety did not match their own (John 8:3–11; 9:13–34).

- **Pugilism** – Some Pharisees tended to believe they were doing God a service by actually persecuting those who might succeed at promoting a religious perspective that differed from their own (Matthew 23:29–34).

- **Trivialism** (spiritual myopia / tunnel vision) – Some Pharisees tended to "strain out gnats" while "swallowing camels"—that is, they tended to focus all of their attention and emotional energy on trivial issues that lacked scriptural support while ignoring those matters that, according to the Bible, mean a great deal to God (Matthew 23:23–24).

- **Formalism / Hypocrisy** – Some Pharisees tended to pose and posture—to pretend to be more spiritually mature than they really were (Matthew 23:25–28).

Given the way Jesus keeps referring to the hypocrisy of the Pharisees and the teachers of the law in his invective against them presented in Matthew 23, it is perhaps safe to say that it was the hypocrisy of many of the Pharisees, more than any other trait or tendency, that created within Jesus so much anger (and anguish) toward the group as a whole.

These, then, are the symptoms of New Testament Pharisaism. These are the actions and attitudes that Jesus confronted in the lives of at least some of the original Pharisees. *Together, these ignoble, unholy patterns of behavior constitute the reason for the bad blood that existed between Jesus and the Pharisees.* If the thesis just stated is accurate, these are the earmarks of an approach to the religious life that Jesus would have his followers (in any age) avoid at all costs.

The question we must all ask ourselves at this point is this: *To what degree are any of these problematic patterns of behavior present in our lives and our churches?* We must be careful here not to fool ourselves. In his masterful work, *Confessions,* Saint Augustine wrote: "The blindness of humanity is so great that people are actually proud of their blindness."[21] Augustine seems to be speaking here of the blinding power of conceit that issues in a profound self-deception. When I read this I think of the many passages in Matthew's Gospel in which Jesus accuses the Pharisees of being spiritually blind (see Matthew 15:14; 23:16, 17, 19, 24, 26). I am reminded also of the following exchange between Jesus and the Pharisees, recorded in John 9:39–41:

> Jesus said, "For judgment I have come into this world, so that the blind will see and those who see will become blind."
>
> Some Pharisees who were with him heard him say this and asked, "What? Are we blind too?"
>
> Jesus said, "If you were blind, you would not be guilty of sin; but now that you claim you can see, your guilt remains."

Could it be that at least some of the historical Pharisees were so self-deceived as to be blind to the presence in their lives of the actions and attitudes we have come to associate with their movement? Could it be that a Pharisaical approach to religion is a rather natural inclination of the fallible human heart? Just how easy is it to become Pharisaical in one's approach toward religion and not realize it? Could it be that we, ourselves, without recognizing it, are guilty of some of these same problematic patterns of behavior? Is there such a thing as "Christian Pharisaism"?

In the next chapter we will consider the highly ironic (and tragic) possibility that too many evangelical congregations are indeed earmarked by more than a few of the same Pharisaical attitudes and actions that Jesus so earnestly called for his followers to steer clear of. But my intention in these pages is not to engage in a witch hunt, nor even to empower some believers to cluck their tongues and shake their heads at the behavior of others. We must continually keep in mind the allure of Pharisaism and our potential for self-deception. *We must be careful not to behave as Pharisees even as we seek to defeat Pharisaism in our churches!*

Notes

1. Lucinda Vardey, *Mother Teresa: A Simple Path* (New York: Ballantine Books, 1995), 185.
2. For example, see Christopher Hitchens, *The Missionary Position: Mother Teresa in Theory and Practice* (London: Verso, 1988).
3. For a fairly concise survey of how each of the four Gospels portrays the Pharisees as the enemies of Jesus see Kathleen Kern, *We Are the Pharisees* (Scottdale, PA: Herald Press, 1995), 32–53. For an even more thorough analysis see Günter Stemberger, *Jewish Contemporaries of Jesus: Pharisees, Sadducees, Essenes* (Minneapolis: Fortress Press, 1995), 21–38, and Donald Riddle, *Jesus and the Pharisees* (Chicago: University of Chicago Press, 1928), 8–54.
4. For example, see Riddle, *Jesus and the Pharisees*, 169, and K. Kohler, "Pharisees," *Jewish Encyclopedia*, vol. 9 (1925), 661–66, cited in A. T. Robertson, *The Pharisees and Jesus* (London: Duckworth and Company, 1920), 4. Rabbi K. Kohler insists, "No true estimate of the character of the Pharisees can be obtained from the New Testament writings, which take a polemical attitude toward them."
5. For example, see E. P. Sanders, *Jesus and Judaism* (London: SCM Press, Ltd., 1985), 264–65.
6. For example, see Kern, *We Are the Pharisees*, 34–35; Jacob Neusner, *From Politics to Piety* (Englewood Cliffs, NJ: Prentice-Hall, Inc., 1973), 68; and Anthony

Saldarini, *Pharisees, Scribes and Sadducees in Palestinian Society* (Wilmington, DE: Michael Glazier, Inc., 1988), 144,158.

7. For example, see Robertson, *The Pharisees and Jesus*, 56–63.

8. Robertson, *The Pharisees and Jesus*, 66–109.

9. Asher Finkel, *The Pharisees and the Teacher of Nazareth* (Leiden, Holland: E. J. Brill, 1964), 132–33.

10. Ibid., 133–34.

11. Ibid., 134.

12. Ibid., 134.

13. Robertson, *The Pharisees and Jesus*, 1.

14. Lewis Smedes, *My God and I: A Spiritual Memoir* (Grand Rapids: Eerdmans, 2003), 88.

15. Kern, *We Are the Pharisees*, 59–76.

16. Ibid., 80–81.

17. Tom Hovestol, *Extreme Righteousness: Seeing Ourselves in the Pharisees* (Chicago: Moody, 1997), 47–176.

18. Robertson, *The Pharisees and Jesus*, 110–59.

19. Most evangelicals make a distinction between "ritualism" and a healthy, necessary engagement in Christian rituals (especially baptism and communion).

20. While legalism is a key attribute of New Testament Pharisaism, and while this book deals specifically with the problem of Pharisaism in evangelical churches, I am aware that another impediment to authentic Christian discipleship occurs when church members adopt an antinomian approach to their faith. Christian antinomianism entails the belief that because of grace it does not matter how the believer lives his or her life; as long as one has "prayed the prayer," he or she is "in," has a place reserved in heaven, and need not be concerned about any kind of interactive relationship between the experiences of salvation and sanctification. As one reads the rest of the New Testament and the writings of the earliest church fathers, it becomes apparent that as the apostles moved out into the Gentile world the problem of religious legalism was joined by the problem of antinomianism. This is not the place to discuss the philosophical roots of antinomianism, nor to elaborate on the emergence of Christian Gnosticism, a heretical version of the Christian faith which seems to have promoted antinomianism among some of its adherents. The reader should simply realize that I am very much aware of the problem of antinomianism (also known as "cheap grace") and that my exposition of the Sermon on the Mount in chapters six to eight of this book will make a strong argument against it.

In sum, Jesus had been accused by the Pharisees of being soft on sin and having a low view of the law. Jesus spiked that idea in no uncertain terms while at the same time encouraging his disciples to avoid adopting an approach to ethics that is mindlessly legalistic, traditionalistic, and ultimately hypocritical. The phenomenon of antinomianism in the life of the early church and in our contemporary era in no way undercuts my argument that Jesus used the Pharisees as an anti-model of Christian discipleship. Not only did the early Christians continue to struggle with legalism (cf. Acts 15; Romans 14; Galatians 3–5; Ephesians 2; Colossians 2; 1 Timothy 4) even as they militated against antinomianism (cf. Romans 3:5–8; 6:1–23; 8:1–14; 1 Corinthians 5; 6:12–20; 10; Galatians 5:16–26; Ephesians 4:17—5:21; Colossians 3:1–11; 1 Thessalonians 4:1–12; 2 Timothy 3:1–9; 2 Peter 2–3; Jude; 1 John (the whole letter!); Revelation 2–3; 22:12–15), but the irony is that one can be Pharisaical about his or her commitment to antinomianism! Even antinomian church members can be dogmatic, judgmental, separatistic, pugilistic, and super-spiritual in the way they relate to those who are not as "enlightened" as they are!

21. Augustine, *Confessions* (New York: Oxford University Press, USA, 1998), 38.

3

AN INCONVENIENT TRUTH

T o what degree is the New Testament Pharisaism described in the previous chapter present in contemporary evangelicalism? Philip Yancey is well known for his prophetic calls for the evangelical church to recognize and deal with the legalism and judgmentalism he sees within it. In his book *What's So Amazing About Grace?* Yancey writes:

> Mark Twain used to talk about people who were "good in the worst sense of the word," a phrase that, for many, captures the reputation of Christians today. Recently I have been asking a question of strangers—for example, seatmates on an airplane—when I strike up a conversation. "When I say the words 'evangelical Christian' what comes to mind?" In reply, mostly I hear political descriptions: of strident pro-life activists, or gay-rights opponents, or proposals for censoring the Internet. I hear references to the Moral Majority, an organization disbanded years ago. Not once—*not once*—have I heard a description redolent of grace. Apparently that is not the aroma Christians give off in the world.[1]

Is it true that many evangelical churches possess pockets of Pharisaism in their midst? If so, what is the effect of this "infection" upon the life and ministry of the local church? What is it that causes many Christians to adopt the very same actions and attitudes that Christ himself protested against in such a fierce, forthright manner? The goal of this chapter is to help us evangelicals come to terms with a truly inconvenient, embarrassing truth: Pharisaism is alive and well in too many of our churches.

The Connection between Pharisaism and Historic Christian Fundamentalism

A careful reading of just about any book chronicling the history of American evangelicalism will serve to underscore two very important points: (1) historic Christian fundamentalism, with its tendency toward dogmatism, separatism, pugilism, legalism, etc., is strikingly reminiscent of the New Testament Pharisaism described in the previous chapter; and (2) despite its attempt to reform its fundamentalist roots, the new evangelicalism that emerged in the mid-twentieth century still possesses some of these fundamentalist/Pharisaical traits. So provocative are these statements that some explanation is in order.

Though some scholars suggest that the foundations of evangelicalism are to be found in the life and thought of the earliest Christians,[2] most church historians trace the roots of what I would call "classic evangelicalism" only as far back as the Protestant Reformation.[3] At the risk of greatly oversimplifying things, allow me to say that the "classic evangelicalism" which emerged as a result of the Protestant Reformation was a multitraditional renewal movement[4] that focused on four key commitments: (1) the notion of a "new birth" experience that was to culminate in a personal, life-altering relationship with Jesus Christ, God's Son and Savior of the world; (2) a conviction that the Bible, as the divinely inspired Word of God, should function as the authoritative guide for Christian faith and practice; (3) a commitment to spread the good news concerning Jesus Christ via the preaching of the gospel and acts of mercy directed at the poor; and (4) a dedication to engage in those spiritual disciplines necessary to maintain one's passionate devotion to Christ and his cause (Bible study, prayer, worship, fellowship, etc.).[5]

Risking further oversimplification, I want to go on to describe the movement known as "theological liberalism" as an attempt by some Christians in Europe and America from the late eighteenth century to the present to accommodate the Christian faith to (a) the emerging findings of natural science (Darwinism), psychology (Freudianism), and economics (Marxism); and (b) an aggressive form of biblical criticism rooted in an unquestioned commitment to the idea that miracles simply do not happen. As a result, theologically liberal scholars came to the conclusion that the Bible is not the divinely inspired "Word of God" but rather a human book that, at best, might function as "an ethical guidebook only."[6] The bottom line is that theological liberalism essentially rejected the four commitments that I am suggesting lie at the heart of classic evangelicalism.

In turn, "Christian fundamentalism" can be perceived as a way some conservative Christians have responded to the phenomenon of theological liberalism. Slowly but surely, the liberal version of Christianity began to take hold in America, the movement coming to be known simply as "modernism." Positions of leadership and influence within Protestant denominations and universities became occupied by adherents of modernism. Whereas some conservative Protestants simply gave up and converted to the modernist version of the Christian faith, there were others who decided to fight back against the tide of theological liberalism.

Christian Smith, an expert in the sociology of religion, writes: "In the first two decades of the twentieth century, this group of Protestant church leaders mobilized a coalition of conservatives to combat modernism in the churches and in the schools. Their two strategic goals were, in the North, to wrest control of the major Protestant—particularly Baptist and Presbyterian—denominations from liberal forces and, in the South, to make illegal the teaching of Darwinian evolution in public schools. In time, these fighting conservatives were labeled 'fundamentalists'—a term coined from a booklet series they published between 1910 and 1915 called *The Fundamentals*—and their movement, 'fundamentalism.'"[7]

Many church historians have offered descriptions of the fundamentalist movement that are reminiscent of what we have come to know as New Testament Pharisaism. For example, in his book *Church History in Plain Language*, Bruce Shelley states that just after the Depression era most Americans thought of fundamentalists as "closedminded, ignorant, belligerent and separatistic."[8] Likewise, in his book *Fundamentalism and American Culture*, George Marsden provides a fairly brief description of early fundamentalism in which a variation of the word "militant" shows up no less than three times: "During this period of its national prominence in the 1920s, fundamentalism is best defined in terms of these concerns. Briefly, it was militantly anti-modernist Protestant evangelicalism. Fundamentalists were evangelical Christians, close to the traditions of the dominant American revivalist establishment of the nineteenth century, who in the twentieth century militantly opposed both modernism in theology and the cultural changes that modernism endorsed. Militant opposition to modernism was what most clearly set off fundamentalism from a number of closely related traditions."[9]

Apparently Marsden conceives of fundamentalism as a militant, pugilistic movement. And in another work Marsden refers not only to the pugilism of the fundamentalists but to their penchant for *separation* as well.[10]

Indeed, history tells us that the fundamentalists, like the ancient Pharisees, became convinced that loyalty to God mandated the practice of separation. Christian Smith makes the observation that by the 1940s the concept of "double separation became the litmus test of purity: a good fundamentalist had to separate not only from modernists and liberals but also from any otherwise-orthodox believer who refused to break all ties with liberals."[11] This meant that any conservative Christian who was reluctant to "come out" or separate completely from any and all association with moderates or liberals could be severely castigated by his or her fundamentalist peers. Considered together, these various citations from the literature devoted to fundamentalism seem to suggest that, *despite their good intentions, a dogmatic, exclusivist, militant mentality was at the heart of historic Christian fundamentalism.*

Going further, in his description of how the separatist strategy of the early fundamentalists affected their ethics, Smith makes reference to the essentially moralistic and legalistic approach to sanctification that came to earmark fundamentalism. He writes:

> The fundamentalist subculture's need to establish and maintain strong identity boundaries prompted the creation of clear behavioral contrasts with "worldliness," defined primarily against progressive cultural expressions of the day. The traditional Christian virtues of charity, humility, patience, and so on were displaced by lists of specific, behavioral rules. What separated God's faithful remnant from the degenerate—besides doctrinal purity, of course—became simply that true Christians did not dance, smoke cigarettes, chew tobacco, drink alcohol, gamble, wear makeup, "bob" their hair, attend the theater, play billiards or cards, or wear immodest clothing. With these subcultural norms, a powerful legalism permeated fundamentalism that maintained its visible separation from the secular world through rigid, self-enforcing, behavioral social control.[12]

In a similar vein, historian Mark Noll makes reference to the "cultural shibboleths that had come to define fundamentalism by the late 1940s."[13] Noll indicates that a partial list of the activities prohibited by the fundamentalists included drinking wine and beer and attending the cinema.[14]

These citations serve to illustrate a very real tendency within fundamentalism to define Christians by what they do not do rather than by what they do. An approach to ethics that focuses on obeying rules rather than the cultivation of virtues certainly seems to incline toward a legalistic approach to sanctification that is quite reminiscent of the ancient Pharisees. Overall, it would indeed appear that the literature devoted to the origin and development of Protestant fundamentalism demonstrates rather conclusively that certain aspects of the Pharisaism of the New Testament are all too present in it. Then again, it is one thing to argue that fundamentalist Christianity tends toward Pharisaism; it is another to conclude that Pharisaism is alive and well in contemporary evangelicalism as a whole.

The Connection between Fundamentalism and Contemporary Evangelicalism

In the 1940s a group of moderate, mostly young evangelicals began to "formulate a critique of their own fundamentalist subculture and a vision for its transformation."[15] This group, which included Billy Graham, was thoroughly committed to a theologically conservative version of the Christian faith and an enthusiastic proclamation of the gospel of salvation as presented in the New Testament. They had also become convinced, however, that "the factionalistic, separatist, judgmental character of fundamentalism itself had become an insurmountable impediment to effectively evangelizing American society for Christ."[16] Therefore, this cadre of conservative Christian leaders took it upon themselves to reform fundamentalism or, to put it differently, to rediscover a form of evangelicalism that on the one hand would be true to the orthodox doctrines of the church but on the other hand would also be intellectually credible and culturally engaged. The movement these men launched has come to be known as the "new evangelicalism."

But here is the problem: the reality seems to be that, despite all good intentions, the new evangelicalism has not managed to free itself completely from many of the traits of Pharisaism that were evident in historic Christian fundamentalism. What is more, this connection between Pharisaism, fundamentalism, and evangelicalism is not simply a historical matter. Many books designed to treat the more recent state of evangelicalism will, in one way or another, make the same connection.

An older example of this type of book is the late Robert Webber's *Common Roots: A Call to Evangelical Maturity*, written in 1978. In this book Webber offered a fairly weighty critique of the new evangelicalism that, perhaps inadvertently, served to indicate the presence of Pharisaism in its midst. Two issues were of particular concern to Webber. The first is evangelicalism's tendency toward sectarianism. "It is a recognizable fact that evangelical Christianity is characterized by a number of divisions: Fundamentalists vs. neo-evangelicals; conservatives vs. progressives; noncharismatics vs. charismatics; covenantalists vs. dispensationalists; Arminians vs. Calvinists; premillennialists vs. amillennialists, to name a few."[17] Webber went on to explain, "Sectarianism is the spirit which regards its own position as the right one. This attitude has kept some evangelicals from associating with other Christians and, thus, from the contribution they could make toward the fullness of evangelical Christianity."[18]

Does this reference to sectarian separatism not seem eerily reminiscent of the interparty infighting we know occurred between the various sects of historic Jewish Pharisaism?

The second issue which concerned Webber is evangelicalism's tendency toward a moral rigorism that ultimately leads to a loveless judgmentalism. Regarding this concern, Webber wrote, "Some of us are characterized by a moral rigorism which demands too much of the church, acting as though the church in its earthly pilgrimage can attain holiness. This attitude is evident in the inflexibility of the contemporary rigorists who, having set high personal standards for church members, act with intolerance and a lack of love toward those who fail to meet these standards."[19]

Obviously, a congregation's inflexibility, intolerance, and lack of love toward those who fail to meet their prescribed standards for holiness is evocative of the way the ancient Pharisees looked down their noses at anyone who did not scrupulously observe the traditions they considered so important.

Though Webber's critique of the new evangelicalism is now thirty years old,[20] it has become increasingly clear that a growing number of conservative theologians and church leaders are convinced that his concerns are still valid. These more recent treatments of contemporary evangelical theology and practice seem to suggest that the old fundamentalism is in some ways still operative in the new evangelicalism. For example, Joel Carpenter's *Revive Us Again: The Reawakening of American Fundamentalism* (1997) puts forward the perspective that throughout the twentieth century American evangelicalism has been influenced to a large degree by the ethos created by historic Christian fundamentalism.[21] Christian Smith, in *American Evangelicalism: Embattled and Thriving* (1998), reminds his readers that the break between the new evangelicalism and the old fundamentalism was neither quick and easy nor absolute and total.[22] In *Renewing the Center* (2000), the late Stanley Grenz made the argument that, especially in the area of theology, many of the impulses of the old fundamentalism remain at work in the new evangelicalism.[23] Richard Mouw's *The Smell of Sawdust* (2000) honestly acknowledges that one of the "three common defects" of evangelicalism is a "separatistic spirit."[24] Yet another work by Robert Webber, *The Younger Evangelicals* (2002), makes the observation that due to concerns over "how Christianity is presented and practiced in a twenty-first-century culture" (by traditional evangelicals) an even *newer* evangelicalism is currently emerging among young adults.[25] Perhaps the currently authoritative work on the topic, *Emerging Churches* (2005), written by Eddie Gibbs and Ryan Bolger, indicates that a significant number of emerging church leaders report having been profoundly disappointed, frustrated, and/or wounded by the fundamentalist attitudes and practices they experienced within traditional evangelical churches.[26] In his controversial book *Reformed and Always Reforming* (2007), Roger Olson forthrightly asserts that the advocacy of many for a "postconservative" evangelical theology is generated by a desire to "continue the reform of fundamentalism" begun but not completed by traditional evangelicals.[27] Finally, Dan Kimball's *They Like Jesus but Not the Church: Insights from Emerging Generations* (2007) makes the point, over and over again, that the biggest problem most young adults have with traditional evangelical churches is the fundamentalist attitudes and behaviors they associate with them.[28]

Believe it or not, the long list presented above could easily be expanded. The point I am making here is that the connection between Pharisaism, fundamentalism, and evangelicalism is readily apparent in various books that chronicle the history of evangelicalism and/or provide contemporary critiques of it. In addition, over the years a smaller number of books have been published which have the specific aim of encouraging evangelical readers to recognize the presence of Pharisaism in their own lives and churches. For example, the title of John Fischer's *12 Steps for the Recovering Pharisee (like me)* makes it fairly obvious that Fischer is of the opinion that contemporary evangelicals can be tempted to embrace a Pharisaical approach to the Christian life. The blurb on the back cover of this popular book begins with these words: "We have met the Pharisees, and they are . . . us."[29]

In her book *We Are the Pharisees,* Kathleen Kern includes a chapter entitled "How Jesus' Critique of the Pharisees Applies to Us." In this chapter Kern comments on the manner in which such Pharisaical traits as self-righteousness, exclusivity, showing off, hypocrisy, hardheartedness, legalism, "gnat-picking," and persecuting prophets manifest themselves in modern evangelical churches.[30]

Something similar can be found in Tom Hovestol's *Extreme Righteousness: Seeing Ourselves in the Pharisees*. After underscoring the fact (several times) that Pharisaism is indeed alive and well in the contemporary evangelical church,[31] and after going so far as to suggest that certain aspects of evangelicalism actually create a fertile soil within which Pharisaism is able to flourish,[32] Hovestol goes on to demonstrate how that self-righteousness, dogmatism, public piety, traditionalism, legalism, separatism, and hypocrisy are all too present in the lives of many evangelical church members.[33]

Finally, in the growing number of books that attempt to offer an apologetic to skeptical non-Christians or "post-Christians," it is not uncommon to find passages that honestly and humbly acknowledge the presence of fundamentalism/Pharisaism in traditional evangelical churches.[34]

Once again, the list of references could go on and on. Hopefully the literary survey just presented is sufficient to make the case that, sadly, Pharisaism is alive and well in many contemporary evangelical churches. The inconvenient truth is that there is an "elephant in the room" that we evangelicals really do need to deal with.

The Negative Effects of Pharisaism upon Evangelical Communities

In her book *Walking on Water: Reflections on Faith and Art*, Madeleine L'Engle comments on how, having lost her way, the presence of Pharisaism very nearly kept her from coming home to her Christian faith. She writes:

In the world of literature, Christianity is no longer respectable. When I am referred to in an article or a review as a "practicing Christian" it is seldom meant as a compliment, at least not in the secular press. It is perfectly all right, according to literary critics, to be Jewish or Buddhist or Sufi or a pre-Christian druid. It is not all right to be a Christian. And if we ask why, the answer is a sad one: Christians have given Christianity a bad name. They have let their lights flicker and grow dim. They have confused piosity with piety, smugness with joy. During the difficult period in which I was struggling through my "cloud of unknowing" to return to the church and to Christ, the largest thing which deterred me was that I saw so little clear light coming from those Christians who sought to bring me back to the fold.[35]

This poignant quote illustrates how damaging a spirit of Pharisaism can be to the life and ministry of a local church.

Theologian Ray Anderson conceives of a sacrament as a sort of tangible expression of the grace of God, a redemptive point of connection between a holy God and sinful human beings. While Anderson describes Jesus as the "primary sacrament," the primary point of connection between God and humanity,[36] he goes on to speak of the church as the continuing sacramental presence of Jesus Christ. He writes, "The church as the body of Christ now lives between the cross and the return of Christ (*parousia*). The original sacramental relation of God to humanity through Jesus Christ is now represented through the enactment of the life of the church itself."[37]

What this means is that the local church, as a tangible expression of the resurrected and ascended Christ (i.e., his body), is intended by God to function as a point of connection (sacrament) between sinful, hurting people and Jesus Christ, who in turn functions as the primary point of connection (sacrament) between them and God. In other words, *the life of a local church is crucial to God's desire to reconcile the world to himself through Christ* (2 Corinthians 5:18–19). But this can only happen, of course, to the degree that a local church is doing a good job of representing Jesus to its world.

It is in this vein that missiologist Charles Van Engen speaks of the local church as a place where the gospel of Christ can be contextualized. He writes, "The Church is a marvelous, mysterious creation of God that takes concrete shape in the lives of the disciples of Jesus as they gather in local congregations and seek to contextualize the gospel in their time and place."[38] Likewise, the multiple authors of the book *Missional Church* define the church as "God's sent people" and argue that the great challenge today is for congregations to move from being churches that support world missions to being *missional* churches—communities of believers that succeed at bringing the good news concerning the kingdom of God to bear against the real ministry needs present in their respective locales.[39]

All of these sources speak of the need for local churches to commit themselves to becoming radically incarnational, hospitable, and winsome in the manner in which they represent the kingdom of God to their respective ministry contexts. This is ultimately what the local church should be about. The problem is that our Pharisaism keeps getting in the way!

In his book *unChristian: What a New Generation Really Thinks about Christianity . . . and Why It Matters,* Barna Group researcher David Kinnaman boldly states that "Christianity has an image problem."[40] Using the data gleaned from a major research project, Kinnaman offers the following sobering observations:

> Our research shows that many of those outside of Christianity, especially younger adults, have little trust in the Christian faith,

and esteem for the lifestyle of Christ followers is quickly fading among outsiders. They admit their emotional and intellectual barriers go up when they are around Christians, and they reject Jesus because they feel rejected by Christians.[41]

Painful encounters with the faith also have a strong influence on what a person thinks of Christianity. In fact, we discovered that one-fifth of all outsiders, regardless of age, admitted they "have had a bad experience in a church or with a Christian that gave them a negative image of Jesus Christ." This represents nearly fifty million adult residents of this country—including about nine million young outsiders—who admit they have significant emotional or spiritual baggage from past experiences with so-called Christ followers. Church leaders are not unaware of this issue. Among pastors of Protestant churches, three-quarters said they often encounter people whose negative experiences create major barriers to their openness to Jesus.[42]

Three out of every ten young outsiders said they have undergone negative experiences in churches and with Christians. Such hurtful experiences are part of the stories of nearly one out of every two young people who are atheists, agnostics, or some other faith.[43]

Kinnaman goes on to stipulate that, of Americans aged sixteen to twenty-nine:

- 87 percent view present-day Christianity as "judgmental";
- 85 percent view present-day Christianity as "hypocritical";
- 70 percent view present-day Christianity as insensitive to others;
- 72 percent view present-day Christianity as out of touch with reality.[44]

Given these statistics, we have no other choice but to acknowledge the possibility that the presence of Pharisaism in too many traditional evangelical churches is wreaking havoc on their ability to function as winsome re-presentations of Christ to their respective communities.

To be more specific, here is a list of some of the negative effects that I am convinced Christian Pharisaism can have upon a local community of evangelical believers:

- The *dogmatism* of the Christian Pharisee produces an unteachable spirit, which in turn makes it difficult for the church member to become an authentic disciple:

- The *egoism* (self-righteousness and spiritual arrogance) of the Christian Pharisee encourages a spirit of pride instead of humility and works against an observance of the "one another" commands scattered throughout the New Testament.

- The *sectarianism* and *pugilism* of the Christian Pharisee causes divisions and hurt feelings within the church family both locally and globally.

- The *super-spirituality* of the Christian Pharisee strikes the still unconverted as either weird or a pathetic attempt to arrest attention and attract admirers.

- The *traditionalism* of the Christian Pharisee makes him or her unwilling to support new and perhaps better approaches to ministry.

- The *formalism* of the Christian Pharisee creates an inordinate concern that ecclesiastical formalities be carried out even when this hinders missional ministry.

- The *ritualism* of the Christian Pharisee can lead eventually to a portrayal of the Christian life as something stale, stagnant, predictable, and boring rather than intimate, interactive, unpredictable, and exciting.

- The *legalism* of the Christian Pharisee ironically produces spiritual insecurity rather than peace and joy and spiritual fatigue rather than a divine sense of empowerment.
- The *separatism* of the Christian Pharisee hinders ministry taking place outside the four walls of the church and produces an unhealthy ghetto mentality within them.
- The *judgmentalism* of the Christian Pharisee does anything but reflect the grace of God to the sinful, hurting people the church should be trying to impact.
- The *spiritual myopia* of the Christian Pharisee causes him or her to engage in gift and ministry projection, to argue about indifferent matters while hurting people are left unreached, and to continually miss the big picture of what the church should really be about.
- The *hypocrisy* of the Christian Pharisee causes the very people the church is trying to reach to want to avoid organized religion like the plague!

Philip Yancey writes:

In his book *Guilt and Grace,* the Swiss doctor Paul Tournier, a man of deep personal faith, admits, "I cannot study this very serious problem of guilt with you without raising the very obvious and tragic fact that religion—my own as well as that of all believers—can crush instead of liberate."

Tournier tells of patients who come to him: a man harboring guilt over an old sin, a woman who cannot put out of her mind an abortion that took place ten years before. What the patients truly seek, says Tournier, is grace. Yet in some churches they encounter shame, the threat of punishment, and a sense of judgment. In short, when they look in the church for grace, they often find ungrace.[45]

Tournier's comments serve to underscore the truth that there is a huge difference between authentic Christianity and mere "churchianity." Authentic Christianity is winsome and attractive; mere churchianity is irksome and off-putting. It is no wonder that so many young Christians, sick of the nominalism present in many evangelical churches, have given up on the local church. *The Pharisee-laden congregation will merely play at being a church, and it will succeed only at pushing people (including its own youthful members) away from the very gospel it is supposed to bear witness to.* Christian Pharisaism is not something that can or should be winked at. Jesus took it seriously; so should we.

Some Possible Root Causes of Christian Pharisaism

Before we can hope to defeat the Pharisaism that infects our churches we need to understand how it gets there. The very idea of a Christian who is also a Pharisee drips with irony. How ironic that the followers of Christ would embrace the traits and tendencies of those whom Jesus so vigorously denounced! What causes this phenomenon? What causes goodhearted people who, presumably, want to be pleasing to God and get the Christian life right to adopt a Pharisaical approach to their walk with Christ?

The basic suggestion of Kathleen Kern, presented in her book *We Are the Pharisees,* is that all Pharisees, whether Christian or Jewish, are simply folks who feel strongly about their beliefs, who are intensely concerned about pleasing God, and who become so caught up in the details of their religious life that they "forget or ignore the real presence of God in their midst."[46]

Tom Hovestol, in *Extreme Righteousness: Seeing Ourselves in the Pharisees,* delves a bit deeper into the issue. As he recounts his own spiritual journey, seeking to identify those formative forces that caused him to drift toward a Pharisaical version of Christianity, he comes to the conclusion that there are aspects of the evangelical subculture that actually serve to instill into the lives of its adherents some of the traits and tendencies of New Testament Pharisaism. For instance, coming to Christ on the coattails of one's parents can produce a feeling of self-righteousness; growing up experiencing little else but personal devotions, church services, and fellowship meetings can produce a sense of isolation and alienation from the surrounding culture; constantly being reminded of what Christians do and don't do can produce a legalistic mindset; recognizing that the key to making one's parents proud is to achieve, conform, and "play by the rules" can reinforce the idea that acceptance is based solidly on performance. It is these formative forces, suggests Hovestol, that cause evangelical church-goers to become Pharisees.[47]

In *12 Steps for the Recovering Pharisee (like me)*, John Fischer's focus is mainly on the Pharisaical tendency toward judgmentalism. His supposition seems to be that Christians behave in a Pharisaical manner essentially because (a) it helps them feel better about themselves; and (b) it provides a sense of clarity (and control) about who belongs to God and who does not.[48]

Similarly, in his book *Those Pharisees*, William Coleman speculates that the root cause of Pharisaism may be a deep-seated fear of offending God.[49] Coleman also refers to the work of psychologist Erich Fromm, who essentially accuses all Christians of being afraid of the freedom to make really important decisions for themselves. According to Fromm, Pharisaical believers take this fear of freedom to the extreme. They abhor the idea that they are free and responsible to make any kind of decision on their own. They crave the psychological security found in a rigid, unambiguous set of rules and rituals. Their sense of certainty is enhanced if they can successfully prescribe this approach to life for everyone around them. It is out of a psychological need for security that they are driven toward a legalistic approach to religious faith, and they feel compelled to foist this legalism on others.

I wonder if the true cause of Pharisaism might rest somewhere in between all the theories just surveyed. *My thesis is that the root cause of Pharisaism is a fear-based craving for spiritual certainty: that is, a psychological safety produced by a sense of certainty regarding spiritual matters (in particular, our status before God).*

In chapter one of this book I suggested that the main motivation of the original Pharisees was to achieve a sense of spiritual certainty. They wanted to be as certain as possible that they were clean before God and were included in his chosen people. I believe it is possible for Christian church members to crave the same thing. I am suggesting that *it is a craving for a psychological safety based on spiritual certitude* that produces within the human heart a legalistic perfectionism that, in turn, produces all the other traits and tendencies of New Testament Pharisaism.

Initial support for this thesis can be found in the well-known story of Martin Luther. In the following quote Luther describes his Christian experience prior to his learning how to entrust his soul to God's mercy and grace:

> Although I lived a blameless life as a monk, I felt that I was a sinner with an uneasy conscience before God. I also could not believe that I had pleased him with my works. Far from loving that righteous God who punished sinners, I actually loathed him. I was a good monk, and kept my order so strictly that if ever a monk could get to heaven by monastic discipline, I was that monk. All my companions in the monastery would confirm this. . . . And yet my conscience would not give me *certainty* [italics added], but I always doubted and said, "You didn't do that right. You weren't contrite enough. You left that out of your confession."[50]

We see that the extreme legalistic perfectionism that tormented Luther prior to his discovery of "justification by faith" derived from his intense desire to be *certain* about his status before God. It was Luther's craving for a sense of spiritual certainty (psychological safety before God), evidently, that drove him at this point in his life toward an essentially Pharisaical approach to the Christian life.

Further support for my thesis can be found in a very interesting work by Margaret G. Alter entitled *Resurrection Psychology: An Understanding of Human Personality Based on the Life and Teachings of Jesus.* According to Alter, many first-century Jews became convinced that the Roman occupation they were forced to endure was an act of divine discipline. It was in order to avoid another outpouring of judgment that some of these Jews—the Pharisees—made a strong commitment to forge out a radical degree of holiness. Thus the Pharisees' meticulous conformity to law became, ironically, not an act of humble obedience but rather a method of seeking control (of themselves, of others, and of God) and a bid for ultimate safety.[51]

Sadly, many modern Christians essentially do the same thing. The compulsive, perfectionistic manner in which many modern Christians approach everything in their lives, including their walk with Christ, is actually a method for seeking control and a bid for ultimate safety in a world filled with frightening ambiguities. Alter explains: "If, in fact, we have nailed down a perfect code to be followed in detail, we do not need to interact with the God of freedom. Indeed, if we possess a code to which we can cling, we embrace an illusion of safety: we know good and evil; we have become 'like God' (Genesis 3)."[52] Alter goes on: "How does this perfectionistic human impulse happen? . . . The longing and anxiety we observe in perfectionistic striving is built into human development and is essentially a painful human longing to be completely safe."[53]

As Alter suggests, the problem with this convoluted attempt to achieve spiritual certainty (psychological safety before God) is that it can actually constitute a form of idolatry. As such, it can lead people away from, rather than toward, a genuine experience of the God who cannot be controlled by any set of rules and rituals. This might explain why Jesus was so vitriolic in his polemic against the Pharisees. He was reacting to what he knew to be a hypocritical, self-serving, idolatrous perversion of the law, which makes real relationship with God impossible. According to Alter, it was their subtle engagement in idolatry that caused Jesus to upbraid the Pharisees with actual anger in his voice.[54]

This might also explain the logic of Jesus' teaching ministry. In a chapter entitled "The Danger of Certainty," Alter asserts, correctly I think, that Jesus was in the habit of continually surprising his hearers with unexpected teachings that served to disrupt their cultural norms and deny the many certainties (rules and rituals) they were using to make themselves feel safe and secure even though they lacked a personal relationship with God. Thus, says Alter, the key to overcoming a compulsive, perfectionistic, fear-based, certitude-craving, legalism-producing, Pharisaical approach to life is to have one's "idolatrous certainties unseated while at the same time coming to recognize that a compassionate God is at the center of the universe."[55]

Alter is not alone in thinking that the root cause of Pharisaism is a desperate quest for spiritual certitude that is ultimately at odds with the New Testament's call for Christ's followers simply to entrust their souls to a God of mercy and grace, learning to live with some spiritual ambiguities in the process. Ray Anderson used to remind his Fuller Seminary students that "A little ambiguity never hurt anyone."[56] As I recall, this was Ray's way of encouraging those of us who studied theology with him to avoid becoming overly dogmatic and arrogant in our doctrinal formulations, always remembering that our present knowledge of God will be "in part," obtained, as it were, "through a glass, darkly" (1 Corinthians 13:12 KJV).

And yet, the saying goes "A *little* ambiguity never hurt anyone." We are not talking here about an embrace of epistemological nihilism—the idea that we cannot possess *any* accurate knowledge at all of God and spiritual truth (see 2 Corinthians 4:6; 10:5; Ephesians 4:13; Colossians 1:10; 2 Peter 1:2–3,8). Nor am I suggesting that there are no core doctrines that lie at the heart of the Christian faith (i.e., Christ's deity and bodily resurrection) which must continually be contended for over against blatantly false teaching (see 1 Timothy 4:16; 6:20–21; 2 Timothy 1:13–14; 4:2–3; Titus 2:1; 1 John 2:24–27; 2 John 7–11; Jude 3–4). That said, could it nevertheless be true that God allows *some* ambiguities to exist in the Christian life in order to confound the human heart's natural inclination to reduce spirituality to nothing but a predictable, controllable set of rules, rituals, traditions, and propositions? Could it be that an authentic, intimate relationship with God in this life actually requires that we learn to exercise a reasonable but still raw trust in his goodness, bigness, and dependability in the face of some purposeful ambiguities? Finally, could it be that this, at least in part, is what motivated Paul to speak so often of the need for Christ's followers to walk by faith (rather than by sight) and to be led by the Spirit (rather than by the flesh's ability to observe the works of the law)?

If the thesis being advanced in these pages is correct, the ultimate antidote for Pharisaism does indeed require that we have our "idolatrous certainties unseated while at the same time coming to recognize that a compassionate God is at the center of the universe." In the chapters that make up part two of this book, I will attempt to demonstrate that this is precisely what we find Jesus doing in his disciple-making ministry (especially in the Sermon on the Mount). And, yes, while in the process of helping his followers gain a breathtaking view of God that would free them from the fear-based bondage of a compulsive, perfectionistic legalism, Jesus would frequently point to the Pharisees as negative examples of what it means to be in the right with God.

Inconvenient or not, the truth is that Pharisaism is alive and well in too many evangelical congregations. If we want to see our churches become truly healthy and effective at representing Christ to the world, we simply must do our best to recover Jesus' method of making disciples.

Notes

1. Philip Yancey, *What's So Amazing About Grace?* (Grand Rapids: Zondervan, 1997), 31.
2. For example, see Robert Webber, *Common Roots: A Call to Evangelical Maturity* (Grand Rapids: Zondervan, 1978).
3. For example, see Earle E. Cairns, *Christianity Through the Centuries*, 3rd ed. (Grand Rapids: Zondervan, 1954), 478.
4. More precisely, the movement we know as "classic evangelicalism" emerged from several post-Reformation renewal movements: German Pietism, English Puritanism, Wesleyan Methodism, Anglican Evangelicalism, English Nonconformism, and American Revivalism. See Mark Noll, *American Evangelical Christianity: An Introduction* (Malden, MA: Blackwell Publishers, 2001), 10–13. See also Cairns, *Christianity Through the Centuries*, 478.
5. For more information regarding the heart of evangelicalism, see Webber, *Common Roots*; Noll, *American Evangelical Christianity*; Donald Bloesch, *The Evangelical Renaissance* (Grand Rapids: Eerdmans, 1973); Alister McGrath, *Evangelicalism and the Future of Christianity* (Downers Grove, IL: InterVarsity, 1995).
6. Cairns, *Christianity Through the Centuries*, 418.
7. Christian Smith, *American Evangelicalism: Embattled and Thriving* (Chicago: The University of Chicago Press, 1998), 6.
8. Bruce Shelley, *Church History in Plain Language* (Dallas: Word, 1982), 458.
9. George M. Marsden, *Fundamentalism and American Culture: The Shaping of Twentieth-Century Evangelicalism, 1870–1925* (New York: Oxford University Press, 1980), 4. This idea that a Pharisaical pugilism is at the heart of fundamentalism is supported by the fact that the publication of *The Fundamentals* (the pamphlets after which the movement is named) was originally inspired by a pugilistic sermon preached by a fundamentalist leader, A. C. Dixon. See George Marsden, *Understanding Fundamentalism and Evangelicalism* (Grand Rapids: Eerdmans, 1991), 118. On another occasion, this same fundamentalist leader was quoted as saying, "Above all things I love peace, but next to peace I love a good fight, and I believe the next best thing to peace is a theological fight" (Marsden, *Understanding Fundamentalism and Evangelicalism*, 101).
10. Marsden, *Understanding Fundamentalism and Evangelicalism*, 66–67.

11. Smith, *American Evangelicalism*, 7.

12. Ibid., 8–9.

13. Noll, *American Evangelical Christianity*, 18.

14. Ibid.

15. Smith, *American Evangelicalism*, 9.

16. Ibid., 9–10.

17. Webber, *Common Roots*, 57.

18. Ibid., 64.

19. Ibid., 60.

20. Three other older works which make the same point as Webber are Donald Bloesch, *The Evangelical Renaissance*, 19–23 (Grand Rapids: Eerdmans, 1973); Donald Dayton, *Discovering an Evangelical Heritage* (Peabody, MA: Hendrickson Publishers, 1976), 1–7; and Donald Bloesch, *The Future of Evangelical Christianity* (Colorado Springs: Helmers & Howard Publishers, 1988), 92–97.

21. Joel Carpenter, *Revive Us Again: The Reawakening of American Fundamentalism* (New York: Oxford University Press, 1997), 237–38.

22. Smith, *American Evangelicalism*, 14.

23. Stanley Grenz, *Renewing the Center* (Grand Rapids: Baker, 2000), 15–16, 81–84.

24. Richard Mouw, *The Smell of Sawdust* (Grand Rapids: Zondervan, 2000), 24–25. Mouw writes, "Our commitment to 'getting the message out,' combined with our emphasis on the local church, has led to considerable 'false-witness bearing' toward other Christians. We have often not felt very accountable to Christian groups who are not immediately visible to us in our local worshiping community or who have not had obvious relevance to our evangelistic activities. And we have even been unspeakably harsh toward Christians with whom we have been closely linked, quibbling over doctrinal minutiae and exhibiting an ungracious and judgmental spirit about the behavior of others."

25. Robert Webber, *The Younger Evangelicals* (Grand Rapids: Baker, 2002), 41. Furthermore, as Webber treats the theme of spiritual formation he seems to imply that traditional evangelicals are guilty of promoting a form of legalism. See pages 173–86.

26. Eddie Gibbs and Ryan K. Bolger, *Emerging Churches: Creating Christian Community in Postmodern Cultures* (Grand Rapids: Baker, 2005), 239–328.

27. Roger Olson, *Reformed and Always Reforming: The Postconservative Approach to Evangelical Theology* (Grand Rapids: Baker, 2007), 68.

28. Dan Kimball, *They Like Jesus But Not the Church: Insights from Emerging Generations* (Grand Rapids: Zondervan, 2007).

29. John Fischer, *12 Steps for the Recovering Pharisee (like me)* (Minneapolis: Bethany, 2000).

30. Kern, *We Are the Pharisees*, 81–101.

31. Tom Hovestol, *Extreme Righteousness: Seeing Ourselves in the Pharisees* (Chicago: Moody, 1997), 12, 35, 45.

32. Ibid., 14–17, 20, 26–27.

33. Ibid., 47–164.

34. For example, see Timothy Keller, *The Reason for God: Belief in an Age of Skepticism* (New York: Dutton, 2008), 52, 56–59, 178–79; Dan Kimball, *They Like Jesus But Not the Church: Insights from Emerging Generations* (Grand Rapids: Zondervan, 2007).

35. Madeleine L'Engle, *Walking on Water: Reflections on Faith and Art* (Colorado Springs: Shaw Books, 2001), 63.

36. Ray Anderson, *The Soul of Ministry: Forming Leaders for God's People* (Louisville: Westminster John Knox Press, 1997), 167–69.

37. Ibid., 169–70.

38. Charles Van Engen, *God's Missionary People: Rethinking the Purpose of the Local Church* (Grand Rapids: Baker, 1991), 17.

39. Darrell Guder, ed., *Missional Church: A Vision for the Sending of the Church in North America* (Grand Rapids: Eerdmans, 1998), 6.

40. David Kinnaman, *unChristian: What a New Generation Really Thinks about Christianity . . . and Why It Matters* (Grand Rapids: Baker, 2007), 11.

41. Ibid.

42. Ibid., 31–32.

43. Ibid., 33.

44. Ibid., 34.

45. Yancey, *What's So Amazing About Grace?* 31.

46. Kern, *We Are the Pharisees*, 18.

47. Hovestol, *Extreme Righteousness*, 14–17.

48. Fischer, *12 Steps for the Recovering Pharisee (like me)*, 10, 16–19.

49. William Coleman, *Those Pharisees* (New York: Hawthorn Books, 1977), 8–9.

50. Quoted in Karen Armstrong, *A History of God* (New York: Alfred A. Knopf, 1974), 276, as cited in Yancey, *What's So Amazing About Grace?* 207.

51. Margaret G. Alter, *Resurrection Psychology: An Understanding of Human Personality Based on the Life and Teachings of Jesus* (Chicago: Loyola University Press, 1994), 24, 31.

52. Ibid., 35.

53. Ibid., 39.

54. Ibid., 31–32.

55. Ibid., 98, 102–3.

56. Anderson attributes this quote to Charles Suhor, deputy executive director of the National Council of Teachers of English, who formulated the law when he discovered "the universe is intractably squiggly," as cited in Paul Dickson, *The Official Rules* (New York: Dell Publishing, 1981), 226.

Part 2

UNDERSTANDING THE
SERMON ON THE MOUNT

4

LOCATION! LOCATION! LOCATION!

Anyone who has ever shopped for real estate has heard that there are three things that must be kept in mind in order to make a good purchase: Location! Location! Location! Something similar can be said about the effective interpretation of the Bible. A key to accurately understanding the intended meaning of any biblical text is to give careful consideration to its "location," or context. Helping us better understand the literary and historical context of the Sermon on the Mount is what the next two chapters are all about.

In this chapter my goal is to provide you with a basic but important introduction to the Gospel of Matthew as a whole. In the next chapter we will explore the relationship between the Sermon on the Mount and the specific Gospel-context in which it is situated. Both chapters are designed to alert us to some contextual features that simply must be kept in mind if we are going to approach the Sermon on the Mount with the right set of interpretive lenses in place. My hope is that by the time you have finished reading these two chapters you will be both willing and eager to entertain my theory that the Sermon on the Mount is all about disciple-making and that Jesus' methodology was to point his followers toward an authentic experience of life in God's kingdom by pointing them away from the actions and attitudes modeled by the Pharisees.

A Basic Introduction to the Gospel of Matthew as a Whole

While all the canonical Gospels (the four Gospels included in our New Testament) present an account of the ministry of Jesus of Nazareth, they do so in slightly different ways. Since the larger context in which the Sermon on the Mount is located is the Gospel of Matthew, it is important for us to become as familiar as we can with it. In the process, I will continually refer to the expert opinion of several important Matthean scholars. While this methodology might serve to endue this chapter (and the next) with a bit of a technical, academic feel, I have chosen to do so with good reason. My contention that the Sermon on the Mount has not always been interpreted in the most accurate manner and that, as a result, the disciple-making methodology of Jesus has largely been lost could be considered somewhat provocative. This requires that I do a good job of showing in these pages that each aspect of my argument actually enjoys the support of a strong number of reputable biblical scholars. While it is certainly permissible for those readers who are less concerned about the technical precision of my argument simply to skip these chapters and jump into my analysis of the Sermon on the Mount, which begins in chapter six, the upside of choosing to make your way patiently through these next two chapters is that you will better prepare yourself to really see what Jesus was up to in his most famous sermon.

How, When, Where, and by Whom Was This Gospel Written?

Obviously, none of the Gospels simply fell to the earth out of heaven. Each of them was composed at a particular time and geographical location.

In the introduction to his commentary on the Gospel of Matthew, Donald Senior provides his readers with a succinct summary of the consensus that exists among most scholars as it relates to the date and place of the first Gospel's composition: "Most interpreters assume that the Gospel of Matthew was written in the final quarter of the first century by a Greek-speaking Jewish-Christian author. The evangelist and his community were probably located in Syria, quite possibly in the city of Antioch. A majority of Matthew's community were Jewish Christians, as was the evangelist himself, but a growing number of Gentile converts were beginning to swell its membership."[1]

This quote is filled with more significance than might at first appear. We will soon see that the theory that Matthew's Gospel was written in Antioch, in the mid-to-late first century AD, in connection with a community of believers that contained both Jews and Gentiles, has the potential to profoundly influence our understanding of the Gospel as a whole and the Sermon on the Mount in particular.

You will notice, however, that in the quote presented above Senior does not specify the identity of the author of the first Gospel. This is not an uncommon practice among New Testament scholars. With regard to the issue of authorship, it is perhaps safe to say that a majority of Matthean scholars would concur with the following view held by commentator Robert Guelich:

"Who was or is 'Matthew'?" Without desiring to enter into that involved discussion about the authorship of the first Gospel, the name *Matthew* as used in this commentary merely denotes the common traditional designation of the Gospel's author. The Gospel itself, of course, comes to us as an anonymous document in spite of the early church's assignment of it to the apostle Matthew, the former tax collector. From the evangelist's writing, we can deduce that he was clearly familiar with Jewish rabbinic circles and customs, while his use of Greek and especially his deliberate choice at times to use the Septuagint (LXX) indicates

his familiarity with "Hellenistic" Judaism. His theological interests reflect a keen awareness of the Old Testament Scriptures, a
profound understanding of Jesus' ministry, and a deep concern
for the current needs and dangers of his own community. As will
be seen, he played a much more active literary role in writing
the Gospel than simply one of compiling an account by using
"scissors and paste."[2]

The important thing to take away from this quote is that, while
the author of this Gospel may or may not have been the tax collector-
turned-apostle named Matthew, he was neither a mere stenographer nor
a mere editor of the recollections and/or writings of others. According to
Guelich, "Matthew" was a genuine author in his own right who was able
to draw from his own knowledge of the Jesus story in order to compose
a Gospel that was designed to address the specific "needs and dangers" of
the community of faith to which he belonged.

Now the fact that the author of the first Gospel evidently possessed
a "profound understanding of Jesus' ministry" and obviously functioned
as more than a mere editor of a variety of oral traditions about Jesus
opens the door (at least in my mind) to the possibility that the author
of the first Gospel was indeed, as tradition has it, the Matthew of the
New Testament. On the other hand, I also agree with those scholars
who insist that, when it comes to the proper interpretation of the first
Gospel, the question of authorship is not nearly as important as the
question of purpose.

Why Was This Gospel Written?

The idea that Matthew wrote his Gospel out of concern for some
needs present in his faith community leads us to wonder about this
Gospel's purpose. It is no secret that Matthew's Gospel is the most
Jewish of the four contained in our New Testament. Nearly all scholars
are in agreement, therefore, that one of Matthew's biggest aims was to

compose a Gospel that would present Jesus as the fulfillment of God's messianic promises to Israel so that more of his countrymen might come to saving faith.

In addition to this evangelistic goal, however, most New Testament scholars also go on to assert that Matthew wrote his Gospel with two other possible goals in mind as well. Matthew may have intended his Gospel to function as an apologetic (doctrinal defense) against the rabbinic Judaism (Pharisaism) with which his church was in conflict.[3] Matthew may also have designed his Gospel to serve his church as a catechesis (a manual for the instruction of new converts in the Christian life). In order to really understand the Sermon on the Mount we need to give some careful consideration to both the catechetic and apologetic goals that Matthew may have had in mind as he wrote his Gospel. (Be warned: because the points I am making in the rest of this chapter are especially crucial to the argument I am making in this book, my references to the opinions of various biblical scholars will be especially numerous!)

Matthew's Gospel as a Catechesis

The idea that Matthew composed a Gospel that would be useful for the training of new converts in the way of Christian discipleship enjoys a remarkably strong consensus among biblical experts.[4] The two biggest reasons for this unusually strong consensus seem to be: (a) the unique manner in which Matthew structured his Gospel; and (b) the emphasis he placed on the dynamic of discipleship.

Matthew's Unique Structure

It appears that Matthew's Gospel was the preeminent one during the earliest era of church history. In his book *Matthew: Evangelist and Teacher*, R. T. France indicates that "in the first century after the writing of our New Testament gospels it was Matthew which quickly established itself as *the* gospel par excellence, the natural place from which to expect to derive the authoritative account of the words and deeds of Jesus."[5]

New Testament scholar Ralph Martin suggests that one of the biggest reasons for the first Gospel's popularity in the early church era was its facility as a teaching tool, which in turn was due to the fact that it contains much teaching-oriented content. According to Martin, "The young in the faith needed instruction, and for this purpose collections of Jesus' teaching on how he expected his followers to live would be of great practical value. Such chapters as Matthew 5–7 (the Sermon on the Mount), 13 (the parables of the kingdom), and 24–25 (apocalyptic utterances) seem to be put together with catechetical interest in view. This would give the First Gospel an obvious value to teachers and converts in the early church."[6]

France offers a similar explanation for Matthew's preeminence early on in the history of the church. After discussing the early church's belief that this Gospel was the first Gospel to be written and was therefore closer to the source, France points out that "it contains proportionately more ethical and pastoral teaching than the other gospels" and that these teachings are "set out in a more obviously systematic way."[7] France goes on to indicate that it is fairly obvious to most scholars that the author of Matthew's Gospel was careful to group his material in such a way as to make it readily accessible for teaching purposes. "Several large sections of the gospel (pre-eminently, of course, the Sermon on the Mount) are devoted to collections of the teaching of Jesus grouped around a common theme. Such sections would provide a suitable framework for teachers in churches. And the character of much of the teaching in Matthew is such as to deal fairly directly with the concerns of a pastor or catechist."[8]

Thus, the view that Matthew deliberately structured his Gospel in such a way as to make it very helpful in the training of new converts enjoys some solid scholarly support.

Matthew's Emphasis on Disciple-Making

As indicated above, a second reason why most New Testament scholars agree that Matthew had a catechetical aim in mind when he wrote his Gospel is because of its emphasis on the dynamic of discipleship. According to New Testament scholar Michael Green, the Gospel of Matthew is all about discipleship. "Matthew's Gospel is strong on discipleship. . . . Decision for Christ inevitably leads to discipleship of Christ. . . . So discipleship is a major concern of Matthew throughout his Gospel. And undoubtedly he intends the readers of his work to apply this truth to themselves."[9]

Green is not alone. Many biblical scholars are convinced that Matthew actually intended his Gospel to function as a document that could help church members better understand what is involved in the life of Christian discipleship. There are two main features of Matthew's Gospel that support this idea.

Matthew's Many Allusions to Discipleship. Some scholars have pointed out the distinctive and extensive manner in which Matthew uses the Greek words that translate into English as the noun "disciple" and the verb "to disciple."[10] The Gospel of Matthew simply uses these particular "discipleship" words in a manner that the other Gospels do not.

Still other scholars have drawn attention to the unique way this Gospel keeps addressing discipleship themes, explaining in the process what it means to be a disciple. These scholars point out that a careful reading of the Gospel will reveal that the bulk of Jesus' teachings is directed at his disciples and focuses on discipleship issues. This tendency of Jesus to speak continually in the direction of his disciples about discipleship issues gives the impression that the Gospel of Matthew, as a whole, is preoccupied with the discipleship dynamic.[11]

In one way or another, it appears that the Gospel of Matthew has a great deal to say about discipleship. It is not going too far to say that most

New Testament scholars agree with Craig Blomberg's assertions that one of Matthew's main themes is discipleship and the church and that the "requirements for discipleship and the constitution of the community of Jesus' followers that became the church dominate Matthew's Gospel as they do no other."[12]

Matthew's Use of Gospel Characters as Exemplars of Discipleship. Another unique feature that testifies to Matthew's interest in discipleship is the way in which the author of this Gospel intended his readers to see authentic Christian discipleship being modeled (or anti-modeled) for them by the characters in his story. Ralph Martin states a view that is held by many other New Testament scholars: in Matthew's Gospel the role of the disciples is to represent "model believers who advance in the school of Christ."[13] Similarly, Michael Wilkins suggests that Matthew portrays the historical disciples of Jesus as realistic examples of discipleship (both good and bad) with which his readers were to relate. "Matthew's portrayal of the disciples both passes on the tradition about the Twelve, and at the same time presents an example of discipleship for his church. The disciples are a positive example of what Matthew expects from his church, a negative example of wrong, and a mixed group who are able to overcome their lackings through the teaching of Jesus. The historical disciples become a means of encouragement, warning, and instruction as examples."[14]

Jack Kingsbury says something akin to this, explaining that Matthew expected the disciples in his Gospel story to be viewed as "typical" of the members of Matthew's church. This connection between the companions of Jesus with the members of Matthew's church is so strong, says Kingsbury, that one can gain insight into what life was like in Matthew's church, and what Matthew believed life would be like in the ideal church, by paying careful attention to Matthew's portrait of Jesus' disciples.[15]

It is in this same vein that Francis Beare asserts that the disciples in Matthew's story not only function as models for Matthew's readers but actually represent them. The view here is that the issues the disciples in Matthew's Gospel have to deal with were issues confronting the members of Matthew's church. Likewise, the questions the disciples put to Jesus in Matthew's Gospel were actually questions being debated in Matthew's faith community. Beare explains: "The disciples are under one aspect the immediate followers of the man of Nazareth, who left home and business to cast their lot with him, and at the same time they are 'stylized' as figures of the Christian believers of Matthew's church."[16]

Now if it is true that Matthew purposefully constructed his Gospel in such a way as to cause his readers to closely identify themselves with Jesus' disciples, this argues for the idea that discipleship is indeed a major theme (and goal) of Matthew's Gospel, the larger document of which the Sermon on the Mount is an important part.

Matthew's Gospel as an Apologetic

Assuming that Matthew did write his Gospel intending for the members of his church to identify with Jesus' disciples so that, in the process, certain discipleship issues that had arisen in their community might be addressed, the question arises, *Just what was going on in Matthew's church that necessitated this pastoral action?* This, in turn, leads us to a consideration of the possibility that Matthew intended his Gospel to function not only evangelistically and catechetically, but apologetically as well.

The Polemic against the Pharisees in Matthew's Gospel

I want to insist that another theme that simply must be kept in mind as we approach the Sermon on the Mount is Matthew's especially hostile treatment of the Jewish religious leaders, especially the Pharisees. Virtually all introductions to the Gospel of Matthew will refer to the anti-Pharisee emphasis that is readily observable within it.[17]

The New International Version of the Gospel of Matthew contains no less than twenty-nine references to the "Pharisees" and another nineteen references to the "teachers of the law," a group which seems to overlap with the Pharisees.[18] Even a cursory examination of the twenty-nine references to the Pharisees in Matthew's Gospel will reveal the harsh manner in which Matthew portrays the antagonists in his story. (Please take time to survey the following passages: Matthew 3:7; 5:20; 9:11, 34; 12:2, 14, 24, 38; 15:1–2, 12; 16:1, 6; 19:3; 21:45–46; 22:15, 34; 23:2–34; 27:62–63.) Such an examination will aptly demonstrate the dramatic tension that the author of the first Gospel skillfully built into his narrative. Given the significant degree of anti-Pharisee polemic that is observable in Matthew's Gospel it is easy to see why most New Testament scholars are of the opinion that, in addition to whatever other intentions Matthew had, one chief purpose for his Gospel was to create a document that would function as an empowering apologetic against the Pharisaic Judaism with which the members of his church were evidently in contact.[19]

Some Possible Scenarios That Would Explain Matthew's Polemic against the Pharisees

So what was going on in Matthew's world that caused him to emphasize in such a pronounced manner the hostility that had existed between Jesus and the Pharisees? Re-creations of the life setting that gave rise to Matthew's Gospel vary from scholar to scholar, but most of these suggested scenarios see Matthew's church experiencing some kind of tension with, as Kingsbury puts it, the Jews "next door"[20] or, as Graham Stanton phrases it, the "synagogue across the street."[21] Were we to wonder about the nature of this tension between church and synagogue, we would find that scholarly opinion falls into two main categories, which I will christen the "Competition" and "Corruption" theories.

The Competition Theory. One view is that in the aftermath of the destruction of Jerusalem and dismantling of the temple in AD 70 both the synagogue and church were emerging institutions that "stood ready to lead the people."[22] Thus, the tension between Jesus and the Pharisees observable in Matthew's Gospel is reflective of a competitive rivalry that existed between Matthew's church and the local Jewish leaders. Matthew scholar Craig Blomberg suggests that Matthew's Gospel was designed to encourage his Jewish Christian audience, who had been labeled as apostate by nearby Jews, to "stand fast in their allegiance to Christ" and to give them some "apologetic ammunition" they could use as they persisted in their attempts to win fellow Jews to faith in Christ.[23]

While not necessarily advocating this theory, Robert Smith explains that "many believe that Matthew's Gospel must be interpreted as a product of the dialog or polemical exchange between leaders of the two communities, as church and synagogue competed for the loyalties of the same people, offering divergent interpretations of the life of Jesus and events of the recent past."[24]

The Corruption Theory. Another view holds that Matthew was concerned that the members of his church were being influenced in a negative manner by their Jewish neighbors. Matthew intended the anti-Pharisee rhetoric in his narrative to serve as a warning to the members of his church with regard to their own walk with Christ. For instance, R. T. France makes the point that the scalding critique leveled against the Pharisees by Jesus in chapter 23 was also designed to warn Christian disciples against engaging in the same hypocritical behaviors.[25]

Another proponent of this perspective is Francis Beare, who asserts that the Pharisees in Matthew's Gospel are to be viewed as "types or figures of the Jewish rabbis and synagogue authorities with whom Matthew was in conflict in his own day." According to Beare, the fact that the disciples are warned to "beware of the leaven of the Pharisees and Sadducees" in Matthew 16:11 suggests that the vigorous manner in which Jesus denounces the Pharisees in Matthew 23 "is partly due to the apprehension of Matthew that the same spirit may show itself in the lives of members of the Christian church."[26] In light of Beare's observations, it would not seem to violate the rules of logic to further suggest that the Pharisees in Matthew's Gospel were intended to function collectively as an anti-model of what Christian disciples should be and do.[27]

Donald Senior uses the phrase "negative example" rather than anti-model, but the meaning is the same. He states, "The point for most of these passages where the Matthean Jesus condemns the religious leaders is not to attack these figures once again but to serve as a negative example for the Christian reader of the Gospel. In other words, warnings about hypocrisy, about misguided interpretation of the law, or failure to act in accord with the gospel are appeals and warnings meant for the Christian of Matthew's community, not for its non-Christian Jewish opponents."[28]

In support of this view, Robert Smith contends that "in his own day Matthew sees Christian leaders displaying the very sorts of behavior and attitudes criticized by Jesus"[29] and that "he trusted his first readers to catch the point of his retelling of Jesus' story and to make the appropriate applications to themselves."[30]

A variation of the "Corruption" theory is that the negative examples Matthew was concerned about were not provided by non-Christian Jews but by Jewish Christians! According to Acts 15:5 some of the members of the church in Jerusalem "belonged to the party of the Pharisees." Evidently this group of Pharisaical believers struggled mightily with the idea that ritual circumcision was not required for one to be "clean" before God. It was likely Pharisaical believers such as these who had gone to Antioch, creating a stir by teaching that "unless you are circumcised, according to the custom taught by Moses, you cannot be saved" (Acts 15:1). Luke goes on to report that at a council convened in Jerusalem to deal with this important question members of this church faction stood up and said, "The Gentiles must be circumcised and required to obey the law of Moses" (Acts 15:5).

Robert Guelich suspects that this dynamic may best explain the *Sitz im Leben*, or life setting, that called the Gospel of Matthew into existence. He puts forward the idea that a flight of Jewish Christians from Jerusalem after its destruction by the Romans in AD 70 brought a cadre of Pharisee-influenced Jewish Christians into Matthew's church located somewhere in Syria, perhaps at Antioch. The presence of these Pharisee-oriented believers reignited the old debate that had been dealt with at the Jerusalem Council back in AD 50 (Acts 15). Guelich states, "Matthew saw their presence as a threat so serious that he reshaped their Jesus tradition (e.g., 5:17–19) to counter and warn his community about these 'false prophets' (7:15–23)."[31]

Regardless of the actual circumstances that motivated Matthew to address the issue of Pharisaism in his church, it appears that he did in fact do so. *The Gospel of Matthew is best understood, then, not just as an apologetic against Jewish Pharisaism at work in the "synagogue across the street," but also as a polemic against the Christian Pharisaism present in the author's own church.*

In Summary

Location! Location! Location! Context *is* crucial! This has indeed been a challenging chapter. We have covered a lot of ground in our attempt to better comprehend the context in which the Sermon on the Mount is located and, in the process, to better understand what Jesus was doing in it. While we will do more of the same in the chapter that follows, we have already observed that Matthew probably had both a catechetical and apologetic purpose in mind when he wrote his Gospel; that disciple-making was a key theme for Matthew; that Matthew expected his readers to identify with the disciples portrayed in his narrative; that Matthew's Gospel as a whole is filled with a polemical tension between Jesus and the Pharisees; and that Matthew was careful to highlight this tension not only because of a competitive rivalry with the "synagogue across the street" but also because Matthew, the pastor, was concerned that the ecclesial pathology that is Pharisaism was corrupting some of the members of his own church!

In the next chapter we will focus our attention on the relationship between the Sermon on the Mount and its larger context—the Gospel of Matthew. In the process we will discover that Matthew, inspired by the Holy Spirit, really did do more than function as a scissors-and-paste editor of materials handed down to him. The author of the first Gospel was a creative stylist who, among other things, knew a thing or two about a literary device known as irony. Perhaps Matthew's skill as a genuine author is yet another reason why his version of the Jesus story proved to be so popular among the first followers of Jesus.

Notes

1. Donald Senior, *Matthew* (Nashville: Abingdon, 1998), 21.
2. Robert Guelich, *The Sermon on the Mount* (Dallas: Word, 1982), 25–26. Guelich's insistence that "Matthew" did more than utilize a "scissors and paste" method when composing his Gospel points to the work of W. D. Davies, who insists that, whoever "Matthew" was, he did more than simply function as a literary editor of various oral traditions concerning Jesus. Davies writes, "We refer to the awareness that we should think of Matthew, and of other composers of the Gospels, not merely as editors, manipulating sources with scissors and paste, so to speak, to produce a mosaic of snippets, but as themselves in a real sense 'authors.' Dependent on a tradition they were, but not passive transmitters of it. By what they preserved, by the way they changed and, above all, arranged, the tradition, they left their impress upon it. This is particularly true of Matthew. No unimaginative compiler or slavish editor, he was a formulator of the tradition, concerned to present it in a specific way to meet the needs of his Church as he understood them." W. D. Davies, *The Setting of the Sermon on the Mount* (Cambridge: Cambridge University Press, 1964), 13.
3. See Michael Crosby, *Spirituality of the Beatitudes: Matthew's Challenge for First World Christians* (Maryknoll, NY: Orbis Books, 1981), 13. Crosby is one of many New Testament scholars who make a strong case for the idea that the goal behind Matthew's Gospel overall was to argue for the authority of Jesus and his church over against the authority of the scribes and Pharisees as exercised in the synagogue.
4. See Michael Green, *The Message of Matthew* (Downers Grove, IL: InterVarsity, 1988), 26; Ernst von Dobschütz, "Matthew as Rabbi and Catechist," in *The Interpretation of Matthew*, ed. Graham Stanton (Philadelphia: Fortress Press, 1983), 26; A. W. Argyle, *The Gospel According to Matthew* (London: Cambridge University Press, 1963), 4; Robert H. Smith, *Matthew* (Minneapolis: Augsburg Publishing House, 1989), 12–13; Donald Hagner, *Matthew 1–13*, Word Biblical

Commentary, vol. 33A (Dallas: Word, 1993), li, lviii; David Hill, *The Gospel of Matthew*, The New Century Bible Commentary (Grand Rapids: Eerdmans, 1972), 44; Donald Guthrie, *New Testament Introduction* (Downers Grove, IL: InterVarsity, 1970), 28; John Drane, *Introducing the New Testament* (San Francisco: Harper & Row Publishers, 1986), 191; Glenn W. Barker, William L. Lane, and J. Ramsey Michaels, *The New Testament Speaks* (New York: Harper & Row, Publishers, 1969), 263; Merrill C. Tenney, *New Testament Survey* (Grand Rapids: Eerdmans, 1985), 157; Everett Harrison, *Introduction to the New Testament* (Grand Rapids: Eerdmans, 1971), 173; Werner Georg Kümmel, *Introduction to the New Testament* (Nashville: Abingdon, 1973), 106–7; L. M. Petersen, "Matthew, Gospel of," in *The Zondervan Pictorial Encyclopedia of the Bible*, vol. 4, ed. Merrill C. Tenney (Grand Rapids: Zondervan, 1976), 129; R. T. France, *Matthew: Evangelist and Teacher* (Exeter, England: Paternoster Press, 1989) ,18; and R. V. G. Tasker, *The Gospel According to St. Matthew: An Introduction and Commentary*, Tyndale New Testament Commentaries, vol. 1 (London: Tyndale Press, 1964), 17–18.

5. France, *Matthew: Evangelist and Teacher*, 17. Also see Ralph P. Martin, *New Testament Foundations: A Guide for Students*, vol. 1 (Grand Rapids: Eerdmans, 1975), 224.

6. Martin, *New Testament Foundations*, 224.

7. France, *Matthew: Evangelist and Teacher*, 18.

8. Ibid. France, 18. In another work, France identifies the five teaching sections thusly: chapters 5–7: teaching about discipleship; chapter 10: teaching about mission; chapter 13: teaching about the kingdom; chapter 18: teaching about relationships among disciples; chapters 24–25: teaching about the future. R. T. France, *Matthew*, The Tyndale New Testament Commentaries (Grand Rapids: Eerdmans, 1985), 60.

9. Green, *The Message of Matthew*, 42–43.

10. For example, see Hagner, *Matthew 1–13*, lxii, and France, *Matthew: Evangelist and Teacher*, 261.

11. For example, see Michael J. Wilkins, *Following the Master: A Biblical Theology of Discipleship* (Grand Rapids: Zondervan, 1992), 190; L. M. Petersen, "Matthew, Gospel of," in *The Zondervan Pictorial Encyclopedia of the Bible*, vol. 4, ed. Merrill C. Tenney (Grand Rapids: Zondervan, 1976), 132; and Jack Kingsbury, *Matthew as Story* (Philadelphia: Fortress Press, 1988), 129–45.

12. Craig L. Blomberg, *Matthew*, The New American Commentary, vol. 22 (Nashville: Broadman Press, 1992), 32.

13. Martin, *New Testament Foundations*, 230.

14. Michael J. Wilkins, "The Concept of Disciple in Matthew's Gospel as Reflected in the Use of the Term *Mathetes*" (PhD diss., Fuller Theological Seminary, 1986), 333–34.

15. Jack Kingsbury, *Matthew* (Philadelphia: Fortress Press, 1986), 82.

16. Francis Beare, *The Gospel According to Matthew* (Oxford: Basil Blackwell Publisher, 1981), 14.

17. For example, see E. P. Sanders, *Jesus and Judaism* (London: SCM Press, Ltd., 1985), 260–61. At the same time, most scholars exhibit a marked and valid concern to make it clear that the vitriol present in Matthew's Gospel is not directed toward the Jewish people as a whole but at their religious leaders specifically, especially the Pharisees. For example, see Kingsbury, *Matthew as Story*, 115; France, *Matthew: Evangelist and Teacher*, 218; Senior, *Matthew*, 30; and Hagner, *Matthew 1–13*, lxxii.

18. France, *Matthew: Evangelist and Teacher*, 220–21.

19. For example, see Georg Strecker, *The Sermon on the Mount: An Exegetical Commentary* (Nashville: Abingdon, 1988), 75; Green, *The Message of Matthew*, 38; Kingsbury, *Matthew*, 101–2; Senior, *Matthew*, 23; Smith, *Matthew*, 20; Herman Ridderbos, *Matthew*, Bible Student's Commentary (Grand Rapids: Zondervan, 1987), 12; Hagner, *Matthew 1–13*, lix; David Hill, *The Gospel of Matthew*, The New Century Bible Commentary (Grand Rapids: Eerdmans, 1972), 67–68; Guthrie, *New Testament Introduction*, 26; Martin, *New Testament Foundations*, 224, 242–43; Harrison, *Introduction to the New Testament*, 173, 176; Robert H. Gundry, *Matthew: A Commentary on His Handbook for a Mixed Church Under Persecution* (Grand Rapids: Eerdmans, 1994), 162; Beare, *The Gospel According to Matthew*, 14; and Guelich, *The Sermon on the Mount*, 26.

20. Kingsbury, *Matthew*, 101.

21. Graham Stanton, "The Gospel of Matthew and Judaism," *BJRL* 66 (1984): 266, quoted in Blomberg, *Matthew*, 35.

22. Smith, *Matthew*, 20.

23. Blomberg, *Matthew*, 35. See also Hagner, *Matthew 1–13*, lix; Guelich, *The Sermon on the Mount*, 26; and W. D. Davies, *The Sermon on the Mount* (Nashville: Abingdon, 1966), 89.

24. Smith, *Matthew*, 20.

25. France, *Matthew: Evangelist and Teacher*, 255–56.

26. Beare, *The Gospel According to Matthew*, 14.

27. See Strecker, *The Sermon on the Mount*, 40, where the author refers to Matthew's use of the Pharisees as an "anti-type" in his Gospel.

28. Senior, *Matthew*, 31.

29. Smith, *Matthew*, 21.

30. Ibid.

31. Guelich, *The Sermon on the Mount*, 26. Guelich seems to be suggesting here that an influx of Jewish Christians from Jerusalem introduced into the community of disciples in Antioch (Matthew's church) a tendency toward legalism (see Acts 15:1–3). It was in order to deal with this encroaching legalism, and to avoid an ecclesial controversy similar to the one reflected in Acts 15, that Matthew deftly composed a version of the Jesus story which, while acknowledging Jesus' high view of the law, also identified the legalism of the Pharisees as an inadequate foundation for Christian ethics and as a false teaching to be avoided. See also Martin, *New Testament Foundations*, 242–43.

5

YOU GOTTA PAY YOUR DUES!

I n his landmark book, *The Scandal of the Evangelical Mind,* historian Mark Noll laments the presence of an anti-intellectualism that persists within contemporary evangelicalism. I am happy to report that in my role as a university professor I am privileged to work with students, ranging in age from eighteen to midlife, who are eager to cultivate their minds and surrender them to God's service. Furthermore, in my role as a pastor I have ministered to and with many parishioners who were anything but anti-intellectual in their thinking. It is also true, though, that I have interacted with some evangelicals who were guilty of intellectual laziness: students who wanted a diploma but not necessarily an education and church members who insisted that it should be sufficient simply to *read* the Bible without having to learn how to *study* it.

The reality is, regardless of the industry or the endeavor, it is axiomatic that to achieve success a person has to pay his or her dues. This is no less true when it comes to interpreting the Bible as it is to any other endeavor. There is a sense in which this is what the previous chapter and this one are all about.

In the previous chapter we began the arduous task of giving some careful consideration to several introductory matters concerning the Gospel of Matthew as a whole—the larger context in which the Sermon on the Mount is located. But to fully understand what Jesus was doing in his most famous sermon, it is necessary to do more than study such introductory matters as the how, when, where, by whom, and why of Matthew's Gospel. To sufficiently pay our dues as biblical interpreters we must also ponder several other unique aspects of Matthew's work, such as the role the Sermon on the Mount plays in Matthew's Jesus-story overall, the fact that Matthew's polemic against the Pharisees shows up in Jesus' most famous sermon, and why it is that in the prelude to the Sermon on the Mount (Matthew 1–4) we see the author making liberal use of irony as a literary device.

In the process of performing these additional investigations we will be amazed, I think, at just how thoughtful and creative an author Matthew really was. My ultimate hope is that by the time you have finished reading this chapter you will not only feel good about having paid your dues but will find yourself chomping at the bit to dive into a thoughtful study of the Sermon itself.

The Important Role the Sermon on the Mount Plays in Matthew's Gospel

We have already established the fact that Matthew was very interested in disciple-making. The goal of this section is to bring attention to the relationship between the Sermon on the Mount and the focus on discipleship that is present in the Gospel overall. My premise is a simple yet bold one: Matthew intended the Sermon on the Mount to play a crucial role in the development of his story about Jesus in general; and, even more importantly, Matthew intended his readers to view the Sermon on the Mount as the heart and soul of Jesus' ministry of spiritual formation in particular. In other words, this is where a true understanding of both Christ and Christian discipleship begins: the Sermon on the Mount.

The Sermon and Matthew's Story about Jesus in General

The idea here is that even though the Sermon on the Mount, from a literary perspective, is essentially just a lengthy speech, the story Matthew tells in his Gospel does not really make sense without it. Many modern readers are not used to thinking of the Gospels as stories in the strict sense of the word: as artistic creations that aim to take the reader on a literary journey. But in *Matthew: Evangelist and Teacher*, R. T. France argues that Matthew's Gospel should be viewed as a drama that exhibits a clear sense of direction. The story Matthew tells steadily builds toward a dramatic climax: an ironic confrontation between Jesus, Israel's Messiah, and the men who functioned as Israel's religious authorities.[1]

In a section entitled "The Place of the Discourses in the Story," France insists that the five rather lengthy speeches Matthew inserts in his story about Jesus, the rejected but victorious king, should not be viewed as clumsy interruptions. Rather, says France, each of these discourses is made up of a compilation of Jesus' teachings focused around a central theme, and each of these themes is designed to "develop the readers' understanding of what has been happening in the story so far, and also to prepare for the development of the plot in the narrative which follows."[2] In other words, each of these discourses (lengthy speeches) plays a crucial role in explaining the theological significance of each stage of Matthew's Jesus story and in moving that story along.

With regard to the discourse known as the Sermon on the Mount, France explains that the literary aim of the early chapters in Matthew's

Gospel is to establish immediately Jesus' unique authority as a teacher and worker of wonders.[3] In the Sermon (chapters 5–7), Jesus teaches the crowd with an air of authority that is contrasted with the teaching of the scribes and Pharisees (see 7:28–29). In the narrative section that follows (chapters 8–9), Jesus backs up his teachings by performing various miracles. According to France, this early establishment of Jesus' authority in both word and deed is "central to the developing presentation of people's varying responses to Jesus which will occupy succeeding chapters."[4] One of the main themes of Matthew's Gospel, according to France, is the "separation between the true 'people of God' who respond to Jesus' message, and the society around who are increasingly seen as in opposition to the 'kingdom of heaven,' and the resultant growth of an alternative society" (i.e., a new, true Israel).[5]

The fact is that the Sermon on the Mount plays a crucial role in the development of this aspect of Matthew's story. Early on in the Gospel, a side has to be taken. Early on, dramatic tension is introduced. *The very first discourse presented in the Gospel of Matthew—the Sermon on the Mount—challenges its readers to make a decision about who Jesus is and whether or not they will put his teachings into practice (see Matthew 7:24–27).*[6]

The Sermon and Matthew's Catechetical/Discipleship Aims in Particular

The idea here is that without the Sermon on the Mount the Gospel of Matthew would lose its value as a disciple-making document. In addition to Matthew's expectation that his readers would be forced by their reading of the Sermon to make a preliminary decision about the nature of Jesus' authority, I am convinced that Matthew intended his readers to view the Sermon as the heart and soul of Jesus' ministry of spiritual formation (i.e., discipleship).

One of the issues hotly debated among Matthean scholars is the relationship between gospel and law in the Sermon on the Mount. Many scholars have suggested that, given the Jewishness of Matthew's Gospel overall (e.g., his concern to demonstrate that many Old Testament prophecies were fulfilled in Jesus' life and ministry),[7] and the way he organized his work around the five major discourse sections, Matthew intended for his readers to see the document as a new Pentateuch presenting a new Moses delivering a new law to a new Israel.[8] Obviously, if any of this was actually in Matthew's mind when he wrote his Gospel, then the Sermon on the Mount, which is the epitome of Jesus' ethical teaching,[9] would have to be considered of supreme importance to the Gospel's disciple-making intent.

But did Matthew really intend that new converts to the Christian faith should see Jesus as a new Moses delivering a new law? Ironically, Robert Guelich makes the same point—that the Sermon on the Mount is about discipleship—by arguing *against* the new Moses/new law motif. According to Guelich, the focus in chapters 5–9 of Matthew is on establishing Jesus as the Messiah. The Christology presented in the Sermon corresponds with the Christology presented in the Gospel as a whole, which is a "fulfillment Christology." Jesus has come to *fulfill* the Old Testament Law and Prophets (Matthew 5:17).[10]

But what does it mean to say that Jesus has come to fulfill the Law and the Prophets? Guelich insists that this does not mean that Jesus has come to simply uphold the law of Moses. Neither does this mean that Jesus has come to set the Old Testament law aside as a new Moses giving a new law. Instead, Jesus has come to announce the arrival and availability of the kingdom of God. *Jesus the Messiah is someone who knows what it means to live under the authority of God's reign and has come to empower his followers to do likewise.*

Going further, I would argue that Jesus' ministry of announcing the arrival and availability of the kingdom has both an indicative (this is the way it is) and imperative (this is what must be done) aspect to it. Jesus himself is the indicative; in his person the kingdom of God has made its appearance among humanity at last. The imperatives of the kingdom are articulated in a bold, powerful manner via the first discourse delivered in Jesus' public ministry: the Sermon on the Mount. But these imperatives are predicated upon the indicative and not the other way around. Put differently, it is on the basis of the prior indicative of who Jesus is and what he has come to do that the Sermon is to be understood as the imperatives of the kingdom. *The Sermon is not a new law per se. It contains, instead, a gracious explanation of how Jesus' followers may live their lives as newly naturalized citizens of God's kingdom.*

Once again, the Sermon on the Mount is about spiritual formation (i.e., discipleship). The strong connection between spiritual formation and the Sermon can also be demonstrated by a comparison of the content of the Sermon on the Mount with that of the other major discourses in Matthew's Gospel. Such a comparison makes it readily apparent that should the Sermon be excised from Matthew's Gospel the reader's understanding of Jesus' spiritual formation program would be drastically reduced. *Indeed, it is hard to conceive of how a version of Matthew's Gospel sans the Sermon on the Mount could have ever achieved a reputation in the early church as a useful catechetical tool.* The material presented in the Sermon is simply crucial to Matthew's catechetical aim and his discussion of discipleship.[11]

The bottom line is that if it is true the Gospel of Matthew was intended to function as a disciple-making document, then the Sermon on the Mount must be considered crucial to its success. When we approach the Sermon on the Mount we should do so expecting to experience Jesus' method of making disciples. The making of disciples is what Jesus' most famous sermon is all about!

The Polemic against the Pharisees in the Sermon on the Mount

We have already taken note of the fact that a unique feature of Matthew's Gospel is the especially blunt manner in which it portrays Israel's religious leaders as a whole, and the Pharisees in particular, as Jesus' main antagonists. Given the fact that of the four canonical Gospels, Matthew's version of the Jesus story is known to be the most Jewish in its style and content, it is ironic that it would also be the one that presents Israel's religious leaders in the worst possible light.

Then again, the principal thesis of this book is that a discipleship curriculum founded upon a proper understanding of the Sermon on the Mount will have the effect of steering disciples away from a Pharisaical approach to the Christian life. I base this conviction on the fact that the Sermon on the Mount, like the Gospel of Matthew as a whole, is thoroughly riddled with an anti-Pharisee polemic. Indeed, my contention is that in the discipleship teaching presented in Matthew's catechetical/apologetic work we see Jesus purposefully and proactively using the Pharisees as an anti-model of what life in the kingdom of God is about. Is this merely a wild idea that I have come up with on my own, or does it enjoy a measure of scholarly support?

Since I will treat this theme in some detail in the next three chapters, all I want to do here is make the important observation that just as it is possible to find New Testament scholars who readily acknowledge the apologetic/polemical nature of the Gospel of Matthew overall, and just as it is possible to find scholars who also see Matthew intending the portrayal of the Pharisees in his narrative to function as a "negative example" of what authentic Christian discipleship looks like, it is also possible to find scholars who will acknowledge that this is precisely what is going on in the Sermon on the Mount. For example, in his book *The Meaning of the Sermon on the Mount*, Hans Windisch includes a chapter entitled "Christ and His Attitude to Judaism." In this chapter Windisch presents a discussion that simply takes for granted the fact that there is within the whole of Jesus' sermon a polemic against the Pharisees that is "sharp and one-sided."[12]

Michael Crosby, an expert on biblical spirituality, embraces a version of the "competition" theory of Matthew's *Sitz im Leben* (historical setting) discussed in the previous chapter. His thesis is that, with the destruction of the temple in Jerusalem in AD 70, Matthew's Jewish-Christian community lacked a sense of spiritual authority. Up to that time, the temple and its ceremonies had played an important role in the spiritual and social lives of this community of faith. With the destruction of the temple, the local synagogue gained in prominence. Spiritual authority for the community was to be found in its strict obedience of the law, the Torah, as interpreted by the rabbis and Pharisees. But by the early eighties the church was beginning to pull away from the synagogue, no longer able to submit to the interpretations of the Jewish leaders and weary of their abuse of authority. This was a time of upheaval and transition; the community was both divided and dividing. Matthew's goal was to reunite his community by focusing their allegiance on Jesus as the rightful authority for both orthodoxy (right belief) and orthopraxy (right behavior). Everything in Matthew's Gospel, from the opening genealogy to the concluding Great Commission, says Crosby, is designed to demonstrate the spiritual authority God had vested in Jesus Christ and which, through him, has been entrusted to his followers: the Christian church made up of both Jews and Gentiles (over against the Jewish synagogue).[13]

The Sermon on the Mount in particular, Crosby insists, displays Jesus' authority in some dramatic ways. First, Matthew positions Jesus "on the mount," deliberately evoking images of Moses' authority.[14] Second, Matthew has Jesus delivering his new ethical code in a way that suggests a special relationship with "the original Lawgiver, the source of all authority." The implication of this suggested relationship is that Jesus possesses the ability like no one else, not even Moses, to explain what is really in the heart of God. Third, Matthew concludes the Sermon by having Jesus sound a call for his hearers to surrender themselves to his teachings and then records the observation of others that Jesus "taught with authority (*exousia*), and not like their scribes."[15]

The bottom line is that Crosby makes a strong case for the idea that the overall goal of Matthew's Gospel was to argue for the authority of Jesus and his church over against the authority of the scribes and Pharisees as exercised in the synagogue. But then Crosby takes the next step and actually brings this understanding of the polemical nature of the Gospel as a whole to the Sermon on the Mount in particular. Actually, Crosby's focus is exclusively on the section of the Sermon known as the Beatitudes (5:3–12). He views the Beatitudes as a summary of the Sermon as a whole, a new moral code offered by Jesus over against that promoted by the scribes and Pharisees.[16] While Crosby's treatment of the content of the Beatitudes is not completely satisfying, his work nevertheless demonstrates support for the idea that the tension that existed between Jesus and the Pharisees in Matthew's Gospel should be taken seriously when interpreting the Sermon on the Mount.

Another commentator who demonstrates a willingness to keep the polemical tension between Jesus and the Pharisees in mind while interpreting the Sermon is J. Dwight Pentecost. In his popular commentary entitled *Design for Living: Lessons on Holiness from the Sermon on the Mount*, Pentecost takes the position that the Sermon was Jesus' response to some key questions that had been put to him by his followers regarding the specific nature of the repentance he had been emphasizing (4:17). The questions being put to Jesus were: "Just what is involved in the repentance you are calling for? Is the righteousness of the Pharisees sufficient for entrance into the kingdom?" According to Pentecost, Christ's answer to this last question was a resounding "No!" Pentecost writes:

"The major portion of the Sermon on the Mount shows the relationship of the King to the Mosaic Law (5:17—7:6). In this portion Christ reveals Himself as the One who fulfills the Law (5:17–20). He then proceeds (5:21–48) to reject the Pharisaic traditional interpretation of the Law. . . . Christ next rejects the Pharisaic practice of the Law (6:1—7:6). . . . He then concludes the sermon, giving instruction to those who would enter the kingdom (7:7–27)."[17]

I encourage you to take note of the anti-Pharisee element in this analysis of the way the Sermon is structured. This same polemical theme shows up in Pentecost's overall summary of what Jesus intended his sermon to accomplish:

> Thus the Lord, in rejecting both the Pharisaic interpretation of the Law and the Pharisaic practice of the Law, brought this multitude to the conclusion "that except your righteousness shall exceed the righteousness of the scribes and Pharisees, ye shall in no case enter into the kingdom of heaven" (5:20). He closed by offering Himself as the narrow way and as the solid foundation through whom they could come into the kingdom and upon which they could stand. The sermon was designed to lead this multitude away from a false concept of righteousness to a true concept of righteousness, from a false hope of entrance into the kingdom to a sure foundation for entrance into Messiah's kingdom.[18]

While Jack Kingsbury does not go so far as to actually suggest that the tension between Jesus and the Pharisees is the hermeneutical key to the Sermon on the Mount, he comes close. Kingsbury views Jesus to be the protagonist of Matthew's story while the religious leaders function collectively as the antagonist. Moreover, Kingsbury sees the conflict between Jesus and the religious leaders to be central to the plot of Matthew's irony-filled story of how Jesus, Israel's Messiah, came to be crucified and then raised from the dead to become Lord of all. With this paradigm firmly in place, Kingsbury argues that, while Matthew's portrayal of the actual outbreak of conflict between Jesus and the religious leaders does not begin until chapter 9, "Matthew leads the reader to anticipate such conflict."[19]

Kingsbury writes: "In the Sermon on the Mount, for example, Jesus predicts persecution for the disciples after the manner of the Old Testament prophets (5:10–12), disparages the righteousness of the scribes and Pharisees as falling short of what is necessary for gaining entrance into the Kingdom of Heaven (5:20), and castigates the 'hypocrites' in the synagogues for performing their acts of piety not in worship of God but so as to win public acclaim for themselves (6:1–18). Following the sermon, Matthew bluntly tells the reader that, in contrast to Jesus, the scribes are 'without authority' in their teaching (7:28–29)."[20]

Implied in this quote is the idea that one of the purposes of the Sermon on the Mount in Matthew's story is to prepare the reader for the conflict between Jesus and the Pharisees due to commence in chapter 9 and to culminate in chapter 27. In other words, *one of the main themes of the Sermon on the Mount—the heart and soul of Jesus' ministry of spiritual formation—is the tension that existed between Jesus and the Pharisees.*

Having discussed the important role that the Sermon plays in Matthew's Jesus story overall, and how the polemic between Jesus and the Pharisees shows up in his most famous sermon, it is time for us to take a careful look at the first four chapters of this Gospel, which together function as Matthew's literary prelude to the Sermon on the Mount.

Irony in Matthew's Prelude to the Sermon on the Mount (Matthew 1–4)

Irony may be defined as *an event or result that is directly opposite of what is expected.* Literary authors will often use irony in order to instill humor or a sense of drama into their work or in an attempt to cause their readers to think more deeply about the topic at hand. At some key points in previous sections I have attempted to draw attention to the presence of irony in Matthew's overall story. In this section I want to point out how Matthew deliberately and liberally utilized irony as a literary device in the first four chapters of his Gospel in order to prepare his readers not only for the ironic nature of the Jesus story in general but also for the amazingly ironic content they would find in chapters 5–7 (the Sermon on the Mount) in particular. As I do so, please remember that we need to keep the members of Matthew's church in mind—always asking, "What theological lessons would they have been picking up from each of these irony-laden incidents?"

The Genealogy of Jesus (Matthew 1:1–17)

Is it not ironic that Matthew, apparently writing to an audience that included Jews, would break with Hebraic patriarchal tradition and include five women in his genealogy of the person he is going to present as the king, the Messiah of Israel? And how terribly ironic is it that two of these matriarchal ancestors of Jesus were Gentiles (Rahab and Ruth)?

The Birth of Jesus (Matthew 1:18–25)

A pregnant virgin! How is that for irony? And how ironic that the long-awaited king of Israel would be born not to wealthy nobility but to poor common folk, and in such sociologically and spiritually scandalous circumstances.

The Childhood of Jesus (Matthew 2)

How ironic that it was a group of Persian magi (astrologers/wise men), rather than Jewish prophets and sages, who initially discerned the birth of Israel's Messiah! How ironic is it that, according to Matthew's account, the only welcoming committee that visited the newborn king of Israel was made up of Gentiles, not Jews? How tragically ironic that the presence in Bethlehem of a child whose name, Jesus, means "one who saves," would precipitate the slaughter of an unspecified number of innocent children. Finally, how ironic is it that, given Israel's history, the land of Egypt would have to provide a safe haven for Israel's infant Messiah, and that he would end up spending the majority of his formative years in Galilee rather than Judea, in Nazareth rather than Jerusalem?

The Baptism of Jesus (Matthew 3)

How ironic is it that in this Gospel we read of the forerunner to Israel's Messiah (John the Baptist) specifically calling out her religious leaders as standing in need of repentance? Even more ironic is the picture Matthew presents of Israel's Messiah standing in a line of sinners waiting to undergo a ritual of repentance that was usually administered to Gentile converts to the Jewish faith![21]

The Temptation of Jesus (Matthew 4:1–11)

How ironic that in order to successfully bind the strongman, Satan, prior to the formal commencement of his messianic ministry, Jesus had to say no to the temptation to make his life all about the pursuit of physical comfort, emotional security, and professional success—the very things for which the political and religious leaders of Israel in his day (especially the Pharisees) were known.[22]

The Relocation of Jesus' Ministry Headquarters (Matthew 4:12–17)

Is it not ironic that Jesus, the Jewish Messiah, would eventually emerge as a political outsider who kept insisting on spending large amounts of time in a rural province that was known more for its Gentile population than for its Jewish one?

The Selection of Jesus' First Disciples (Matthew 4:18–22)

How ironic that the very first, most important disciples Jesus recruited were a handful of Galilean fishermen rather than a cadre of high-performing rabbinical students!

The Remarkably Rapid Rise of Jesus' Popularity (Matthew 4:23–25)

Finally, how ironic is the fact that Jesus—essentially a ministry outsider with a lack of formal rabbinic credentials—was nevertheless able to attract a huge crowd of curious seekers from regions far and wide?

I believe that, in one way or another, all of the ironic situations just listed were deliberately included by Matthew in the first four chapters of his Gospel in order to prepare his readers for the ironic content they would discover as they made their way through Jesus' Sermon on the Mount.

And we have yet to give sufficient attention to what may be the greatest irony of all: the very coy manner in which Matthew refers in these first four chapters of his Gospel to those folks who would function as the main antagonists in his Jesus story.[23] Perhaps the greatest irony present in the first four chapters of Matthew is that *this Gospel does not record any antagonistic encounters between Jesus and the religious leaders prior to the Sermon on the Mount.* It is highly ironic that even though New Testament scholars are virtually unanimous in asserting that Matthew's Gospel is the more anti-Pharisaical, Mark's Gospel introduces the polemical tension between Jesus and the Pharisees much more quickly than does Matthew (see Mark 2:13–17; 2:18–22; 2:23–28; 3:1–6). On the other hand, it should also be noted that Mark does not present his readers with any sort of "Sermon on the Mount" in his Gospel. This raises the question: *Could it be that Matthew intended the Sermon on the Mount to serve the same literary purpose as Mark's detailed descriptions of these several hostile encounters between Jesus and the Pharisees?* According to this view, Matthew's literary purpose for the Sermon on the Mount was, among other things, to establish for his readers the sense of antagonism between Jesus and the Pharisees that developed early on in Jesus' public ministry.[24]

Given the ironic nature of the events described in the first four chapters of his narrative, it is reasonable to assume that Matthew intended for his readers to develop, at this point in his Gospel presentation, two basic assumptions: first, even more ironies are likely to be forthcoming; and second, Israel's religious leaders are not likely to be portrayed in a positive light. *Indeed, the thesis at work in this chapter (and the three that follow) is that the Sermon on the Mount is filled with irony, and that most of these ironies owe their existence to some belief or behavior of the Pharisees.*[25]

In Summary

In this chapter we have made several observations that are crucial to a proper interpretation of the Sermon on the Mount. First, we observed that the Sermon is all about disciple-making. Not only is the Sermon on the Mount crucial to any catechetical or disciple-making purpose Matthew had in mind for his Gospel, it is not going too far to say that this particular teaching is Matthew's way of presenting to the world the heart and soul of Jesus' ministry of spiritual formation. Second, we observed that the polemical tension between Jesus and the Pharisees that is so readily apparent in the Gospel as a whole is present in the Sermon also. Third, we observed how Matthew seems to have used the literary device of irony in his prelude to the Sermon on the Mount (chapters 1–4) in order to prepare his readers for the greatest irony of all: Jesus' use of the very popular Pharisees as negative examples of what it means to be his disciple and a son or daughter of God's kingdom.

When combined with the contextual observations presented in the previous chapter, I would suggest we have some fairly strong support for my contention that the Sermon on the Mount can and should be utilized as the foundation for a disciple-making curriculum that serves to steer people away from Pharisaism and toward an authentic experience of life in the kingdom of God. In the next three chapters we will put this thesis to the test as we examine the content of Jesus' most famous sermon section by section. But to inspire you to continue this journey with me I want to bring this chapter to a close by pointing out one other important reality concerning the Sermon on the Mount: the fact that over the years many scholars and parish leaders have seen fit to comment on the remarkable value of this Sermon when it comes to the spiritual and ministry formation of Christ's followers. For example, British churchman John R. W. Stott writes, "The Sermon on the Mount is probably the best-known part of the teaching of Jesus, though arguably it is the least understood, and certainly it is the least obeyed. It is the nearest thing to a manifesto that he ever uttered, for it is his own description of what he wanted his followers to be and to do."[26]

Speaking even more specifically of the Sermon's relevance, Stott suggests that it addresses such pertinent themes as a Christian's character (5:3–12); a Christian's influence (5:13–16); a Christian's righteousness (5:17–48); a Christian's piety (6:1–18); a Christian's ambition (6:19–34); a Christian's relationships (7:1–20); and finally, a Christian's commitment (7:21–27).[27]

Guy Greenfield, pastoral counselor and former professor of Christian ethics, also speaks of the value of the Sermon as a discipleship curriculum. In fact, Greenfield goes so far as to suggest that contemporary pastors are actually being remiss if they fail to expose their church members to the content of the Sermon on the Mount in a catechetical setting.

> This first use of the Sermon on the Mount by the Matthean church should be suggestive for use today. How many converts in our contemporary churches are discipled with the content

of the Sermon on the Mount? Memorizing the Sermon on the Mount is one thing and is not enough. Understanding it and applying it to the modern believer's everyday living situation are something else. A class for new converts taught by the pastor could profitably be built around the themes of the Sermon on the Mount.

If C. H. Dodd was right that in the very earliest period of the church's life there were two forms of preaching, namely proclamation (kerygma) and teaching (didache), then should we not ask if our contemporary churches are properly maintaining this needed balance? Have too many pastors majored in proclamation and minored on teaching? No wonder that the typical church has over half its membership on inactive status, baptized but weak in Christian living and witness. The Sermon on the Mount could serve as a pastoral corrective if seriously taught and applied.[28]

Finally, Matthean scholar E. T. France has this to say about the value of the Sermon on the Mount as a discipleship curriculum:

The wide range of material included in that magnificent collection of teaching which we call the Sermon on the Mount is united by its focus on the nature and demands of discipleship. It deals with the true character and rewards of discipleship (5:3–10), the distinctiveness of the disciple (5:11–16), the ethics of discipleship in relation to current understanding of the ethical demands of the law (5:17–48), the disciple's religious observance (6:1–18) and his choice of priorities between the claims of God and of earthly concerns (6:19–34), his attitude to fellow disciples (7:1–6, 12) and to God as his Father (7:7–11); it then concludes with four contrasts between true and false discipleship (7:13–27), which serve to challenge the readers to examine their own standing as followers of Jesus as well as to discern the genuine and spurious among those who are attached to the church. The appropriateness of this collection for use in teaching in the church was quickly recognized; it remains to this day a favourite resource of preachers and teachers who wish to turn the attention of their congregation to what it means to live consistently as a follower of Jesus, and there can be little doubt that Matthew so intended it.[29]

- Core values rooted in Jesus' understanding of the kingdom
- A high regard for the law as an abiding indication of God's will for his people
- A hermeneutic that goes beyond a hyper-literal, legalistic, ultimately self-serving approach to God's Word
- Wisdom concerning the proper manner in which to engage in spiritual disciplines
- Encouragement to forge a sanctified sense of ambition (i.e., a theologically informed perspective concerning work, money, and things)
- Sage advice regarding the most effective way of helping other people
- An understanding of the crucial importance of prayer when living in community
- Vital warnings regarding false shepherds
- A reminder of the decisive need for a radical, personal, enduring commitment to the lordship of Jesus Christ

These are some of the things that a discipleship curriculum based on the Sermon on the Mount can provide the members of evangelical churches. In addition, such a curriculum can help defeat the Pharisaism that is literally causing the evangelical movement to sputter, stutter, and stumble at this critical time in the history of the church—living as we are in an important era of transition between modernity and postmodernity.

I congratulate you on your willingness to slog through these last two chapters, paying your hermeneutical "dues" in the process. Now we are prepared to dive into an informed study of Jesus' most famous sermon. We now have the interpretive lenses in place that will enable us to see what Jesus was really doing in the Sermon on the Mount, and I trust that we are also sufficiently motivated to do so.

In the next chapter we will focus our attention on Matthew 5 and the way in which Jesus directed his followers toward an authentic experience of Christian discipleship by pointing them away from the attitudes and actions modeled by the Pharisees. Are you ready for even more irony? I hope so, because—as the saying goes—you ain't seen nothin' yet!

Notes

1. R. T. France, Matthew: Evangelist and Teacher (Exeter, England: Paternoster Press, 1989), 149.
2. Ibid., 155. See also George Ladd, *A Theology of the New Testament* (Grand Rapids: Eerdmans, 1974), 218–19.
3. France, *Matthew: Evangelist and Teacher*, 155. See also Robert Guelich, *The Sermon on the Mount* (Dallas: Word, 1982), 27–28.
4. France, *Matthew: Evangelist and Teacher*, 155. See also Craig L. Blomberg, *Matthew*, The New American Commentary, vol. 22 (Nashville: Broadman Press, 1992), 24–25.
5. France, *Matthew: Evangelist and Teacher*, 155–56, 164. See R. T. France, *Matthew*, The Tyndale New Testament Commentaries (Grand Rapids: Eerdmans, 1985), 54.
6. France, *Matthew: Evangelist and Teacher*, 165.
7. Donald Guthrie, *New Testament Introduction* (Downers Grove, IL: InterVarsity, 1970), 21–22.
8. The Pentateuch is how biblical scholars refer to the first five books of the Old Testament, traditionally held to have been written by Moses. Thus, some scholars believe that the five discourses presented in Matthew's Gospel are an intentional allusion to the Pentateuch. For example, see Blomberg, *Matthew*, 23; France, *Matthew: Evangelist and Teacher*, 255; Michael Green, *The Message of Matthew*

(Downers Grove, IL: InterVarsity, 1988), 30; A. W. Argyle, *The Gospel According to Matthew* (London: Cambridge University Press, 1963), 4; Davies, *The Sermon on the Mount*, 31–32; Guthrie, *New Testament Introduction*, 23, 31.

9. Jack Kingsbury, *Matthew as Story* (Philadelphia: Fortress Press, 1988), 106. See also Guthrie, *New Testament Introduction*, 32, and Davies, *The Sermon on the Mount*, 31–32.

10. Guelich, *The Sermon on the Mount*, 28.

11. Perhaps this is why Daniel Patte felt the need to write two entire books exploring the connection between discipleship and the Sermon on the Mount! See Daniel Patte, *Discipleship According to the Sermon on the Mount* (Valley Forge, PA: Trinity Press International, 1996; and Daniel Patte, *The Challenge of Discipleship: A Critical Study of the Sermon on the Mount as Scripture* (Harrisburg, PA: Trinity Press International, 1999. See also William Klein, *Become What You Are: Spiritual Formation According to the Sermon on the Mount* (Tyrone, GA: Authentic Publishing, 2006); David B. Howell, *Matthew's Inclusive Story: A Study in the Narrative Rhetoric of the First Gospel* (Sheffield, England: JSOT, 1990), 255–56; France, *Matthew: Evangelist and Teacher*, 155; Kingsbury, *Matthew as Story*, 132; Ralph P. Martin, *New Testament Foundations: A Guide for Students*, vol. 1 (Grand Rapids: Eerdmans, 1975), 224; and Guelich, *The Sermon on the Mount*, 15.

12. Hans Windisch, *The Meaning of the Sermon on the Mount* (Philadelphia: Westminster Press, 1951), 140.

13. Michael Crosby, *Spirituality of the Beatitudes: Matthew's Challenge for First World Christians* (Maryknoll, NY: Orbis Books, 1981), 6–7.

14. Ibid., 7. See also Donald Hagner, *Matthew 1–13*, Word Biblical Commentary, vol. 33A (Dallas: Word, 1993), 86.

15. Crosby, *Spirituality of the Beatitudes*, 7.

16. Ibid.

17. J. Dwight Pentecost, *Design for Living: Lessons on Holiness from the Sermon on the Mount* (Grand Rapids: Kregel Publications, 1999) 15–16.

18. Ibid., 16.

19. Kingsbury, *Matthew as Story*, 118.

20. Ibid.

21. I cannot help but direct your attention to a quote by James Torrance that speaks to me not only of the power of Jesus' incarnation but of his baptism into our sinful condition as well. Dr. Torrance writes: "Christ does not heal us by standing over against us, diagnosing our sickness, prescribing medicine for us to take, and then going away, to leave us to get better by obeying his instructions—as an ordinary doctor might. No, he becomes the patient! He assumes that very humanity that is in need of redemption, and by being anointed by the Spirit in humanity, by a life of perfect obedience for us, by dying and rising again, our humanity is healed in him." James Torrance, "The Vicarious Humanity of Christ," in *The Incarnation-Ecumenical Studies in the Nicene-Constantinopolitan Creed A.D. 381*, ed. Thomas

F. Torrance (Edinburgh: Handsel Press, 1981), 141; cited in Ray S. Anderson, *An Emergent Theology for Emerging Churches* (Downers Grove, IL: InterVarsity, 2006), 94.

22. More will be said about the Pharisees' preoccupation with renown, personal comfort, and wealth in chapter seven.

23. Kingsbury, *Matthew as Story*, 115.

24. See also Luke 5:17—6:11. I'm indebted to Andrew Sloan, this book's editor, for making the helpful observation that Luke's readiness to refer to the tension between Jesus and the Pharisees before presenting his
"Sermon on the Plain" (Luke 6:17–49) would seem to support the thesis that Matthew, over against both Mark and Luke, did indeed intend his "Sermon on the Mount" to introduce his readers to the antagonism that existed between Jesus and the Pharisees.

25. At a couple of places in the Sermon Jesus also seemed to point out problematic beliefs and behaviors associated with the "pagans" (5:47, 6:7, 6:32). Evidently it was Jesus' habit, when doing spiritual formation, to direct his disciples' attention periodically to some anti-model, contrasting the negative example with some aspect of life in the kingdom. At the same time, I intend to show in the pages following that when Jesus did refer to the pagans it had the effect of highlighting an ironic similarity between them and the Pharisees!

26. John R. W. Stott, *Christian Counter-Culture: The Message of the Sermon on the Mount* (Downers Grove, IL: InterVarsity, 1978), 15.

27. Ibid., 19.

28. Guy Greenfield, "The Ethics of the Sermon on the Mount," *Southwestern Journal of Theology* 35 (1992): 19.

29. France, *Matthew: Evangelist and Teacher*, 253.

6

COMING KINGDOM-CORRECT: JESUS, THE PHARISEES, AND DISCIPLE-MAKING IN MATTHEW 5

According to rap parlance, to *come correct* is "to represent the real, to do something the way it should be done."[1] In the earliest days of Jesus' public ministry, his main message had been "Repent, for the kingdom of heaven is near" (Matthew 4:17). It is not illogical to assume that his hearers would have wanted to know what kind of repentance Jesus was talking about and what it meant to enter the kingdom. Coming correct with regard to the kingdom of God (i.e., coming kingdom-correct) is what the Sermon on the Mount is all about.

Once again, the major premise guiding this book is that, properly understood, the Sermon on the Mount has what it takes to function as the foundation of a disciple-making curriculum that will effectively steer people away from Pharisaism and toward an authentic experience of kingdom living. While space will not allow an exhaustive treatment, my goal in the next three chapters is to provide at least a cursory demonstration of how, in Matthew 5–7, we are able to see Jesus making kingdom-correct disciples, using the Pharisees as anti-models (negative examples) in the process.

Irony in the Sermon's Prologue (Matthew 5:1–2)

The first two verses presented in chapter 5 are technically not a part of the teaching Jesus delivered on the mount or hillside.[2] Still, there are some issues addressed here that are not without interpretive significance. This brief passage reads this way:

> Now when he saw the crowds, he went up on a mountainside and sat down. His disciples came to him, and he began to teach them, saying . . .
>
> (Matthew 5:1–2)

I want to suggest that it does not take long for the careful reader to discern that Matthew's use of irony in the four chapters leading up to the Sermon will most certainly be present within the Sermon itself.

The Significance of the Sermon's Setting

The "crowds" spoken of in 5:1 appear to be the same "crowds" referred to at the end of chapter 4 (4:23–25). Matthew seems to present to us the idea that even though Jesus had up to this point been proclaiming and demonstrating the availability of God's kingdom in the synagogues of Galilee, the crowds of hurting people following Jesus had swelled in number to such an extent that he was only able to meet with them in large open spaces. With great compassion Jesus had been ministering to these crowds by performing various kinds of healings and exorcisms, demonstrating the power of the kingdom in the process. At some point, however, Jesus must have sensed that these crowds of curious seekers needed to know more about what it meant to live one's life under the rule and reign of God. He therefore made the decision to do what was necessary to cause this outdoor healing service to segue into a preaching/teaching service. The text tells us that, seeing the crowds, Jesus "went up on a mountainside and sat down" (Matthew 5:1). Biblical scholars report that it was customary for rabbis to teach from a seated position. Thus, when Jesus assumed this posture, his disciples came to him understanding that he wished to teach.[3]

But the text specifically tells us that Jesus "went up on a mountainside." How significant was this hillside setting? In what appears to be Luke's version of this same sermon (Luke 6:17–49), we are specifically informed that it was delivered on a level place (Luke 6:17). Could it be that Matthew had a theological/rhetorical reason for having his readers picture Jesus delivering this sermon on a mountainside?[4]

In a previous chapter we took note of the fact that many scholars believe Matthew's reference to Jesus going up on a mountainside to teach was intentionally reminiscent of Moses receiving and issuing the Old Testament law on Mount Sinai. These scholars are convinced that the purpose of the Sermon on the Mount in Matthew's story was to establish quickly and efficiently the authority of Jesus, Israel's messianic king. Therefore, it is held that Matthew's portrayal of Jesus assuming a Moses-like posture and then delivering a teaching that rang with a special sense of authority (Matthew 7:28–29) was filled with theological and rhetorical significance.[5]

If this is true, then we run into yet another occasion where Matthew's story exudes a very strong sense of irony. However aware of the suggested rhetorical/theological significance of the Sermon's hillside setting a typical first-century Jewish reader of this Gospel might have been, he or she would not have expected to hear Jesus do anything more than simply reiterate the highly venerated law of Moses. *But what Jesus had actually come to do was to establish a new covenant altogether, a covenant that would differ significantly from the one that Moses had initiated.* The difference between gospel and law is magnificent, as this quote from Carl Vaught indicates: "Moses went up onto a mountain where the first covenant came to focus in the first Law. Matthew, writing with Hebrew apologetic purposes in view, wishes to remind us of this fact, and thus he sketches a picture of Jesus going up onto a hillside to begin his teaching. However, this time what is at stake is a new covenant; on this occasion, what is involved is a new Law; in this context, what Jesus formulates is the Law the prophet Jeremiah mentions when he says: 'One day I will write a new law on your hearts' (Jeremiah 31:33)."[6]

Could it be that Matthew (and/or Jesus himself) did invest the hillside setting with this sort of New Covenant significance? If so, we need to recognize the tremendous importance of the teaching we are about to study and to approach it with the same sense of reverence, awe, and appreciation that, on their best days, earmarked the attitude of the ancient Jews toward the law of Moses.

And yet, in our case, the sense of reverence, awe, and appreciation with which we approach the Sermon is heightened by the fact that this teaching does not present us with laws written in stone that we must strive to obey in our own strength. No, a big part of what makes the New Covenant "new" (and different) is that an authentic, Spirit-empowered "reading" of the Sermon on the Mount is the process by which God writes his law upon our hearts, the means by which Jesus instills within his followers the grace necessary to actually discern and do the will of God. *I am convinced that a sincere, prayerful study of this discipleship teaching, engaged in under the right circumstances (genuine Christian community), has the power to change us at the core of our being.* The Sermon on the Mount is Jesus' way of planting the seed of kingdom life deep within those who have made the decision to follow him.[7] This really is good news!

The Significance of the Sermon's Audience

Another item of interpretational significance derives from the fact that Matthew's prologue makes it clear that, despite the presence of the "crowds," the Sermon is really directed at Jesus' "disciples." Look at Matthew 5:1–2 again:

> Now when he saw the crowds, he went up on a mountainside and sat down. His disciples came to him, and he began to teach them, saying . . .

When we modern readers see the word "disciples" in the biblical text we may tempted to think of "the Twelve" (Matthew 26:14) whom Jesus also designated "apostles" (Mark 3:14). But the larger context of Matthew 5:1–2 and 7:28–29 makes it clear that Jesus' original audience was made up of a much larger group of followers.[8] We have already acknowledged that Matthew intended *his audience* (the members of his church) to identify themselves with Jesus' disciples. The fact that in Matthew's story *Jesus' audience* was comprised not just of the Twelve but of a larger body of disciples probably would have encouraged Matthew's church members to identify themselves with those whom Matthew portrays as sitting on the hillside listening to Jesus' most famous sermon.

And yet, at the same time, it is important for us to understand that Matthew's church members—Matthew's audience—would have, like us, possessed some prior information that the "audience on the mount" would have lacked. Matthew's church members would have read his Gospel (or heard it read to them) from a vantage point *after* Jesus' public ministry, arrest, death, resurrection, and ascension had all played out. They would have possessed what narrative theologian Jerry Camery-Hoggatt refers to as "prior information" and the "outside repertoire of cultural information that is necessary if the interpreter is to fill in the gaps in the story and organize the parts into a coherent and meaningful whole."[9] This means that as Matthew fashioned his discourse he could assume that *his audience*, the readers of his Gospel, possessed some knowledge about Jesus' life and ministry that *Jesus' audience* on the mount did not.[10]

This observation is important for a couple of reasons. First, it means that as we modern interpreters go about the task of uncovering the meaning of the Sermon on the Mount we do *not* do so by asking the question "What do I hear Jesus saying at this point in the Sermon?" Nor should we wonder "What did the 'audience on the mount' hear Jesus saying at this point in the Sermon?" No, the correct interpretive question is "Given the outside repertoire of cultural information Matthew knew was at their disposal, how did he intend his readers (the members of his church) to interpret what Jesus was saying to his audience on the mount at this point in the Sermon?"

Second, this observation is important because it explains why, at several points along the way, Jesus seems to say things in the Sermon that would not have made sense to his audience on the mount but would have made sense to Matthew's audience—his church members. This ironic feature of Matthew's Gospel begs for further explanation.

Here and there in Matthew 5–7 the modern interpreter will come across a passage that simply assumes the audience on the mount knew what Jesus was saying, even though the text itself does not seem to provide sufficient clues for an unambiguous interpretation. This is a telltale sign that Matthew was, ironically, actually telling his story with his readers (his church members) in mind. Matthew assumed that his readers possessed the "outside repertoire of cultural information" necessary for them to correctly "fill in the gaps in the story and organize the parts into a coherent and meaningful whole." In other words, Matthew could allow ambiguities to exist in his story line because he trusted that his readers would be able, given the prior information they possessed, to "disambiguate" the text.[11]

Now it just so happens that a crucial bit of prior information that Matthew would have assumed the readers of his Gospel already possessed was an understanding of the very real polemical tension that had existed between the historical Jesus and the historical Pharisees.[12] Matthew could assume this because he knew that his readers were already familiar with the Jesus story in its oral form, and possibly with the Gospel of Mark.[13] Therefore, this literary-critical discussion of the distinction that needs to be made between Jesus' audience and Matthew's audience turns out to be quite important indeed. This means that *some of Matthew's allusions in the Sermon on the Mount to the Pharisees as anti-models of authentic Christian discipleship could be quite implicit while still being recognizable by his intended audience—the members of his church.* We will need to keep this fact in mind as we proceed to make our way through the remainder of Jesus' most famous discipleship teaching, filled as it is with irony after irony.

Irony in Matthew 5:3–12 – The Christian's Character

Jesus began his sermon by advocating a set of actions and attitudes— the core values of the kingdom of heaven. I want to suggest that the Beatitudes, as a whole, constitutes a description—a declaration even—of the kind of people who are truly blessed, the kind of people who are to be envied because they are truly approved of by God.[14]

From an exegetical standpoint, I believe the key to understanding the basic meaning of each of the beatitudes is to recognize the Old Testament passages that would have likely informed Jesus' understanding of what it means to be blessed by God.[15] This hermeneutical method helps us narrow the range of possible meanings Jesus might have intended when he uttered this list of core values. For example, if we take seriously the idea that Jesus had Isaiah 57:15 and 66:1–2 in mind when he spoke of being "poor in spirit," it might help us conclude that this core value calls for his followers to recognize their radical need for God in their lives, rather than to assume that material things can provide soul satisfaction or that they can live truly God-pleasing lives in their own strength and on the basis of their own resources (for contrast, see Luke 16:13–15).

Likewise, if we take Isaiah 61:1–3 into consideration when interpreting what Jesus meant when he pronounced blessing upon those who "mourn," it might help us conclude that this core value calls for Jesus' followers to be the kind of people who, instead of minimizing their sin and continually justifying themselves before God and others, are profoundly aware of and grieved by the presence and effect of sin in their own lives (for contrast, see Luke 18:9–14).

If we take Psalm 37:1–11 seriously when contemplating what it means to be "meek," it might lead us to conclude that this core value calls for Jesus' followers to keep trusting in God to protect and provide for them rather than feel the need to return tit for tat or engage in conspicuous, shameless self-promotion (for contrast, see Matthew 23:1–12).

If we conclude that Jesus might have had Psalms 42:1–2 and 63:1–5 in mind when he indicated that truly blessed people are those who "hunger and thirst for righteousness," then we might hear Jesus calling for his followers to cultivate proactively an insatiable appetite for an intimate, interactive, prophetic relationship with God rather than rest content with a religion based on legalistic and ritualistic performance (for contrast, see Matthew 23:23–24).[16]

If we decide that Micah 6:6–8 and Zechariah 7:9–10 were Old Testament passages that informed Jesus' pronouncement of blessing upon the "merciful," then we may understand this beatitude as Jesus' way of encouraging (empowering) his followers to cultivate a capacity for compassion, rather than harsh judgmentalism, in their dealings with others (for contrast, see Matthew 9:10–13).

If we decide that the beatitude which speaks of the "pure in heart" being blessed by God was inspired by Jesus' familiarity with Old Testament passages such as Psalm 24:3–6, then we may safely assume that Jesus expects his followers to avoid hypocrisy, possess integrity, be sincere in their professed devotion to God, and engage in spiritual disciplines for the right reasons rather than as a mere show designed to impress others (for contrast, see Matthew 23:25–28).

If we decide that Psalm 34:11–21 had anything to do with the blessing Jesus pronounced upon the "peacemakers," then we can conclude that Jesus expects his followers to refuse to return evil for evil and to promote peace rather than strife and conflict (for contrast, see Matthew 23:29–32).

Finally, if we come to the conclusion that such passages as Psalms 22, 69, and 119 were formative in Jesus' understanding of the blessing that awaits those willing to be "persecuted because of righteousness," then it becomes apparent that in this last-but-not-least beatitude Jesus is calling for his followers to be willing to endure hostility at the hands of others because of their loyalty to God and his kingdom cause (for an amazing contrast, see Matthew 23:33–39).

However one interprets the precise meaning of a particular beatitude, many commentators have remarked on the unexpected, ironic nature of this list of God-approved actions and attitudes. More than one commentator has observed that these core values of the kingdom[17] are quite contrary to the prevailing notions of blessedness (i.e., success and happiness) present in most societies.[18] This level of irony would probably be apparent to even the casual reader, since Matthew was careful to include so much irony in the chapters leading up to the Sermon. The counterintuitive aspects we run up against in Matthew's presentation of Jesus' genealogy, birth, childhood, baptism, and temptation; the manner in which Jesus relocated his ministry headquarters and selected his first disciples; the remarkably rapid rise of his popularity—all serve to alert readers that the Jesus story before them is going to be less than completely predictable. Furthermore, the contrasting biblical references which I inserted parenthetically in my treatment of the Beatitudes all serve to indicate that *the New Testament Gospels (especially the one penned by Matthew) portray the Pharisees as religiously minded folk whose lives are completely lacking when it comes to the core values of the kingdom!*

Most commentators fail to reckon with the fact that the Beatitudes also functioned as the introduction to Jesus' sermon.[19] Any effective preaching pastor will verify how important a good sermon introduction is. In a sermonic setting, one only has a few scant seconds to arrest the attention of the listening audience and convince them to give the forthcoming message a fair and, hopefully, enthusiastic hearing. One classic way to capture the attention of an audience is to begin a sermon by saying something shocking, unexpected, ironic. A startled, curious audience is much more likely to pay close attention to what a preacher is saying than one that is fast becoming bored and disinterested.

What I am suggesting here is that Jesus knew exactly what he was doing when he began his Sermon with the Beatitudes. Matthew's readers would have readily understood that these core values of the kingdom would have been extremely shocking to Jesus' hearers—his "audience on the mount"—not just because they seemed to contradict the prevailing notions of happiness and success in their society, but also because the "outside repertoire of cultural information" they possessed would have allowed them to recognize that *each and every one of these attitudes and actions was noticeably absent from the lives of most of the scribes and Pharisees of their day!*[20]

Matthew's readers would have, therefore, recognized a tremendous irony at work in Jesus' sermon introduction. They would have found it very difficult to associate such qualities as spiritual poverty, meekness, purity of heart, peacemaking, etc. with the typical separatist Pharisee. Indeed, it is likely that Matthew's readers would have immediately recognized that the lifestyle of the typical Pharisee was completely antithetical to the lifestyle Jesus was commending via this list of kingdom core values.[21]

On the other hand, Matthew's readers also would have known how very popular, despite their separatism, the scribes and Pharisees had been with the *am-ha-aretz* (people of the land) in Jesus' day—how they were viewed by the common folk as spiritual heroes.[22] Thus, this sermon introduction would have been understood by Matthew's readers as a supremely effective way for Jesus to gain immediately the rapt attention of his large audience while also forecasting what the dual theme of his sermon would be: an explication of life in God's kingdom and the nature of authentic Christian discipleship over against the beliefs and practices of the Pharisees.[23]

Irony in Matthew 5:13–16 – The Christian's Influence

In this next section of the Sermon, Matthew's readers would have understood Jesus to be communicating to his hearers the good (but ironic) news that if they were to live their lives in accordance with the core values he had just articulated—especially the last one, which pronounced blessing upon those willing to endure persecution because of their commitment to him—they (rather than the Pharisees) would be the ones who would end up functioning as the true heroes of God's kingdom.

This interpretation is supported by the following exegetical observations. First, throughout this passage Jesus seems to purposefully direct his hearers' attention away from the Pharisees and teachers of the law back toward themselves by his emphatic use of the pronouns "you" and "your."[24] Take a look at what this passage (backing up to verse 11 in order to get the full effect) looks like with all of the second-person pronouns emphasized:

Blessed are *you* when people insult *you*, persecute *you* and falsely
say all kinds of evil against *you* because of me. Rejoice and be
glad, because great is *your* reward in heaven, for in the same way
they persecuted the prophets who were before *you*.

You are the salt of the earth. But if the salt loses its saltiness,
how can it be made salty again? It is no longer good for anything,
except to be thrown out and trampled by men.

You are the light of the world. A city on a hill cannot be
hidden. Neither do people light a lamp and put it under a bowl.
Instead they put it on its stand, and it gives light to everyone in
the house. In the same way, let *your* light shine before men, that
they may see *your* good deeds and praise *your* Father in heaven.

(Matthew 5:11–16, italics added)

Eleven times in six verses Jesus directs his hearers' attention toward
themselves. I believe Jesus was trying to help his audience experience
a radical paradigm shift. Before this, the Pharisees and teachers of the
law would have been viewed by these common folk as Israel's spiritual
heroes. At the very least, they were the ones who promoted themselves as
defenders of the faith, loyal protectors of God's honor, fierce proponents
of the religious traditions handed down by their rabbinic masters. In
other words, the day before Jesus preached the Sermon on the Mount it
would have been the Pharisees and teachers of the law who would have
been viewed as the salt of the earth and the light of the world. But Jesus'
use of second-person pronouns in Matthew 5:11–16 effectively changed
all that.

Second, a careful reading of this passage will show Jesus subtly por-
traying the Pharisees and teachers of the law not as heroes to be admired
but as villains to be avoided. We have just seen how Jesus informs his
hearers that becoming his followers will invite persecution. He goes on

to say, however, that this experience of persecution for his sake should, ironically, be considered a badge of honor and a privilege to be rejoiced over in that it assures a heavenly reward and puts the devoted disciple in the same class of spiritual heroes as the Old Testament prophets. Take another look at Matthew 5:11–12, this time with the third-person references emphasized:

> Blessed are you when *people* insult you, persecute you and falsely say all kinds of evil against you because of me. Rejoice and be glad, because great is your reward in heaven, for in the same way *they* persecuted the prophets who were before you.

This raises the important interpretive question: Who are the "people" Jesus is talking about here? Who did Jesus envision as those who would eventually insult and persecute his followers?

Jesus obviously expected his hearers to know who he was talking about, and yet Matthew makes no effort in the text to identify them. This is one of those passages, referred to above, where the modern interpreter must conclude that, because Matthew had his readers in mind, he could allow the presence of ambiguity in the text.[25] Matthew's readers would have been familiar with the antagonist role the Jewish leaders (especially the Pharisees) played in the real-life persecution of Jesus and his first followers. Indeed, they themselves may have experienced insult and persecution from the "synagogue across the street." Thus, they possessed the "outside repertoire of cultural information" that was necessary for them to fill in the gaps in the story and understand that in 5:11–12 Jesus was referring to the Pharisees, as Matthew 10:17 and 23:29–36 would later verify.[26] Far from being Israel's spiritual heroes, the Pharisees would prove to be the primary persecutors of Christ's followers in the earliest era of Christian history.

The third bit of exegetical support for the perspective that Jesus was, ironically, referring to his loyal followers as spiritual heroes in the making derives from the fact that Jesus proceeds in the Sermon (5:13–16) to explain to his hearers that their commitment to continue living their lives according to the core values of the kingdom despite the experience of fierce persecution will cause them to become profoundly productive in terms of the economy of the kingdom. They will begin to function as spiritual salt and light. Their good deeds, performed over Christ's signature (i.e., in his name), will cause others around them to want to likewise become members of God's kingdom.[27] In other words, they will become what the Pharisees and teachers of the law are not: truly productive agents of the kingdom of God.[28] How ironic that the people most influential in God's kingdom economy turn out to be not the super-spiritual Pharisees but the impious members of the *am-ha-aretz* who have become devoted disciples of Jesus![29]

But in order to be effective the salt has to remain salty (pure) and the light must not be hidden (out of fear of persecution). It is imperative that Christ's followers learn how to imitate him in the way they interact with God and others. Thus, Jesus goes on in the remainder of his sermon to speak of Christian ethics, spirituality, ministry, and integrity.

Irony in Matthew 5:17–48 – The Christian's Righteousness

Because this section of the Sermon is somewhat lengthy and dense, I am going to bracket off verses 17–20 and verse 48 and treat them as separate texts.

Matthew 5:17–20

Actually, these four verses stand at the very heart of Matthew 5, and perhaps of the Sermon as a whole. Jesus makes it very clear in this passage that he has not come to abolish the Law or the Prophets, but to fulfill them.[30] He goes on to insist, in a somewhat dramatic manner, that he has a high rather than low view of the Law. He then concludes this paragraph with the startlingly ironic statement that unless the righteousness of his hearers surpasses that of the Pharisees and teachers of the law (scribes) they "will certainly not enter the kingdom of heaven" (5:20).

Matthew's readers would have readily understood why Jesus seems a bit defensive here, even though thus far in the narrative nothing has been said about him possessing a low view of the Law. According to Mark's Gospel, by this time in the story of Jesus' ministry the Pharisees had already begun to consider Jesus guilty of blasphemy (Mark 2:1–12), of impiety (because of his associations with sinful people—Mark 2:13–17), of not doing enough to keep his disciples from breaking the Sabbath (Mark 2:23–28), and of breaking the Sabbath himself (Mark 3:1–6). Very soon they would publicly accuse him of being in league with the devil (Mark 3:22). Matthew likely assumed that his readers possessed this "prior information" and were therefore able to fill in the gaps and disambiguate his text. Matthew expected his readers to know, or at least surmise, that the Pharisees and teachers of the law had come to view Jesus as a rogue rabbi who, because he had (in their opinion) a frighteningly "low" view of the Law of Moses, was therefore soft on sin.

What is more, it is probable that the Pharisees and teachers of the law had begun to float a rumor to this effect. This interpretive suggestion is supported by William B. Tolar, a professor of biblical backgrounds. Commenting on Matthew 5:17–20, he writes, "The scribes and Pharisees regarded themselves as keepers, interpreters, and teachers of God's law. Through the years they had developed a complex system of rules and regulations (their interpretations of scripture) which they equated with God's laws. The Pharisees had so completely identified their interpretations of scripture with scripture itself, they could not distinguish between the two and therefore regarded Jesus as a dangerous revolutionary and wanted to kill him (see John 5:18). In their bitter and blind resentment of Jesus they had probably started rumors that he was intentionally destroying the laws of God."[31]

To reiterate, *Jesus appears to be on the defensive in 5:17–20 because he was!* This explains why the latent polemical tension that up to this point had been merely implicit in the text suddenly becomes stunningly explicit. In Matthew 5:20 (the one verse which, more than any other, could qualify as the interpretive key to the Sermon as whole), Jesus says: "For I tell you that unless your righteousness surpasses that of the Pharisees and the teachers of the law, you will certainly not enter the kingdom of heaven." [32] This warning uttered by Jesus would have seemed the epitome of irony to his listeners. Keeping in mind the popularity and hero status that the Pharisees and teachers of the law enjoyed in Jesus' day,[33] it would have been quite unexpected and provocative for Jesus' "audience on the mount" to hear him say that the righteousness exhibited by the super-spiritual, hyper-scrupulous Pharisees and teachers of the law actually fell short of the mark of what God was looking for in his people. Of course, because of their pre-understanding of Jesus' historical critique of the hypocrisy present in the lives of the Pharisees and teachers of the law, Matthew's readers would have understood that the irony present in the text at 5:17–20 was a rhetorical device designed to highlight the tension that existed between Jesus and the Pharisees and to prepare the reader for the next section of Jesus' sermon.[34]

Matthew 5:21–47

It is possible to view Matthew 5:21–47 as a collection of texts that are connected not only by proximity but also by a common, unifying theme. As just indicated, in Matthew 5:20 (perhaps the interpretive key to the entire sermon) Jesus makes the startling statement that he fully expects his followers, as newly naturalized citizens of God's kingdom, to manifest a righteousness that far surpasses that of the Pharisees and teachers of the law. At this point in the Sermon, Jesus proceeds to provide his hearers with no less than six examples of how—ironically—the strict, legalistic, hyper-literal hermeneutical approach of the Pharisees and teachers of the law had caused them to miss the heart of God and to forge a lifestyle that, while adhering to the letter of the Law, was nevertheless lacking in true righteousness.

The scholarly consensus is that Jesus' frequent refrain, "You have heard that it was said" (5:21, 27, 31, 33, 38, 43), refers to the teaching of the scribes and Pharisees—the teachers and leaders of the synagogue.[35] *In each case, Jesus boldly counters the ethical teaching of the Pharisees and teachers of the law with his own announcement of the kind of behavior that God is really looking for.* Matthew's readers would have understood that in the course of providing his hearers with these six antitheses ("You have heard that it was said . . . But I tell you . . .") Jesus was not just demonstrating that it is possible to focus on the letter of the Law and still miss the spirit of it; he was also indicting the Pharisees for several hypocritical actions and attitudes.[36] This is what happens when religious people treat the Bible as a moral rule book rather than as a means by which the prayerful reader might grow in his or her ability to discern the heart of God in this or that ethical situation. The truth is that an innate, fallen tendency to look for loopholes will cause even the most super-spiritual church member to minimize in self-serving ways the ethical imperatives found in Scripture. This is what the Pharisees had been doing, and Jesus was about to bring attention to their hypocrisy and faux righteousness in a very public manner.[37]

Space will not allow a thorough exposition of these six antitheses. Still, I want to do my best in these pages to give you a rough idea of how I see Jesus teaching his disciples kingdom ethics by contrasting a true righteousness before God with that of the Pharisees.

Jesus' Teaching concerning Murder. In 5:21 Jesus reminds his hearers of an ethical teaching they had received from their teachers (the Pharisees and teachers of the law):

> You have heard that it was said to the people long ago, "Do not murder, and anyone who murders will be subject to judgment."

The Pharisees and teachers of the law would have based their teaching on Old Testament passages such as Exodus 20:13 and 21:12, which strictly forbid the act of premeditated murder. Since the letter of the Law simply said "You must not murder people," a strict, hyper-literal, legalistic, loophole-oriented, self-serving interpretation of this command would have allowed the Pharisees to conclude that *as long as they did not literally kill anyone, it was OK for them to write people off as useless, assassinate their characters, hurl hurtful epithets their way, and mentally wish them dead.*[38]

But in Matthew 5:22 Jesus goes on to explain the kind of behavior God is really looking for:

> But I tell you that anyone who is angry with his brother will be subject to judgment. Again, anyone who says to his brother, "Raca," is answerable to the Sanhedrin. But anyone who says, "You fool!" will be in danger of the fire of hell.

According to Jesus, an ethic that is truly in touch with the heart of God calls for Christ's followers to do much more than refrain from committing literal murder. We can and must avoid committing mental and verbal murder as well.[39]

Jesus' Teaching concerning Adultery. In 5:27 we find Jesus reminding his hearers of another ethical teaching that had been delivered to them by the Pharisees and teachers of the law:

> You have heard that it was said, "Do not commit adultery."

This teaching would have been based upon Old Testament passages such as Exodus 20:14 and Leviticus 20:10. Since the letter of the Law simply said "You must not sleep with another person's spouse," a strict, hyper-literal, legalistic, loophole-oriented, self-serving interpretation of this command would have allowed the Pharisees to conclude that *it was OK to turn people into sexual objects and leer at them lustfully as long as they did not go on to act physically on the impulse.*[40]

But in Matthew 5:28 we find Jesus going beyond the mere letter of the Law to reveal the spirit behind it:

> But I tell you that anyone who looks at a woman lustfully has already committed adultery with her in his heart.

This insightful passage indicates that we do not actually have to sleep with someone other than our mate in order to be guilty of the sin of adultery in God's eyes. According to Jesus, an ethic that is truly in touch with the heart of God calls for Christ's followers to do much more than refrain from literally sleeping with other folks' spouses. We can and must avoid committing spiritual adultery as well.[41]

Jesus' Teaching concerning Divorce. In 5:31 Jesus moves on to another ethical issue he considered important when he reminds his hearers that, according to the Pharisees and teachers of the law,

> It has been said, "Anyone who divorces his wife must give her a certificate of divorce."

This teaching would have been based primarily upon a strict interpretation of Deuteronomy 24:1–4, which essentially instructed the men of Israel not to send their wives packing without the proper paperwork, and not to remarry them once they had been married to other men. A strict, hyper-literal, legalistic, loophole-oriented, self-serving interpretation of this command would have allowed the Pharisees to conclude that *as long*

as they did not sleep with women they were not married to at the time—as
long as they legally divorced and remarried before switching partners—they
were free to experience sexual intimacy with many women over a lifetime.[42]

But Jesus confronted this kind of behavior when he went on to say:

But I tell you that anyone who divorces his wife, except for
marital unfaithfulness, causes her to become an adulteress, and
anyone who marries the divorced woman commits adultery.

(Matthew 5:32)

Jesus evidently wanted his hearers to understand that marriage is
serious business in God's eyes. Divorce should not be the first thing we
think of when we become frustrated with our spouse or when we see
someone else we think we would rather be with. This powerful passage
says that to divorce one person in order to be with another is tantamount
to the sin of adultery. According to Jesus, an ethic that is truly in touch
with the heart of God calls for Christ's followers to allow the Holy Spirit
to help us avoid the hardness of heart that usually makes divorce seem
like such a necessity. Empowered by the transformative experience of
grace, we can and must work hard to keep our marriages intact, rather
than separate what God has joined together. (That this is the correct way
to understand Jesus' meaning here is supported by what we hear Jesus say
about divorce in Matthew 19:1–9.)

Jesus' Teaching concerning the Importance of Keeping Oaths. In
5:33 Jesus moves on to talk about another important ethical issue: truth
telling. He begins by reminding his hearers of another teaching they had
received from the Pharisees and teachers of the law:

Again, you have heard that it was said to the people long ago,
"Do not break your oath, but keep the oaths you have made to
the Lord."

This teaching would have been based on Old Testament passages such as Numbers 30:2, Deuteronomy 6:13, and Exodus 20:7. Taken together, we might conclude that the letter of the Law simply calls for the people of Israel to be careful to keep the oaths they take before God since these verbal promises have been made either to him or in his name. Matthew 23:16–22 would suggest that, over time, the Pharisees had adopted a strict, hyper-literal, legalistic, loophole-oriented, self-serving interpretation of these commands that allowed them to conclude that *as long as they did not actually use the name of God when swearing an oath or making a promise, they were legally and morally free not to make good on their pledges.*[43]

Jesus condemned this tendency to twist the truth, not only in his denunciation of the Pharisees and teachers of the law in 23:16–22, but also here in the Sermon on the Mount:

> But I tell you, Do not swear at all: either by heaven, for it is God's throne; or by the earth, for it is his footstool; or by Jerusalem, for it is the city of the Great King. And do not swear by your head, for you cannot make even one hair white or black. Simply let your "Yes" be "Yes," and your "No," "No"; anything beyond this comes from the evil one.[44]
>
> (Matthew 5:34–37)

According to Jesus, an ethic that is truly in touch with the heart of God calls for Christ's followers to avoid the use of slippery speech altogether. Rather than engage in an elaborate, complicated, and calculating swearing of oaths, we can and must simply say what we mean and mean what we say. Any attempt to manipulate others by fancy or misleading rhetoric is simply evil.

Jesus' Teaching concerning the Pursuit of Justice. Moving on to an-other important ethical topic, in 5:38 Jesus reminds his hearers of another teaching they had received from the Pharisees and teachers of the law:

> You have heard that it was said, "Eye for eye, and tooth for tooth."

This is the concept referred to in Latin as *lex talionis*, the law of retaliation—of tit for tat—which would have been based upon Old Testament passages such as Leviticus 24:19–20: "If anyone injures his neighbor, whatever he has done must be done to him: fracture for frac-ture, eye for eye, tooth for tooth. As he has injured the other, so he is to be injured." Interpreted in isolation from other mitigating passages, such as Leviticus 19:18 and Zechariah 7:9, a strict, hyper-literal, legalistic, loophole-oriented, self-serving interpretation of Leviticus 24:19–20 would have allowed the Pharisees to conclude that *it was morally justifi-able (perhaps even mandated) for them to return tit for tat to anyone who in any way brought them harm, discomfort, or inconvenience.*

While the culture of Jesus' day would have perhaps refrained from the practice of literally lopping off limbs, gouging out eyeballs, knocking out teeth, etc.,[45] it is easy to see how the legalistic mindset of the Pharisees and teachers of the law could have made them very litigious—extremely eager to see any harm, damage, or slight redressed in a court of law.[46] Indeed, the letter of the Law might have seemed to them to actually re-quire that civil lawsuits be rigorously engaged in whenever necessary, not only for the sake of the health of the society but out of strict obedience to God's Law as well. Moreover, it is easy to see how a strict, legalistic mindset, when combined with a natural human tendency toward the maintenance of one's rights and property, would have produced within the Pharisees a certain reluctance to go out of their way to forgive or show compassion to others.

But in Matthew 5:39–42 Jesus announces the kind of behavior God is really looking for:

> But I tell you, Do not resist an evil person. If someone strikes you on the right cheek, turn to him the other also. And if someone wants to sue you and take your tunic, let him have your cloak as well. If someone forces you to go one mile, go with him two miles. Give to the one who asks you, and do not turn away from the one who wants to borrow from you.

According to Jesus, an ethic that is truly in touch with the heart of God calls for Christ's followers to recognize that they do not have to respond tit for tat to anyone who hurts them in some way. Neither should they feel the need to be stingy with their time, energy, and resources. Jesus' followers can and must learn how to forgive and show compassion to others.

Jesus' Teaching concerning the Proper Treatment of One's Enemies. In the final antithesis provided by Jesus he draws his listeners' attention to one final ethical teaching they had received from their teachers, the Pharisees and teachers of the law:

> You have heard that it was said, "Love your neighbor and hate your enemy."

> (Matthew 5:43)

The first half of this teaching would have been based on Leviticus 19:18, which calls for God's people to love their neighbors as themselves. With regard to the second half of the teaching referred to by Jesus—the instruction to hate one's enemies—I know of no passage in the Old Testament that explicitly calls for this behavior. The only Old Testament passage I can find that might be construed as scriptural support for this practice would be Psalm 139:21–22: "Do I not hate those who hate you,

O LORD, and abhor those who rise up against you? I have nothing but hatred for them; I count them my enemies." Though the Old Testament contains other passages that specifically call for God's people to help their enemies rather than hate them (for example, Exodus 23:4–5; Proverbs 25:21–22), it appears that the Pharisees and teachers of the law preferred to base their ethic on passages such as Psalm 3:7; 18:32–42; 55:15; 69:19–28; 71:9–13; 118:5–12; and on Psalm 139:19–22, where the psalmist is either (a) using poetic hyperbole in order to express his radical devotion to God; (b) expressing (as a vassal) his loyalty to Yahweh (his sovereign) in a manner common to the ancient Near East; or (c) is honestly venting the frustration he felt toward those he considered his enemies. Regardless, a strict, selective, hyper-literal, legalistic, loophole-oriented, self-serving interpretation of Psalm 139:21–22 would have allowed the Pharisees to conclude that *as long as they did their best to love their neighbors and friends, it was morally appropriate for them to hate those they considered their enemies.*

But then Jesus came along in his Sermon on the Mount and confronted this practice of selective loving in no uncertain terms:

> But I tell you: Love your enemies and pray for those who persecute you, that you may be sons of your Father in heaven. He causes his sun to rise on the evil and the good, and sends rain on the righteous and the unrighteous. If you love those who love you, what reward will you get? Are not even the tax collectors doing that? And if you greet only your brothers, what are you doing more than others? Do not even pagans do that?

> (Matthew 5:44–47)

Since this particular passage presents the underlying rationale for why Jesus' disciples can and must function as salt and light (Matthew 5:13–16) by rejecting the teachings of the Pharisees and teachers of the law (see Matthew 16:6–12) and engaging instead in all the loving, merciful, compassionate behaviors he has called for thus far in his Sermon (Matthew 5:20–47), I want to humbly offer the following paraphrase of what I hear Jesus saying in it:

> The Pharisees and teachers of the law talk a lot about being God's children, but they are not really. For example, while they correctly teach that it is important for you to obey the Old Testament command to love your neighbor, they mistakenly teach that it is appropriate for you to hate your enemies. They do not understand that it is precisely this ability to pray God's blessing upon those who are out to get them that separates those who are truly God's kids from those who only think they are.
>
> What the Pharisees do not understand is that your heavenly Father (or Abba) is a very loving being! His very essence is love. It just flows out of him indiscriminately. This explains why, for example, the sun does not shine and the rain does not fall on good, righteous people only, but on evil, unrighteous folks as well.
>
> What kind of heavenly reward do you think you will deserve for having spent your life loving only those who loved you first? Even self-centered CEOs, sociopathic gang members, and fanatical terrorists are capable of taking care of their own. How could that kind of selective caring serve to distinguish the true child of God from the person who lacks the presence of God's Spirit in his or her life?
>
> No, in order for you to really function as the light of the world and the salt of the earth you will have to do better than the Pharisees and teachers of the law, who routinely murder folks with their mouths, commit adultery in their hearts, change marriage partners like suits of clothes, use slippery

speech to manipulate one another, respond tit for tat to those who injure or inconvenience them, and hate their enemies. I am here to tell you that what God really wants is for you to let me help you become profoundly loving people, just like your Father in heaven.

Are you able to discern the "underlying rationale" which I am suggesting emanates in an implicit manner from Matthew 5:42–47? If not, hopefully the next section of our survey of the Sermon will make it plain.

Matthew 5:48

The key to understanding and embracing my paraphrase of 5:44–47 is found in 5:48. Jesus had previously made the startling statement that he fully expects his followers to manifest a righteousness that surpasses that of the Pharisees and teachers of the law (5:20). After providing his hearers with a litany of examples of the kind of self-serving righteousness that God is *not* looking for, he concludes this section at 5:48 with a somewhat startling call for his followers to be perfect even as their heavenly Father is perfect.

This particular verse has been the subject of much debate. Seizing on the translation of the Greek word *teleios* into English as "perfect," some commentators have concluded that Jesus never really expected his followers to attempt to put the ethical teachings presented in the Sermon into actual practice, at least not in an effort to thereby forge an acceptable righteousness before God.[47] The idea here is that Jesus was deliberately calling for his followers to do the impossible precisely so that they, in despair, would recognize their complete inability to create in their own strength a righteousness that would meet God's high ethical standards. Thus, they would be forced to come to Jesus the Messiah, acknowledging their radical dependence on his imputed righteousness.

To some degree I concur that the Sermon on the Mount was intended to have this effect. It is important for Christ's followers to recognize their need to experience the imputed righteousness of Christ (see Romans 3:19–24; 2 Corinthians 5:21) and to remember that prior to the return of Christ he or she will always be *simil justus et peccator* (simultaneously righteous and sinful). However, I also agree with Carl Vaught who, in his book *The Sermon on the Mount: A Theological Interpretation*, reminds his readers that there are other ways of understanding what Jesus had in mind when he used the word *teleios* to describe the goal of his ethic. Vaught writes:

> It is important to focus on the Greek word that is translated "perfection" in this passage. The word *telios* is the term from which we get the word *telos,* or "end." As a result, the word translated "perfection" means the end toward which a developing being is oriented so that when it reaches that end, it will finally be mature, and by implication, be what it was meant to become. . . . "Be engaged," Jesus says, "in the task of becoming what you were meant to be, reaching the *telos,* the purpose, the goal, and the maturity for which you were intended." In these terms, the Sermon on the Mount intends to bring the followers of Jesus into a kingdom that has both come and is coming and into a way of life that makes it possible for us to live in terms of the end toward which we ought to be directed.[48]

According to the view put forward by Vaught, Jesus' call for his followers to be perfect even as their heavenly Father is perfect is as much a promise as it is a command. The idea is that we belong to a loving, compassionate God who delights in empowering his children to likewise behave in loving, compassionate ways. The message of Jesus to his followers is "You can do this. You can become so secure in your experience of God's love and grace that you are able to pass this same love and grace on to others, even your enemies. This is precisely what I expect you to spend the rest of your lives as my disciples learning how to do."[49]

The question is if Matthew's readers would have understood Jesus in this way. I believe that the members of Matthew's church would have been more aware than the modern interpreter of what the Greek word *teleios* would mean in this context. Perhaps even more to the point, they would have possessed a more thorough understanding of the relationship between law and gospel in the theology of Jesus (and Paul).[50] Equipped with a profound understanding of the empowering nature of grace, they would have taken very seriously Jesus' call for them to internalize the radical love of their heavenly Abba so that they, like him, might actually manifest a righteous, loving, gracious lifestyle that differed drastically from the faux righteousness of the Pharisees and teachers of the law.[51]

In *What's So Amazing About Grace?* Philip Yancey tells a story about a friend who rode a bus to work and overheard a conversation between a young woman sitting next to him and her neighbor across the aisle. The woman was reading M. Scott Peck's best-selling book, *The Road Less Traveled*. According to Yancey's friend, the conversation went like this:

> "What are you reading?" asked the neighbor.
>
> "A book a friend gave me. She said it changed her life."
>
> "Oh yeah? What's it about?"
>
> "I'm not sure. Some sort of guide to life. I haven't gotten very far yet."
>
> She began flipping through the book. "Here are the chapter titles: 'Discipline, Love, Grace, . . .'"
>
> The man stopped her. "What's grace?"
>
> "I don't know. I haven't gotten to Grace yet."[52]

The sad truth is that there are a lot of people in evangelical churches who have not gotten to grace yet. This is a huge issue because grace is a powerful, life-transforming force. Grace is the difference between genuine Christianity and every other religion. Grace is the difference between Pharisaism and authentic kingdom living. We simply must learn to embrace God's grace!

I suspect that despite all the ethical imperatives Jesus delivered, this is the biggest lesson he intended his hearers on the hillside to grasp. I also suspect Matthew was eager for the members of his church to catch hold of it as well. Learning to embrace grace is the crucial first step to coming kingdom-correct. As we have seen, this was something the Pharisees had been unable or unwilling to do. In the next chapter we will turn our attention to Matthew 6 and the way Jesus courageously continued to use the Pharisees as anti-models of even more discipleship dynamics.

Notes

1. *Rap Dictionary*, s.v. "Come correct," http://www.rapdict.org/Come_correct (accessed December 2, 2008).
2. While most Matthean scholars are of the opinion that what is presented in Matthew 5–7 is actually a compilation of various teachings uttered by Jesus during his public ministry, brought together by Matthew in order to accomplish his catechetical/apologetic aims (see Archibald M. Hunter, *A Pattern for Life: An Exposition of the Sermon on the Mount* [Philadelphia: Westminster Press, 1965], 11; Donald Hagner, *Matthew 1–13*, Word Biblical Commentary, vol. 33A [Dallas: Word, 1993], 83; Michael Green, *The Message of Matthew* [Downers Grove, IL: InterVarsity, 1988], 88–89), my exegetical analysis will take Matthew's story at face value, as if the Sermon on the Mount was a specific discreet speech made by Jesus early on in his public ministry. This is evidently the way Matthew wished his readers to experience it.
3. Carl G. Vaught, *The Sermon on the Mount: A Theological Interpretation* (Albany, NY: State University of New York Press, 1986), 6. See also D. A. Carson, *The Sermon on the Mount: An Evangelical Exposition of Matthew 5–7* (Grand Rapids: Baker, 1978), 14; Hagner, *Matthew 1–13*, 85–86.
4. Though anything is possible, I find it difficult to believe that Matthew and Luke are reporting on completely different occasions since Jesus delivered essentially the same sermon. In my mind it is more likely that these two inspired authors felt the freedom to share the same Jesus story in slightly different ways in order to emphasize the theological truths that their respective communities needed to hear.
5. For example, see Sinclair Ferguson, *The Sermon on the Mount: Kingdom Life in a Fallen World* (Carlisle, PA: Banner of Truth Trust, 1997), 6.
6. Ibid.
7. For a succinct and accessible survey of the various ways in which the Sermon on the Mount has been approached over the years, see William Klein, *Become What*

You Are: Spiritual Formation According to the Sermon on the Mount (Tyrone, GA: Authentic Publishing, 2006), 18–26, Ultimately, Klein opines that while a perfect obedience to the ethical teachings presented in the Sermon awaits the appearance of the kingdom at the end of the age, Jesus expects his followers to take his ethical teachings seriously here and now. The indwelling of God's Spirit makes it possible for sincere Christ-followers to render kingdom obedience here and now. Hence the name of the book: *Become What You Are*. See pp. 31–32, 37–38. My approach differs from Klein's only in the sense that I tend to emphasize more the performative nature of Jesus' utterances in his most famous sermon. In other words, I would underscore the idea that the Sermon is a speech act which, when prayerfully listened to, actually exercises a transformative effect upon the sincere listener/disciple.

8. In Matthew's Gospel the Twelve have not been selected yet (see Matthew 10:1–4). In Luke's version, the Twelve have already been chosen by this time in the story, but Luke is careful to make the distinction between the Twelve and a larger body of followers whom he refers to as "disciples" (see Luke 6:12–20).

9. Jerry Camery-Hoggatt, *Speaking of God: Rhetoric of Text, Rhetoric of Sermon* (Peabody, MA: Hendrickson, 1995), 41.

10. Jack Kingsbury, *Matthew as Story* (Philadelphia: Fortress Press, 1988), 38.

11. In *Speaking of God*, Camery-Hoggatt speaks of the need for interpreters of biblical texts to "disambiguate," to resolve the ambiguities present in a biblical text by "filling in the gaps" in a way that the original author obviously intended. See p. 89.

12. I am endorsing here the view that the New Testament's portrayal of the Pharisees is historically trustworthy. See my treatment of this debate in chapter two.

13. Archibald M. Hunter, *A Pattern for Life: An Exposition of the Sermon on the Mount* (Philadelphia: Westminster Press, 1965), 13. Hunter posits that when Matthew sat down to write his Gospel he had before him the Gospel of Mark, "Q," and "M." "Q" refers to a hypothetical source some scholars believe both Matthew and Luke made use of, along with the Gospel of Mark, when they composed their Gospels. "M" refers to a hypothetical "sayings source" only Matthew used.

14. See Carson, *The Sermon on the Mount*, 16; David Hill, *The Gospel of Matthew*, The New Century Bible Commentary (Grand Rapids: Eerdmans, 1972), 110.

15. We need to remember that a truly high (orthodox) Christology takes the humanity of Jesus as seriously as his divinity. While still retaining his essential deity, a truly human Jesus (made possible by the incarnation) would have developed his theology the way other Jews of his day would—by studying the Old Testament Scriptures (see Luke 2:52)!

16. I am indebted to Dallas Willard (lecture presented in Fuller Seminary Doctor of Ministry seminar, "Spirituality and Ministry," Sierra Madre, CA., June 20, 2002) for the idea that Jesus possessed an "intimate, interactive" relationship with God and desired to teach his disciples how to do likewise.

17. Carson, *The Sermon on the Mount*, 16. Carson refers to the Beatitudes as "norms of the kingdom."

18. John R. W. Stott, *Christian Counter-Culture: The Message of the Sermon on the Mount* (Downers Grove, IL: InterVarsity, 1978), 40. See also E. Stanley Jones, *The Christ of the Mount* (New York: Abingdon, 1931), 54–85; D. Martyn Lloyd-Jones, *Studies in the Sermon on the Mount*, vol. 1 (Grand Rapids: Eerdmans, 1971), 35–36; J. Dwight Pentecost, *Design for Living: Lessons on Holiness from the Sermon on the Mount* (Grand Rapids: Kregel Publications, 1999) 33; Craig L. Blomberg, *Matthew*, The New American Commentary, vol. 22 (Nashville: Broadman Press, 1992), 101–2; Green, *The Message of Matthew*, 91; Ferguson, *The Sermon on the Mount*, 17, 44.

19. In his commentary on the Sermon, A. Tholuck does make reference to the role of the Beatitudes as the introduction of Jesus' sermon. A. Tholuck, *Commentary on the Sermon on the Mount* (Philadelphia: Smith English and Co., 1860), 62. See also Blomberg, *Matthew*, 95.

20. W. D. Davies, *The Sermon on the Mount* (Nashville: Abingdon, 1966), 86.

21. See Georg Strecker, *The Sermon on the Mount: An Exegetical Commentary* (Nashville: Abingdon, 1988), 40, where the author argues that the demand of purity that is present in the "pure in heart" beatitude is "turned indirectly against the attitude of the Pharisees, who are pictured as the antitype in Matthew's Gospel." See also Vaught, *The Sermon on the Mount*, 15–16, where the author suggests that the key to understanding the "poor in spirit" beatitude is to reflect upon Jesus' parable of the Pharisee and the tax collector praying in the temple (Luke 18:10–14). See also Ferguson, *The Sermon on the Mount*, 47.

22. William Coleman, *Those Pharisees* (New York: Hawthorn Books, 1977), 27. See also Marcel Simon, *Jewish Sects at the Time of Jesus* (Philadelphia: Fortress Press, 1967), 10; W. D. Davies, *Introduction to Pharisaism* (Philadelphia: Fortress Press, 1967), 17.

23. Some scholars believe that Matthew deliberately structured his Gospel so that each major section is thematically connected to another major section in a chiastic, concentric, or symmetrical manner. Most versions of this structural theory connect the Sermon on the Mount with the denunciation of the Pharisees in chapter 23. For example, see Robert H. Gundry, *Matthew: A Commentary on His Literary and Theological Art* (Grand Rapids: Erdmans, 1994), 166; Hagner, *Matthew 1–13*, lii; R. T. France, *Matthew: Evangelist and Teacher* (Exeter, England: Paternoster Press, 1989), 148. Thus, this theory lends support for the idea that as the Matthean Jesus enunciated the blessings contained in the Beatitudes he had the failings of the Pharisees in mind.

24. Davies, *The Sermon on the Mount*, 86; Blomberg, *Matthew*, 101.

25. See Kingsbury, *Matthew as Story*, 39, where the author explains that Matthew expected his readers (church members) to possess information that the rhetorical hearers of Jesus did not. Kingsbury goes on to identify specifically 5:11–12 as an example of a passage where Matthew felt the freedom to allow some ambiguity to exist in the text he had composed.

26. Hagner, *Matthew 1–13*, 95.

27. Robert Guelich, *The Sermon on the Mount* (Dallas: Word, 1982), 125, 129.

28. Hill, *The Gospel of Matthew*, 115. Hill suggests that Jesus' reference in 5:13 to salt losing its saltiness was designed to serve as a warning to the disciples not to follow the path of Israel who ought to have been the salt of humankind but had lost all its savor and saltiness. Support for this idea can be found in the fact that later in the story (21:33–45) Jesus would spell out his frustration with the low level of ministry productivity rendered by Israel's religious leaders. See also Hagner, *Matthew 1–13*, 99, 101.

29. Guelich, *The Sermon on the Mount*, 127.

30. R. T. France is careful to point out that when Jesus referred to "the Law or the Prophets" he was actually referring to the Old Testament Scriptures as a whole; the third element in the Hebrew scriptures, the "Writings," did not need to be specifically included. R. T. France, *Matthew*, The New International Commentary on the New Testament (Grand Rapids: Eerdmans, 2007), 181.

31. William B. Tolar, "The Sermon on the Mount from an Exegetical Perspective," *Southwestern Journal of Theology* 35 (1992): 4–12.

32. See Hagner, *Matthew 1–13*, 83, where Hagner cites Joachim Jeremias' view that 5:20 can be considered the "theme" of the Sermon.

33. According to Craig Blomberg (*Matthew*, p. 105), among Jesus' contemporaries the scribes and Pharisees "were a paradigm of the greatest righteousness imaginable within Judaism." See also John Wick Bowman and Roland W. Tapp, *The Gospel from the Mount* (Philadelphia: Westminster Press, 1957), 63.

34. Hagner (*Matthew 1–13*, p. 110) suggests that 5:17–20 is filled with irony in that Jesus is using "the language of the Pharisees" ("not the smallest letter, not the least stroke of a pen") to make the point that "he alone, and not the Pharisees, can interpret the Torah finally and authoritatively."

35. Tolar, "The Sermon on the Mount from an Exegetical Perspective," 7. See also Stott, *Christian Counter-Culture*, 72.

36. Clarence Bauman, *The Sermon on the Mount: The Modern Quest for Its Meaning* (Macon, GA: Mercer University Press, 1985), 156. Bauman cites the view of Karl Bornhäuser that each and every antithesis presented in 5:21–48 constituted an implicit indictment of a specific Pharisaic teaching or practice. See also Guelich, *The Sermon on the Mount*, 17; Stott, *Christian Counter-Culture*, 78–80; Green, *The Message of Matthew*, 92–97; Bowman and Tapp, *The Gospel from the Mount*, 64–105.

37. I want to suggest that it is even possible that Matthew intended his readers to see, on the one hand, a loose but direct relationship between these six indictments and the seven woes pronounced upon the Pharisees in chapter 23 and, on the other hand, a loose, inverse (ironic) relationship between this list of indictments and the set of kingdom core values (the Beatitudes) with which Jesus began this sermon.

38. William Barclay, *The Gospel of Matthew*, The Daily Bible Study Series (Philadelphia: Westminster Press, 1975), 1:138.

39. In Matthew 5:23–26 Jesus goes on to indicate how important it is for his followers to recognize that their relationship with God is impacted by their relationship with their peers.

40. Vaught, *The Sermon on the Mount*, 79–81. See also Dallas Willard, *The Divine Conspiracy: Rediscovering Our Hidden Life in God* (San Francisco: HarperSanFrancisco, 1998), 158ff. for a discussion concerning "The Destructiveness of Fantasized Desire."

41. In Matthew 5:29–30 Jesus underscores the gravity of sin in general and the importance of what he has just said about spiritual adultery in particular by speaking, sarcastically, of the need to do whatever is necessary to avoid sin, even to the point of gouging out one's right eye and/or cutting off one's right hand. To my knowledge, all contemporary scholars contend that Jesus did not mean for his followers to take the instructions presented in these verses literally. For example, see Carson, *The Sermon on the Mount*, 44; Blomberg, *Matthew*, 109; Barclay, *The Gospel of Matthew*, 1:148.

42. Bible commentator William Barclay tells us that in Jesus' day this question of divorce and remarriage was being hotly debated. Barclay implies that there were many Pharisees who embraced the idea that a man could divorce and remarry as often as he liked, as long as he did it legally. One rabbinical school, the school of a rabbi named Shammai, taught that the only legal grounds for divorce was adultery. But there was another school, the school of a rabbi named Hillel, which taught that a man could divorce his wife for any reason at all—for such things as spoiling his dinner by putting too much salt in his food, going out in public with her head uncovered, talking with men in the streets, developing a reputation as a brawling woman, speaking disrespectfully of her husband's parents in his presence, or simply being troublesome or quarreling with her husband too much. According to Barclay, a certain Rabbi Akiba [*sic*] actually taught that a man could legally divorce his wife even if he simply "found a woman whom he considered to be more attractive than she." Barclay, *The Gospel of Matthew*, 1:152. See also Vaught, *The Sermon on the Mount*, 85–86, 88; Jacob Neusner, *From Politics to Piety* (Englewood Cliffs, NJ: Prentice-Hall, Inc., 1973), 114. Neusner confirms the report that Rabbi Aqiba [*sic*] maintained that a man could divorce his wife if he found a prettier woman!

43. According to William Barclay, "The Jews divided oaths into two classes, those which were absolutely binding and those which were not. Any oath which contained the name of God was absolutely binding; any oath which succeeded in evading the name of God was held not to be binding. The result was that if a man swore by the name of God in any form, he would rigidly keep that oath; but if he swore by heaven, or by earth, or by Jerusalem, or by his head, he felt quite free to break that oath. The result was that evasion had been brought to a fine art." Barclay, *The Gospel of Matthew*, 1:159. See also Vaught, *The Sermon on the Mount*, 93–94.

44. Barclay explains: "The idea behind this was that, if God's name was used, God became a partner in the transaction; whereas if God's name was not used, God had nothing to do with the transaction. The principle which Jesus lays down is quite

clear. In effect Jesus is saying that, so far from having to make God a partner in any transaction, no man can keep God out of any transaction. God is already there. The heaven is the throne of God; the earth is the footstool of God; Jerusalem is the city of God; a man's head does not belong to him; he cannot even make a hair white or black; his life is God's; and, therefore, whether God is actually named in so many words or not, does not matter. God is there already." Barclay, *The Gospel of Matthew*, 1:159–60.

45. There is some question as to how strictly and frequently *lex talionis* was actually applied even in ancient Israel. See Barclay, *The Gospel of Matthew*, 1:164.

46. Barclay informs us that the rabbis eventually began the practice of assessing the monetary value of injuries rendered and requiring reparation. Barclay, *The Gospel of Matthew*, 1:164–65. On the other hand, cultural anthropologist Bruce Malina suggests that first-century Mediterranean Judeans were highly concerned about the maintenance of honor in the larger social realm and would have considered it highly dishonorable to seek redress in civil court from one's equals (as if one could not deal with one's equals otherwise). I do not take this to mean, however, that there existed a social pressure to give in to one's adversaries rather than go to court, but rather that one's honor depended upon one's ability to settle interpersonal disputes in some deft way that avoided both going to court and giving in. If Malina's insight is valid, and my interpretation of him is accurate, this means that it would have been even more ironic and countercultural for Jesus to encourage his followers to settle interpersonal disputes by simply giving and forgiving. This "giving and forgiving" approach to conflict resolution would have gone against the grain of both the Pharisees' Scripture-mandated litigiousness and the sense that one's honor required the ability to handle interpersonal grievances deftly without going to court or giving in. Bruce Malina, *The New Testament World: Insights from Cultural Anthropology* (Louisville: Westminster John Knox Press, 2001), 43.

47. For example, according to D. A. Carson (*The Sermon on the Mount*, 153), the interpretive position held by Lutheran orthodoxy is that "the Sermon is an impossibly high ideal designed to make men aware of their sin and turn to Christ for forgiveness."

48. Vaught, *The Sermon on the Mount*, 11.

49. Note that in Luke's version of this exhortation (Luke 6:36) the call is for Jesus' disciples to be merciful as their (heavenly) Father is merciful.

50. This understanding of the difference between law and gospel would have been even more profound if, as many scholars believe, Matthew's community was located at or near Antioch where, according to the Book of Acts, the apostle Paul himself had ministered for some time.

51. Ferguson, *The Sermon on the Mount*, 114, 116. Ferguson insists that the "heart of the problem" with the Pharisees was that they did not know God as their heavenly Father (*Abba*).

52. Philip Yancey, *What's So Amazing About Grace?* (Grand Rapids: Zondervan, 1997), 29.

7

WEIGHT WHERE IT COUNTS: JESUS, THE PHARISEES, AND DISCIPLE-MAKING IN MATTHEW 6

I once read somewhere that to make a sailboat both safe and maneuverable a huge weight must be attached to its hull. The fact that a sailboat is heaviest below the water line means that no matter what happens to it—even if the wind and waves cause the boat to tip over completely—it will eventually right itself. When it comes to sailboats, it is crucial for there to be a weightiness about them that is not readily observable to onlookers.

The same thing holds when it comes to Christian disciples. In Matthew 6 we find Jesus calling for his followers to possess both a secret and a simple life. In the first half of the chapter (verses 1–18) Jesus instructs his followers to reject the ostentation of the Pharisees and, instead, to engage in devotional practices in a particular manner and with a particular motive. In the second half of the chapter (verses 19–34) the Teacher exhorts his disciples to reject the materialism of the Pharisees (see Luke 16:14) and, instead, to make the pursuit of God's kingdom and righteousness their greatest goal. In Matthew 6 as a whole we find Jesus encouraging his followers to take a careful look at their lives in order to make sure that they, unlike the Pharisees, are "heaviest below the water line": that they possess a spirituality that, while weighty, is not readily observable to onlookers.

Irony in Matthew 6:1–18 – The Christian's Piety

In this section Jesus continues to engage in the spiritual formation of his followers while also pointing out the deficiencies of the Pharisees. But now the focus is not on the ethics of the Pharisees but rather on their hypocritical piety.

Three Devotional Disciplines: Giving, Prayer, and Fasting

Three times in this section of the Sermon Jesus makes reference to some publicly pious "hypocrites" who are guilty of engaging in three key devotional disciplines (almsgiving, prayer, and fasting) in a wrong manner and with a wrong motive. Here are the pertinent passages:

> So when you give to the needy, do not announce it with trumpets, as the hypocrites do in the synagogues and on the streets, to be honored by men. I tell you the truth, they have received their reward in full.

> (Matthew 6:2)

> And when you pray, do not be like the hypocrites, for they love to pray standing in the synagogues and on the street corners to be seen by men. I tell you the truth, they have received their reward in full.

> (Matthew 6:5)

When you fast, do not look somber as the hypocrites do, for
they disfigure their faces to show men they are fasting. I tell you
the truth, they have received their reward in full.

(Matthew 6:16)

Once again, Matthew's readers would have had no problem understanding the identity of the "hypocrites" referred to in these passages.
Despite the fact that the word "Pharisee" does not appear in this section of the Sermon, it is not unusual for scholars and commentators
to identify the hypocrites as Pharisees.[1] This identification is possible
for several reasons. First, in the remainder of Matthew's Gospel Jesus
refers specifically to the Pharisees as hypocrites no less than eight times
(Matthew 15:7; 22:18; 23:13,15, 23, 25, 27, 29). Second, Jesus' main
criticism of the hypocrites here in Matthew 6 is their pursuit of the attention and admiration of others instead of God. In the other Gospels we
read how Jesus indicted the Pharisees and teachers of the law for being
guilty of the same thing (Mark 12:38–40; Luke 20:46–47; John 5:44).
Third, in Matthew 6:5 Jesus refers to hypocrites "standing in the synagogues," and we know it was the Pharisees who based their operations out
of the synagogues and who ruled over them (see Matthew 23:2–3; John
12:42). Fourth, as we will soon see, our knowledge of the devotional
practices of the Pharisees alerts us to the fact that many of them were
indeed guilty of the problematic devotional practices Jesus refers to in
this section of his sermon. Scottish New Testament interpreter William
Barclay, in particular, provides a wealth of information when it comes to
the devotional practices of the Jews in Jesus' day. According to Barclay,
the devout Jew (Pharisee) could be guilty of drawing attention to himself
as he gave to the poor both in the synagogues and in the marketplace;[2]
turning his daily prayer times into ritualistic recitations of pre-written
liturgical prayers;[3] and going to great lengths on Mondays and Thursdays

(their fast days) to let everyone around him know that he was going without food for reasons of piety.[4] Put all this together and it argues for the fact that when Jesus taught his followers how *not* to give, pray, and fast, he had the Pharisees in mind.

Jesus goes on to make it very clear that he is not condemning an engagement in devotional disciplines per se. Far from it. His point is that while he expects his followers to engage in the very same spiritual disciplines as those practiced by the Pharisees, these devotional disciplines should be performed in a particular *manner* and with a particular *motive* that differed drastically from that of their supposed religious teachers.

With regard to the issue of *manner*, Jesus tells his disciples that they should give to the poor, pray, and fast—but in secret rather than in public, before God alone. They should not parade their piety about, nor should they exude an air of super-spirituality. Whenever possible, Jesus' followers should allow the spiritual discipline of secrecy (purposefully hiding one's piety or good works from the attention of others) to impact the way they engage in their other devotional practices.

With regard to the issue of *motive*, Jesus is critical of the Pharisees' preoccupation with being viewed as especially pious and spiritual in the eyes of their peers. After each reference to the practice of the Pharisees, Jesus comments in what appears to be a very sarcastic manner: "they have received their reward in full." He then goes on to call for his followers to practice their spiritual disciplines with the right motive in place: that is, *in order to please and commune with their heavenly Abba in a personal way, trusting that by doing so they are putting themselves in a position to receive a truly worthwhile reward.*

Though Jesus does not elaborate on the nature of this reward in his sermon, the issue is well worth wondering about. In his commentary on the Gospel of Matthew, Barclay offers that the Christian disciple can expect to be rewarded in at least three ways for his or her service to the Lord: (a) with a sense of *inner satisfaction* for having done the right thing despite the costs involved, and with the feeling of spiritual *contentment* that this experience of soul satisfaction brings; (b) with *still more work to do* now that we have proved ourselves capable of it; and (c) with *the vision of God*. When Barclay refers to the "vision of God" he seems to be describing what theologians refer to as the beatific (or heavenly) vision—the experience of beholding God with joy and delight rather than fear and dread after this life is over.[5] I want to suggest, however, that there is a sense in which the vision of God is, like his kingdom, something that is both already and not yet.[6] There is a sense in which we can experience, at least in part, the vision of God (an intimate experience of his presence) here and now in this present state of existence.

Furthermore, we need to consider the possibility that *this is essentially what Christian discipleship is all about!* One of the main things that set the historical, human Jesus apart from all other human beings was the way he was able to live his day-to-day life continually beholding God, continually sensing his empowering presence, continually communing with him in an intimate, interactive way. In his very real humanity, Jesus loved God so very much because he knew him so very well. This communion with a loving, compassionate, and gracious God empowered the human Jesus to behave in loving, compassionate, and gracious ways toward his neighbors—the rest of the human race. It is precisely this ability to know and love God and our neighbors that Jesus wants to help his apprentices acquire. And just as Jesus evidently felt the need to engage in such spiritual disciplines as giving, prayer, fasting, solitude, service, celebration, worship, fellowship, etc. in order to experience an ongoing communion with God, so should we.

In other words, I am suggesting that we need to recognize the connection between Matthew 6:1–18 and Matthew 5:48. It is by engaging in the devotional practices referred to in 6:1–18 (in the right manner and for the right reason) that Christ's followers are empowered to obey 5:48: to be perfect even as their heavenly Father is perfect, to become loving, compassionate, and gracious children of a loving, compassionate, and gracious God. The Pharisee's approach to spirituality knows nothing of this quest for personal communion and transformation. The Pharisee's quest is for a religious certitude to be achieved by obeying rules and observing rituals in a meticulous manner. Sadly, the payoff for the Pharisee is nothing more than a sense of self-righteousness that has to be bolstered continually by the admiration of others. How sad and yet how common this quest is, even in evangelical churches.

The Lord's Prayer

Jesus' insistence that his followers engage in spiritual disciplines in a particular manner and with a particular motive (contra the Pharisees) shows up again in his sidebar seminar on prayer (6:5–15). I want to suggest that the model prayer Jesus provides his hearers in the Sermon on the Mount was designed to disabuse his disciples of whatever lessons about prayer they had picked up from the Pharisees and teachers of the law (as well as any pagan models they had encountered).

First, we have reason to believe that the Pharisaical tendency when engaging in the act of prayer was to think that the longer and more complicated the prayer the better. Matthew Green reports that "verbosity in prayer was a common ancient failing."[7] In support of this observation, Green cites Rabbi Levi as teaching, "Whoever is long in prayer is heard."[8] And yet Jesus' model prayer encourages brevity, ingeniously covering a lot of spiritual territory in an amazingly succinct manner. The New International Version's rendition of this powerful, paradigmatic prayer (excluding the traditional ending recorded in the text note) contains only fifty-two words!

Second, William Barclay indicates that the Pharisaical tendency to make their prayers long and complicated could also result in their becoming nothing more than ritualistic recitations and occasions for ostentation. Commenting on the ancient Jewish practice of prayer and how these prayers tended to become formalized, Barclay explains that the daily recitation by pious Jews of the *Shema* (Deuteronomy 6:4–9; 11:13–21; Numbers 15:37–41) every morning and evening, and the eighteen prayers known collectively as the *Shemoneh 'esreh* ("The Eighteen") every morning, afternoon, and evening, "had every chance of becoming a vain repetition, which men mumbled through like some spell or incantation."[9]

Then, going on to explain how the Jewish practice of prayer in Jesus' day could degenerate into a pursuit for peer approval, Barclay writes:

> The Jewish system of prayer made ostentation very easy. The Jew prayed standing, with hands stretched out, palms upward, and with head bowed. Prayer had to be said at 9 a.m., 12 midday, and 3 p.m. It had to be said wherever a man might be, and it was easy for a man to make sure that at these hours he was at a busy street corner, or in a crowded city square, so that all the world might see with what devotion he prayed. It was easy for a man to halt on the top step of the entrance to the synagogue, and there pray lengthily and demonstratively, so that all men might admire his exceptional piety. It was easy to put on an act of prayer which all the world might see.[10]

Barclay's observations serve to underscore the idea that when Jesus encouraged his followers not to pray in an empty, repetitious, attention-getting manner, he had the prayer practices of the Pharisees as well as the pagans in mind.

Third, Michael Green points out that Jesus' instruction for his disciples to use the designation "Abba" in prayer was highly unusual and therefore ironic.[11] Green writes: "It begins with the word of intimacy, *Father*. In the Aramaic Jesus spoke, that would be 'Abba,' Jesus' own characteristic address to God. Nobody had ever addressed God like that.

The word was used by little children of their daddy. And Jesus, who alone had that intimacy or relationship with God as his dear daddy, gives his disciples the right to come in on the same level of intimacy, and call God Abba. Amazing!"[12] When Jesus taught his disciples to begin their prayers by addressing God as their heavenly Abba, his disciples recognized that he was taking them into a new devotional dimension—instructing them to do something they had never heard the Pharisees do.

Fourth, while the Pharisees tended to think of the kingdom of God as a geopolitical reality to be achieved at some point in the future, what we find in the "Lord's Prayer," as in Jesus' teaching overall, is the idea that the kingdom of God is the experience of living one's life under the reign of God. Though the full and complete experience of living under the loving lordship of God will not occur until the age to come, both Jesus and Paul seem to suggest that there is a sense in which we are able to enter and experience the kingdom of God here and now (see Mark 12:28–34; Luke 17:20–21; Colossians 1:13–14; 1 Thessalonians 2:11–12).

Thus, Jesus teaches his followers in his sermon to begin their prayers by invoking the power and presence of God's kingdom in a worshipful manner ("Our Father in heaven, hallowed be your name, your kingdom come, your will be done on earth as it is in heaven"). Having done this, prayer is a simple matter of letting our heavenly Abba know what we are in need of, trusting in his great love for us. According to Jesus, we should feel the freedom to bring to God any concerns we have about *provision* ("Give us today our daily bread"), *pardon* ("Forgive us our debts, as we also have forgiven our debtors"), *personal guidance* ("And lead us not into temptation"), and *protection* ("but deliver us from the evil one").

Please notice not only how simple and uncomplicated this model prayer is, but how personal and intimate (though not individualistic) it is. The Lord's Prayer makes no sense apart from the idea that the persons praying it view themselves as beloved children of a loving, compassionate, and gracious God. To the degree that this way of looking at oneself in relation to God was foreign to the Pharisees, this prayer would have made no sense to them. Indeed, the more dogmatic and fastidious Pharisees of Jesus' day might have considered his teaching on prayer to be not just ironic, but downright blasphemous!

If it is true, as I am suggesting, that the key to defeating Pharisaism (and to living in the power of God's love for ourselves and others)[13] is to maintain an intimate, interactive relationship with God as one's heavenly Abba, then to engage in prayer as Jesus instructed in the Sermon on the Mount is strong and necessary medicine. This empowering idea that God is a loving, compassionate, gracious Abba is reinforced every time the Lord's Prayer is uttered in a thoughtful manner.

What about Jesus' reference to the way the pagans pray?

And when you pray, do not keep on babbling like pagans, for they think they will be heard because of their many words. Do not be like them, for your Father knows what you need before you ask him.

(Matthew 6:7–8)

It is possible that all Jesus was doing here was being careful to steer his listeners away from the pagan practice of babbling on and on in prayer—a practice his audience on the mount might have been exposed to through their association with either the Gentiles who lived in Galilee or the occupying Roman soldiers. However, it is also possible to interpret Jesus' reference to the pagans as part of his polemic against the Pharisees. If Matthew could count on his audience (his church members) being familiar with the verbose manner in which the Pharisees engaged in prayer, then what we find in 6:7–8 is an implied linkage between the garrulous prayer practice of the Pharisees and that of the pagans. Talk about irony! How ironic (and significant) that Jesus would compare the self-righteous separatist Pharisees to Gentile unbelievers![14] And all of this is important for the training of Christian disciples so that they might avoid Pharisaism and enjoy life in the kingdom of God.

Irony in Matthew 6:19–34 – The Christian's Ambition

This section of the Sermon is all about money and things and the proper attitude Christ's followers should adopt toward them. From a purely human perspective, what Jesus says here about how his disciples should relate to money and things could be considered highly ironic. Furthermore, my contention is that here, as in the rest of the Sermon, Jesus has the Pharisees in mind as negative examples.

The Interpretive Key to This Section: The Pharisees' Love of Money

At a critical point in Matthew 6:19–34 Jesus warns his hearers that they cannot serve both God and money:

No one can serve two masters. Either he will hate the one and love the other, or he will be devoted to the one and despise the other. You cannot serve both God and Money.

(Matthew 6:24)

Given the natural human tendency to ground one's sense of psychological and physical security upon one's financial well-being, any encouragement at all to prioritize God over money could be considered highly ironic. But the irony does not end there. The Gospel of Luke contains a parallel passage that is nearly identical to Matthew 6:24. However, the very next verse in Luke's version of this passage states rather matter-of-factly that, because the Pharisees "loved money," this encouragement from Jesus to prioritize God over money earned him their scorn. Luke

16:14 reads: "The Pharisees, who loved money, heard all this and were sneering at Jesus."

Since Matthew was writing to an audience that was comprised of at least some Jews, he apparently did not feel the need to explain the many Semitisms (Hebraic or Aramaic idioms) present in his story, nor to provide his readers with the kind of background information about the Pharisees that we find here in Luke 16:14.[15] Could it be that the Pharisees' love of money was well known to Matthew's readers? This idea is supported by Matthew 23:25, where Jesus refers to the teachers of the law and Pharisees as hypocrites who are "full of greed and self-indulgence."

In his book *Design for Living: Lessons on Holiness from the Sermon on the Mount*, J. Dwight Pentecost explains that the reason behind Jesus' discussion of money in the Sermon was precisely the fact that the Pharisees of Jesus' day were "characterized not only by hypocrisy but also by greed."[16] Pentecost presses on to insist that the reason why the Pharisees were so scrupulous about their almsgiving, praying, and fasting was that they viewed these devotional practices as the means by which they might gain God's favor and experience financial blessing.

> The Pharisees built a system in which they sought to enrich themselves by doing things the Law demanded. The Pharisee, as our Lord said in Matthew 6, gave to the poor, prayed incessantly, and fasted twice a week. But he did it to obtain material prosperity from God. He wanted to bind God to pour out blessing on him because of his righteousness. The Pharisees misapplied a scripture verse [Deuteronomy 28:3–6] to convey their concept toward material possessions: "Whom the Lord loveth, He maketh rich." The acquisition of material wealth became the greatest goal in life for the Pharisees. It was a sure sign their righteousness satisfied God and that God had rewarded them by pouring material blessing upon them.[17]

If Pentecost's explanations are accepted, then it would appear that the Pharisees' love of money would have been widely known among the Jews and that Matthew would have been justified in simply expecting his Jewish readers to understand that when Jesus warned his literal disciples against an inordinate love of money and things he had the negative example of the Pharisees in mind. Thus, it may very well be that recognizing the implicit polemic against the Pharisees present in this section of the Sermon is key to a proper interpretation of it!

A Reading of Matthew 6:19–34 with This Interpretive Lens in Place

Without going into too much detail, let us explore how Jesus' teaching about the Christian's ambition might be interpreted if we choose to see it as an implicit critique of the Pharisees' love of money and their tendency toward greed and self-indulgence.

Matthew 6:19–24 is made up of three main exhortations, each of which is followed by a rationale. In this powerful passage Jesus exhorts his followers to invest their lives in the cause of the kingdom rather than in the hoarding of material wealth. The rationale provided by Jesus for this action is that (a) material wealth can slip through our fingers due to theft or decay; (b) to focus all of our attention on the pursuit of material things is to allow our souls to be filled with darkness rather than light (the experience of delusion and depression rather than illumination and inspiration); and (c) it is simply not possible to have two ultimate priorities in life (i.e., we cannot serve God and money).

In Matthew 6:25–32 Jesus exhorts his followers to avoid the natural tendency to worry over such matters as food, drink, clothing, and longevity. Jesus seems to have in mind here a person who is preoccupied not only with living long but also with living well, especially when it comes to food and clothing. The rationale for rejecting such mundane preoccupations is that (a) life is about more than eating well and looking good; (b) these are the kinds of concerns with which the pagans are frenetically preoccupied; and (c) sincere followers of Christ have a heavenly Father who knows their day-to-day needs and who possesses the ability to feed and clothe them in remarkably ample ways.

Given what Jesus has to say here about not stressing over food and clothing, and given our assumption that throughout the Sermon Jesus has the Pharisees and teachers of the law in mind as negative examples, it should not surprise us to read elsewhere in the Gospels of Jesus criticizing the Pharisees for their love of banqueting, their focus on their apparel, and their reputation for taking advantage of poor people, especially widows, in order to maintain their opulent, self-indulgent lifestyles (see Matthew 23:5–6, 25; Luke 11:43; 20:45–47). Is it not likely then that both Jesus' hearers and Matthew's readers would have heard in Jesus' exhortation for his disciples not to stress over food and clothing an implicit critique of the lifestyle of many of the Pharisees?

In Matthew 6:33–34 Jesus exhorts his followers to reject worry altogether and, instead, to focus all their attention on a moment-by-moment pursuit of an intimate, interactive relationship with God and the righteous kind of life such a commitment accomplishes. According to Jesus, it is possible for his followers to worry less about the future and to live more in the present. This kind of worry-free living is possible because (a) God's providence really is something his kids can count on; and (b) the fact is that whatever trouble tomorrow brings, God's grace will be sufficient to help Jesus' followers deal with it.

Then again, as we discovered in chapter one of this work, the ability simply to trust God was not the strong suit of the Pharisees. Their legalistic approach to religion was motivated by a deep need for spiritual certainty and control (which produced for them a sense of psychological safety). Instead of simply resting in the love of a gracious God, they felt the need to earn and deserve his favor instead. Though Luther's example proves otherwise (see chapter three), the attempt to earn God's favor can appear to provide more spiritual certainty than does simply trusting in his love, mercy, and grace. How ironic that such a foundation for the religious life, focused as it is on the ability of our flesh to fulfill God's righteous requirements and produce spiritual and psychological security, can end up causing us (out of fear) to cater to our flesh's craving for financial security as well. Once again, it is possible to argue that as Jesus exhorts his disciples to reject worry and to live worshipfully instead, he may have had the Pharisees as anti-models in mind.

Rather than being heaviest below the water line—rather than possessing a spiritual and moral weightiness in the depth of their souls—Jesus accused the Pharisees and teachers of the law of being hypocrites who were full of greed and self-indulgence (Matthew 23:25). It is quite likely that it was the horrible example set by the Pharisees before their contemporaries that prompted Jesus to include in his discipleship training the strong exhortations concerning the Christian's piety and ambition that we find in Matthew 6. In the next chapter we will consider the possibility that Jesus' teachings concerning the Christian's *relationships* and *commitment* were likewise prompted by the terrible example set by the Pharisees—the very people who had previously been viewed as spiritual heroes. How very predictable at this point: even more irony in Jesus' Sermon on the Mount!

And yet I cannot bring myself to conclude this chapter without encouraging my readers to ask themselves a crucial question: Do you recognize the presence of any hint of Pharisaism in your own devotional practices, relationship to things, or tendency toward worry? We evangelicals talk a lot about being justified by faith, but the way we actually live day to day often gives the lie to the assumption that our "faith" in Christ necessarily involves an "existential trust" in God's ability to take care of us no matter what adversities might come our way.

I recently read in a work of fiction a statement that caused me to do a double take: "Trust is the fruit of a relationship in which you know you are loved."[18] Our ability to really trust in God is rooted in our having internalized at the core of our being the message that we are profoundly loved by him. In our endeavor to see how Jesus used the Pharisees as negative examples of what it means to experience life in God's kingdom, we must not fail to hear, existentially, what Jesus is saying to *us* about how much we are loved by his (and our) heavenly Abba.

This is how we obtain weight where it counts. This is how we become heaviest below the water line. This is how we manage to stay afloat during a spiritual journey that sometimes requires us to pass through some pretty stormy weather. And this is how, as the next chapter will reveal, we become the kind of people who can minister in a truly effective way to others in Jesus' name.

Notes

1. For example, see: Robert Guelich, *The Sermon on the Mount* (Dallas: Word, 1982), 278–79; John R. W. Stott, *Christian Counter-Culture: The Message of the Sermon on the Mount* (Downers Grove, IL: InterVarsity, 1978), 126; John Wick Bowman and Roland W. Tapp, *The Gospel from the Mount* (Philadelphia: Westminster Press, 1957), 111; see Sinclair Ferguson, *The Sermon on the Mount: Kingdom Life in a Fallen World* (Carlisle, PA: Banner of Truth Trust, 1997), 112–13.
2. William Barclay, *The Gospel of Matthew*, The Daily Bible Study Series (Philadelphia: Westminster Press, 1975), 1:187–88.
3. Ibid., 1:191–97.
4. Ibid., 1:235.
5. Ibid., 1:184–85.
6. The idea that the New Testament teaches that the kingdom of God is, at the same time, both already and not yet was popularized decades ago by New Testament scholar George Eldon Ladd. See his many works on the subject, especially *A Theology of the New Testament* (Grand Rapids: Eerdmans, 1974) and *The Gospel of the Kingdom* (Carlisle, England: Paternoster Press, 1959).
7. Michael Green, *The Message of Matthew* (Downers Grove, IL: InterVarsity, 1988), 99.

8. Ibid.

9. Barclay, *The Gospel of Matthew*, 1:192.

10. Ibid., 1:197. It is true that the prayer Jesus gave his disciples as a model for their praying can and has been turned into a liturgical instrument that is routinely offered up by Christians in a formalistic manner. But I would contend that while there can be genuine value in a meaningful, thoughtful, heartfelt recitation of the "Lord's Prayer," given the historical and biblical context in which it was delivered to us, Jesus never meant for this model prayer to become a substitute for the kind of personal, intimate interaction with God which Jesus seems to have modeled for his disciples during his own prayer times.

11. Though the Greek text of Matthew 6:9 uses the word *Pater*, it is likely that in the Sermon Jesus actually used the Aramaic *Abba*. Regardless, the point is that Jesus instructed his disciples to address God in a manner more intimate than was the rabbinical custom.

12. Green, *The Message of Matthew*, 100.

13. Please note that the idea that our experience of God's love can and should inform the way we relate to others is supported by Matthew 6:14–15, where we find Jesus linking the disciple's experience of being forgiven by God with his or her willingness to extend forgiveness to others.

14. Could it be that Jesus was doing something similar in Matthew 5:47 and 6:32?

15. It should be pointed out that neither did Matthew feel the need to include the background information about the Pharisees' ceremonial washing presented in Mark 7:3–4. Evidently, Matthew knew that his implied readers (the members of his church) already possessed this "outside repertoire of cultural information."

16. J. Dwight Pentecost, *Design for Living: Lessons on Holiness from the Sermon on the Mount* (Grand Rapids: Kregel Publications, 1999), 148–49.

17. Ibid., 150. Notice also the emphasis reflected in this quote upon the search for certainty.

18. William P. Young, *The Shack* (Los Angeles: Windblown Media, 2007), 126.

8

"I'D RATHER SEE A SERMON": JESUS, THE PHARISEES, AND DISCIPLE-MAKING IN MATTHEW 7

My friend Mike was on a family vacation in Europe. While he was standing in front of an Internet café in London, a woman approached him. After determining that he spoke English, she posed the question, "If you were to die tonight, do you know where you would spend eternity?"

Recognizing this as an attempt by the woman to begin an evangelistic conversation, Mike indicated that he knew without a shadow of a doubt that he would spend eternity in heaven. Predictably, the woman went on to ask the follow-up question: "How do you know you will spend eternity in heaven?"

Once again Mike gave the "correct" response: "I know I will spend eternity in heaven when I die because I have put my trust in Jesus Christ as my personal Lord and Savior."

Hearing this, the woman did not express joy at meeting a brother in Christ. Instead, she admonished him. "Do you see all these other people walking up and down the street? Why aren't you sharing the gospel with them?"

Mike, who has done his share of personal witnessing, expressed thanks for the reminder that he should be sensitive to any witnessing opportunities the Lord opened up for him in the course of his holiday travels. Not satisfied, the woman pressed him further, fairly demanding that he join her in her street witnessing then and there.

Sensing a bit of drivenness at work in this woman, Mike made the comment, ever so gently, that it was good to know that their experience of salvation did not hinge on religious works, not even the work of street witnessing. Hearing this, the woman became visibly upset. Vigorously shaking her head from side to side, she asserted, "No, the Bible tells us that we must *work out our salvation* in fear and trembling."

The conversation continued for a while, but finally the woman gave up and walked away in a huff. In Mike's words, "I got the feeling that the lady went away thinking that I was the devil!"

I hope you are able to recognize, sadly, the Pharisaical actions and attitudes at work in this woman's life. Instead of rejoicing that she had found a brother in Christ and sharing with him a mutually encouraging season of fellowship, the legalism, judgmentalism, and pugilism at work in her life had the effect of turning the encounter into a heated conflict. It does not have to be this way.

Irony in Matthew 7:1–12 – The Christian's Relationships

Most commentators treat Matthew 7 as if it were made up of a hodgepodge of disparate bits of discipleship instruction, a potpourri of leftover discipleship principles. But whether Matthew 5–7 represents an actual sermon Jesus preached in one session or a composite created by Matthew of various discipleship teachings delivered by Jesus at various times and places during the course of his ministry, I cannot bring myself to believe there is no inner logic to Matthew 7 that connects it thematically to what we have already read in Matthew 5 and 6. Let me suggest that keeping the polemic between Jesus and the Pharisees in mind is the key to discerning such a connection. Just as Jesus has used the Pharisees as anti-models for his disciples in terms of their ethics, piety, and ambition, he does so in 7:1–12 with regard to their relationships.[1]

To be more precise, I am convinced that this part of the Sermon on the Mount is ultimately about the disciple's ministry formation. If Jesus did not intend at this point in his sermon to address the issue of how his apprentices can and should be effective in their attempts to minister to others, then he did not do so at all. This is an idea I find untenable given what Jesus had to say in 5:13–16 about the need for his followers to function as salt and light.

Moreover, is it not true that ministry is ultimately about relationships? Is this not the way Jesus went about doing ministry: making friends for God (e.g., Luke 19:1–9)? Is it not true that any local church's ability to represent the kingdom of God in its ministry context depends upon the willingness and ability of its members to create and maintain healthy relationships with one another and those who have yet to join the community of faith?

Thus, we observe that this particular section of the Sermon begins and ends with words of instruction about how the followers of Jesus are to relate to others. In 7:1 Jesus addresses the importance of the disciple's *attitude* toward others (contra the Pharisees). In 7:12 Jesus addresses the importance of the disciple's *actions* toward others (also contra the Pharisees). In between, Jesus can be seen identifying at least five things his followers must do or not do if they want to make a difference for him in the lives of other people.

First, Jesus states that in order to be really effective at helping other people his followers (unlike the Pharisees) must not be in the habit of writing folks off in a critical, judgmental manner.

> Do not judge, or you too will be judged. For in the same way
> you judge others, you will be judged, and with the measure you
> use, it will be measured to you.
>
> (Matthew 7:1–2)

Many scholars are careful to point out that there is a crucial difference between judging in the sense of evaluating and analyzing and judging in the sense of condemning. It is one thing to make critical judgments when necessary; it is altogether another to live one's whole life as a judgmental person.[2]

It doesn't take a genius to figure out that Christ's followers are not going to be able to imitate his ministry of making friends for God if they tend to be, like the Pharisees, quite judgmental of everyone who does not already have his or her life in order. And yet, even sincere Christ-followers can be guilty of this. When are we going to get it through our heads that people don't respond well to being judged and condemned? When are we going to wake up to the fact that when we criticize, judge, and condemn other people, they usually respond by criticizing, judging, and condemning us in return? When are we finally going to figure out that, no matter how benevolent our motive might be, if we approach people in a way that is negative and highhanded, the people we are supposedly trying to help are not going to listen to us?

Philip Yancey tells us that Ernest Hemingway's mother was a devout but ungracious church member who detested her famous son's libertine life and after a time refused to allow him in her presence. Yancey writes:

> One year for his birthday, she mailed him a cake along with
> the gun his father had used to kill himself. Another year she

wrote him a letter explaining that a mother's life is like a bank. "Every child that is born to her enters the world with a large and prosperous bank account, seemingly inexhaustible." The child, she continued, makes withdrawals but no deposits during all the early years. Later, when the child grows up, it is his responsibility to replenish the supply he has drawn down. Hemingway's mother then proceeded to spell out all the specific ways in which Ernest should be making "deposits to keep the account in good standing": flowers, fruit or candy, a surreptitious paying of Mother's bills, and above all a determination to stop "neglecting your duties to God and your Savior, Jesus Christ."[3]

Yancey concludes the story by saying, "Hemingway never got over his hatred for his mother or for her Savior."[4] So what categories do we file this story under? We could file it under "Condemnation," "Judgmentalism," "Legalism," "Ungrace," and "How *Not* to Get People to Listen to Us."

Second, Jesus goes on to instruct his followers that they (unlike the Pharisees) must not set out to "fix" others while denying the dysfunction in their own lives.

> Why do you look at the speck of sawdust in your brother's eye and pay no attention to the plank in your own eye? How can you say to your brother, "Let me take the speck out of your eye," when all the time there is a plank in your own eye? You hypocrite, first take the plank out of your own eye, and then you will see clearly to remove the speck from your brother's eye.
>
> (Matthew 7:3–5)

It is easy to assume that Jesus, having been raised in a carpenter's shop, was familiar with the dilemma of someone getting a speck of sawdust stuck in his eye. He envisions this poor person being accosted by a "helper" who offers to remove the speck even though he has a two-by-four sticking out of his own eye! Jesus' rhetoric is hyperbolic to the point of comic absurdity.

We should note that Jesus refers to the person who tries to fix other people without first addressing the obvious dysfunction in his or her own life as a *hypocrite*. More than one biblical scholar has suggested that this reference meant that Jesus originally had the Pharisees in mind when he brought this teaching.[5] The point Jesus is making is that it would be hypocritical (Pharisaical) for his followers to go around trying to fix everyone else's problems without humbly acknowledging that they have some serious issues of their own that need to be dealt with first.

Third, Jesus proceeds to instruct his followers not to try to force their help on people who are not (yet) in a position to really understand and appreciate the ministry that is being offered to them.

> Do not give dogs what is sacred; do not throw your pearls to pigs. If you do, they may trample them under their feet, and then turn and tear you to pieces.

> (Matthew 7:6)

A lot of people puzzle over the meaning of this verse, but I believe that Jesus' intended message becomes clear when we are careful to look at it in its context. Remember, Matthew 7:1–12 is all about what it takes to engage in effective ministry. Having warned his followers to avoid the Pharisaical practice of trying to "fix" other people without first dealing with their own issues, he goes on to state fairly clearly that even then effective ministry might not take place, at least not right away. Timing is important when it comes to effective ministry. Not everyone is "ready" at any given point in his or her spiritual journey to receive the ministry that Christ's followers are able and willing to provide. *It does no good to try to force ministry on folks who are resistant to it, because at this time in their lives they do not see their need for it.*

The value of this interpretation is that it understands what Jesus says in 7:6 to be part of the larger discussion of ministry effectiveness going on in 7:1–12. Jesus paints two word pictures here: one that evokes the image of a pack of ravenous dogs and one that causes his hearers to imagine a herd of hungry pigs. Understood in isolation from the rest of the passage in which it is located, this reference to dogs and pigs might give the impression that Jesus is violating his own teaching about not being judgmental—that he is referring to some people as dogs and pigs in a dismissive, exclusive, condemning manner. The other possibility, a view I am not alone in holding,[6] is that in 7:6 Jesus is actually exhorting his followers not to waste their time trying to share the gospel with people who are adamant in their resistance to it, a point Jesus was careful to make more than once in his ministry (see Matthew 10:11–16).

Some biblical interpreters go on to suggest that in his reference to dogs and pigs Jesus actually had the Pharisees in mind—that Jesus was warning his followers not to try to convince the Pharisees of the truthfulness of the gospel message until such a time as they would be ready to hear it.[7] This is another point which Jesus evidently felt the need to make more than once in the course of his disciple-making ministry (see Matthew 15:12–14).

Fourth, it is as a part of this discussion of ministry effectiveness that Jesus presses on to encourage his followers to always remain persistent in their practice of prayer.

> Ask and it will be given to you; seek and you will find; knock and the door will be opened to you. For everyone who asks receives; he who seeks finds; and to him who knocks, the door will be opened.
>
> Which of you, if his son asks for bread, will give him a stone? Or if he asks for a fish, will give him a snake? If you, then, though you are evil,[8] know how to give good gifts to your

children, how much more will your Father in heaven give good gifts to those who ask him!

(Matthew 7:7–11)

At first glance, this encouragement to persist in prayer does seem like a non sequitur (i.e., a statement that does not logically follow from what preceded it). Perhaps 7:1–12 is a hodgepodge of unrelated discipleship instructions after all! On the other hand, it may be that Matthew expected his readers would be able to disambiguate the text and make the connection between the reality of ministry roadblocks in the form of hardened hearts and the power of prayer to burst such hardened hearts wide open.

What I am suggesting is that Jesus' reference to the power of persistent prayer, located where it is in this passage, was designed to let Matthew's readers know that there is always something the sincere Christ-follower can do when she encounters a person who simply does not appreciate and value the message of the gospel or when she feels that she does not possess the gifts necessary to accomplish the ministry task at hand. Even though it is unwise and unproductive for the Christian worker to keep preaching at and sharing with ministry-resistant persons, this does not mean that we must give up on these hard-to-reach folks. Instead, the fully trained disciple recognizes that there are times when the most powerful thing she can do is go to prayer. When viewed in the context in which it is located, the teaching on prayer contained in 7:7–11 seems to be saying that when we Christ-followers pray we are petitioning a loving heavenly Father who cares greatly about us and the people we are trying to reach, and who can be counted on to open closed doors and release whatever gifts are necessary for us to succeed in the ministry assignments we have undertaken.

Ironically, sometimes the hardened heart that must burst open in order for effective ministry to take place is not that of the recipient of the ministry but of the giver. Perhaps the most important ministry gift we Christ-followers must possess to be effective in ministry is the gift of empathy. This is a point my former seminary professor, Lewis Smedes, was careful to make in his book *My God and I: A Spiritual Memoir.* According to Smedes, as important as *what* we do is *how* we do it. The key consideration here, of course, is the Christian virtue of love. Smedes writes, "Take our duty to tell the truth, for instance. Without love, we are likely to spout the truth with no regard for its effect on the person to whom we tell it. But if we have love, or empathy, we can put ourselves in the other person's shoes, and this will give us a better chance of seeing the right time and the right way to tell her the truth."[9] Smedes goes on to clarify:

> How do we know the right time and the right way to tell the truth? How do we know when and how to tell a person that she is dying, or that her son has gotten himself in jail, or that her husband has lost his job, or that she has made a fool of herself, or that her little child has an incurable disease, or that his wife is having an affair? What we need more than anything else is the Spirit of love to open our eyes and ears to see and hear what is really going on in the heart and mind of the person to whom we are talking.[10]

The truth is that effective ministry requires a discernment that flows from a Spirit-empowered empathy. I believe my former mentor would have agreed with my contention that we access this kind of Spirit-empowered empathy primarily through prayer. The reference to prayer in 7:7–11 is *not* a non sequitur! For a variety of reasons, persistence in prayer is crucial to the ministry effectiveness of Christ's followers.

Fifth, what I have just written about the tremendous importance of empathy explains why Jesus concludes his instructions on ministry effectiveness with a call for his followers (unlike the Pharisees) to learn to treat other people with the love, respect, dignity, and sensitivity that they themselves would hope to receive.

> So in everything, do to others what you would have them do to you, for this sums up the Law and the Prophets.
>
> (Matthew 7:12)

This verse is hugely important to a proper understanding not only of Jesus' teaching on ministry effectiveness but of the Sermon on the Mount as a whole. J. Dwight Pentecost sees in Matthew 7:12 the conclusion of Jesus' call for his followers to manifest a righteousness that surpasses that of the Pharisees and teachers of the law.[11] Pentecost goes on to insist that this verse, also known as the Golden Rule, constitutes a deliberate, ironic inversion of rabbinic teaching.[12] In other words, even as Jesus enunciated the Golden Rule he had the Pharisees as an anti-model in mind!

More importantly, this interpretation bids us recognize the night-and-day difference that exists between the Golden Rule as it is presented in its negative and positive forms. It really is amazing what Jesus is calling for here. I routinely tell my college students that when they lay their heads on their pillows at night, the day-ending question they should be asking themselves is not *Was I careful not to hurt, offend, or injure anyone today?* No, the question that all of us, as sincere Christ-followers, should be asking each evening is this: *Who did I help today? Who did I show God's love to?*

Jesus seems to suggest that it is possible for his followers to become people whose hearts are so full of the love of God that they cannot help but proactively demonstrate his love to everyone they meet. This is what it means to function as salt and light (see Matthew 5:13–15). This is what causes people who come into contact with sincere Christ-followers to want to glorify the God these Christian workers say they serve (see

Matthew 5:16). It is hard to conceive of a more fitting conclusion to Jesus' teaching concerning the ministry effectiveness of his disciples.

But Matthew 7:12 does even more: it brings Jesus' hearers back once again to the realization that what he is calling for in his sermon can never be accomplished by his followers acting in their own strength.[13] This is what made it so imperative that the religious program of the Pharisees—dependent as it was on the strength of the flesh, focused as it was on external issues, and productive as it was of an attitude of smug, super-spiritual self-righteousness—be so thoroughly deconstructed in Jesus' disciple-making teaching.

The lifestyle portrayed in Jesus' Sermon on the Mount simply cannot be achieved by sincere religious people doing their best to obey God's commandments. This way of life calls for the kind of changed hearts spoken of by the Old Testament prophets (e.g., Ezekiel 11:19–20; 36:26–27; Jeremiah 24:7; 31:31–34) and the New Testament apostles (e.g., Romans 2:28–29; Hebrews 8:7–12). Jesus seems to presume the presence of changed, empowered hearts residing within his disciples. As I stated in an earlier chapter, I believe that a careful, prayerful study of the Sermon on the Mount can produce this very thing.

In sum, Matthew 7:1–12 is anything but a hodgepodge of disparate bits of discipleship instruction or a potpourri of leftover discipleship principles. This is a potent section of the Sermon in which Jesus provides his followers with five no-nonsense exhortations designed to help them experience genuine ministry effectiveness (contra the harsh, super-spiritual, insensitive, ultimately ineffective ministry approach of the Pharisees).

Furthermore, as we have already noted, Jesus' teaching on ministry effectiveness begins with the exhortation for his followers to avoid being judgmental and condemning in their attitudes toward others and ends with the exhortation to minister to others in the very same way they would want to be ministered to. It seems to me that this more sensitive, personal, and relational approach to ministry would rule out the pushy, impersonal method of evangelism practiced by the woman who accosted my friend on the street during his European vacation. Evidently, F. D. Bruner would agree. Commenting on the negative effects of an insensitive, aggressive evangelism he writes: "There is a form of evangelism that urges Christians to use every opportunity to share the gospel. Unfortunately, insensitive evangelism often proves harmful not only to the obdurate whose heart is hardened by the undifferentiating evangelist, but harmful also to the gospel that is force-fed. . . . Aggressive evangelism gets converts and counts them, but we are never able to count those turned away from the gospel for the numbers of the offended are never tallied."[14]

The numbers of the offended are never tallied. Ultimately, the lesson of Matthew 7:1–12 is that we Christ-followers will be more effective in ministry if we avoid acting like Pharisees in the process.

Irony in Matthew 7:13–27 – The Christian's Commitment

In the same way that Matthew was careful to portray Jesus utilizing a formal introduction to the Sermon, we also find Jesus utilizing a formal conclusion. Most communicators would concur that the purpose of a sermon conclusion is twofold: (a) to reemphasize the main themes of the message preached; and (b) to press for a decision.[15] This is essentially what we find Jesus doing in his conclusion to the Sermon on the Mount.

In this final section of the Sermon, I see Jesus warning his hearers about three things that could cause them, spiritually speaking, to sabotage their own success. First, Jesus warns his hearers that they need to be willing to take the road less traveled despite its loneliness and rigor: that is, they need to choose carefully between two life-paths.

> Enter through the narrow gate. For wide is the gate and broad
> is the road that leads to destruction, and many enter through it.

But small is the gate and narrow the road that leads to life, and only a few find it.

(Matthew 7:13–14)

Second, Jesus also warns his listeners of the need to remain continually on guard against spiritual predators who, ironically, present themselves as spiritual models: that is, they need to be on the lookout for the right kind of spiritual fruit.

Watch out for false prophets. They come to you in sheep's clothing, but inwardly they are ferocious wolves. By their fruit you will recognize them. Do people pick grapes from thornbushes, or figs from thistles? Likewise every good tree bears good fruit, but a bad tree bears bad fruit. A good tree cannot bear bad fruit, and a bad tree cannot bear good fruit. Every tree that does not bear good fruit is cut down and thrown into the fire. Thus, by their fruit you will recognize them.

Not everyone who says to me, "Lord, Lord," will enter the kingdom of heaven, but only he who does the will of my Father who is in heaven. Many will say to me on that day, "Lord, Lord, did we not prophesy in your name, and in your name drive out demons and perform many miracles?" Then I will tell them plainly, "I never knew you. Away from me, you evildoers!"

(Matthew 7:15–23)

Third, Jesus is careful to warn his hearers that they need to recognize how foolish, how really stupid, it would be for them to listen to his teachings without actually putting them into practice: that is, they need to build their lives on the firm foundation.

Therefore everyone who hears these words of mine and puts them into practice is like a wise man who built his house on the rock. The rain came down, the streams rose, and the winds blew and beat against that house; yet it did not fall, because it had its foundation on the rock. But everyone who hears these words of mine and does not put them into practice is like a foolish man who built his house on sand. The rain came down, the streams rose, and the winds blew and beat against that house, and it fell with a great crash.

(Matthew 7:24–27)

Now that we have gained an overview of the three warnings with which Jesus concluded his most famous sermon, I want us to consider the possibility that, even here, it is likely that Matthew's readers would have sensed that Jesus had the Pharisees in view.

The Religion of the Pharisees Was the Broad Road

With regard to the first warning (the need to choose between the two life-paths), John R. W. Stott puts forward the idea that the broad road alluded to in 7:13 refers to an approach to religion that involves such Pharisaical characteristics as superficiality, self-love, hypocrisy, mechanical religion, false ambition, and censoriousness.[16] Likewise, J. Dwight Pentecost argues that Jesus had Pharisaical religion in mind when he warned his followers to avoid the broad way.

> The Lord made it very clear that the righteousness of the Pharisees would never bring the people into fellowship with God (Matthew 5:20). This was a crushing blow to the Pharisees and to those who had trusted Pharisaic righteousness to make them acceptable to God.
>
> After the Lord dismissed the righteousness of the Pharisees, He explained why He repudiated it. Pharisaic interpretation of the Law was wrong, for the Pharisees had concluded the only

thing that mattered to God was what man did; if a man behaved himself outwardly, he was acceptable to God even though his heart was unclean. Jesus dismissed the Pharisee's practice of the Law, for, if one does not understand the holiness of God, and its demands, he will never conform to those standards in his conduct. Perverting the demands of the holiness of God, the Pharisees countenanced all manner of false practice and yet deemed themselves righteous. Our Lord refers to this, man's religion, as the "broad way."[17]

Is Pentecost justified in suggesting that the Pharisees were preoccupied with outward behaviors versus inward motivations? I find support for this argument in two key Matthean passages. In Matthew 15:1–20, Jesus boldly criticizes the Pharisees' myopic stress on ceremonial hand-washing and kosher diet. In Matthew 23:25–28, we find Jesus accusing the Pharisees of hypocritically engaging in impression management, endeavoring to maintain a façade of piety when the interior of their lives is actually filled with greed, self-indulgence, and all sorts of wickedness. Thus, I firmly believe that it is appropriate to view the Pharisees as preoccupied with what could be considered an external, ceremonial righteousness. As Pentecost points out, this amounts to a man-centered religion that ends up allowing for ethical behaviors that grieve the heart of God. As a result, it may very well be that Jesus had the Pharisees in mind when he warned his followers to avoid the broad road.

What, then, did Jesus have in mind when he spoke of the "narrow road" (Matthew 7:14)? While Pentecost agues that the narrow way refers to Jesus himself, he does not specify just how this way is taken. This is a point of controversy among evangelicals. Some argue that the experience of salvation can be separated from discipleship, while others strenuously object to this bifurcation. My personal conviction is that we opt for the narrow road over the broad road when we surrender ourselves to Christ's loving lordship, truly embarking on a lifetime of apprenticeship to Jesus as our master-teacher (see Matthew 7:21).[18]

The Pharisees Were the False Prophets, the Wolves in Sheep's Clothing

With regard to the second warning (the need to be on the lookout for the right kind of fruit), Jesus warns his audience to steer clear of false prophets, saying: "They come to you in sheep's clothing, but inwardly they are ferocious wolves" (7:15). The text does not explicitly identify whom Jesus had in mind when he spoke of these "false prophets." Some scholars have proposed that Jesus/Matthew had Gentile charismatic enthusiasts in mind;[19] but it is hard to imagine, given the Gospel's likely historical setting, how either Jesus' hearers or Matthew's readers would have made that connection. On the other hand, another interpretive possibility is that Jesus had the Pharisees (and their descendants) in mind as he referred to wolves in sheep's clothing, and that Matthew expected his readers to understand this to be the case. I can offer at least three reasons why I believe this may well be what Jesus/Matthew had in mind.

First, the obvious allusion to the hypocrisy—the outside-inside disparity—at work in the false prophets reminds us that in another place (Matthew 23:27–28) Jesus accuses the Pharisees of being hypocrites: "whitewashed tombs, which look beautiful on the outside but on the inside are full of dead men's bones and everything unclean."

Second, we should note that in 7:16 Jesus indicates that the false prophets can be detected by the bad "fruit" they produce. Jesus states rather clearly that it is impossible for false prophets to produce authentically good fruit. The fact is that in three other sections of Matthew's Gospel the Pharisees are indicted for their inability to bear good fruit (3:7–10; 12:33–34; 21:43–45). It is not unlikely that Matthew's readers already would have been aware of Jesus' profound lack of appreciation for the Pharisees' ministry fruitfulness.

Third, it also needs to be pointed out that even if Jesus did have charismatic enthusiasts in mind when he warned of the false prophets in 7:15–23, an enthusiasm for *charismata* (spiritual gifts) does not preclude the adoption of a Pharisaical approach to the Christian life. Indeed, as a Pentecostal I can verify that it is possible to argue that an overemphasis upon charismatic gifts and ministries, not grounded in a solid Pauline theology of the Spirit, could very well serve to inculcate within the "charismatic enthusiast" such Pharisaical traits and tendencies as self-righteousness, spiritual arrogance, judgmentalism, hyper-piety, dogmatism, pugilism, and trivialism (spiritual myopia or tunnel vision). In support of this last observation, Robert Guelich specifies that the false prophets referred to by Jesus in 7:15–23 signified *Jewish charismatic enthusiasts who also possessed a Judaizing agenda.*[20]

Guelich and I are not alone in our contention that when Jesus referred to the false prophets in 7:15–23 he had the Pharisees and their descendants in mind. After explaining how Ezekiel refers to Israel's princes and prophets as wolves ready to fleece and destroy God's flock, misrepresenting God in the process (Ezekiel 22:27–28), J. Dwight Pentecost argues, "In Israel there were religious leaders, who called themselves God's shepherds, who had destroyed hearts and were intent on enriching themselves by feeding on the flock. The Lord frequently spoke of the Pharisees as those who were greedy for both power and material gain. They wanted the power that belonged to God's shepherd, Messiah; they wanted to enrich themselves at the expense of the flock."[21]

Perhaps this is a good time for us to acknowledge the fact that Pharisaism is a spiritual dynamic that can be present in the lives of church leaders (as well as church members). All of us who are leaders of God's flock need to ask ourselves a crucial question: *To what degree is a spirit of Pharisaism at work in my own walk with Christ?*

The Religion of the Pharisees Was the Faulty Foundation

Finally, with regard to the third warning (the need to build on the right kind of foundation), Pentecost suggests that when Jesus referred to the foolish man who built his house upon the sand he had in mind those auditors who, after hearing his teaching, would nevertheless choose the man-made religion of the Pharisees because it, ironically, seemed less demanding and difficult. "Some in the multitudes who heard the word of Christ and weighed the demands of Christ made upon them in order to enter His Kingdom concluded the way was too difficult, too narrow, and turned again to the broad, easy way the Pharisees presented to them. They turned to the way of the Pharisees as a result of the decision to reject the Word of Christ."[22]

Pentecost argues here that the only real alternative to the way of Christ is the religion of man—some form of Pharisaism. Since he views the "audience on the mount" essentially as a group of religiously minded seekers (Why else would they be there?), he concludes that any failure on their part to embrace an authentic discipling relationship with Jesus would have been a tacit embrace of Pharisaic religion.[23] This raises a set of fascinating questions concerning the makeup of the typical evangelical congregation. Just how pervasive is the spirit of Pharisaism in our churches? Could it be that there really are only two alternatives when it comes to conservative Christianity: authentic discipleship or Pharisaism? Could it be that Pharisaism is far more prevalent in our churches than we have cared thus far to realize?

To summarize, the three observations presented above seem to at least suggest the possibility that in his conclusion, as elsewhere in the Sermon on the Mount, Jesus was using the Pharisees as an anti-model for the kind of kingdom actions and attitudes he intended to cultivate in the lives of his followers. If this is to be granted, then we must acknowledge that Pharisaism is not simply a nuisance to be endured by evangelical church leaders; it is an unacceptable, spiritually dangerous alternative to genuine Christian discipleship that must be aggressively addressed, compassionately condemned, and decisively defeated.

Irony in Matthew 7:28–29 – The Sermon's Epilogue

Following the Sermon's conclusion, Matthew reports the crowds' reaction to it. The immediate response of Jesus' audience to his teaching ministry was extremely favorable. His hearers were greatly impressed with the sense of spiritual authority with which he taught, over against "their teachers of the law." Even if this was only an immediate response that would eventually wane, a certain irony is discernable here. How ironic that even though Jesus was essentially a ministry outsider—an upstart teaching novice who had actually intensified the demands of God's law upon his hearers—the crowd still preferred his teaching ministry over that of recognized trained professionals who specialized in lessening God's ethical demands! Thus, even in Matthew's epilogue to the Sermon on the Mount the polemic against the scribes and Pharisees is maintained. Perhaps Matthew expected that this final, overt allusion to the polemical tension between Jesus and the Pharisees would reassure his readers that they had been prudent to fill in the previous gaps in his story line with that polemical tension in mind.

This rough sketch of what an interpretation of the Sermon on the Mount might look like if one were to keep the polemical tension between Jesus and the Pharisees consistently in view reveals that the Sermon is filled with a plethora of ironies, and that most of these ironies owe their existence to the beliefs and behaviors of the Pharisees. The thesis of this book is that Matthew's goal in the Sermon on the Mount was to show Jesus spelling out for his followers what life looks like when it is being lived in the strength of the kingdom. To illustrate the alternative (ritualism, traditionalism, legalism, separatism, etc.), Matthew has Jesus frequently (sometimes implicitly, sometimes explicitly) directing the attention of his disciples to the Pharisees, who collectively serve as a negative example of kingdom living. In other words, Matthew's polemical purpose in the Sermon on the Mount is clear: to encourage the members and leaders of his church to steer clear of Pharisaism.[24] Matthew Green comes close to saying this very thing when he writes:

> To follow Jesus demands a totally different way of life, and is vital for the people of God. Right at the outset of his ministry Jesus lays it on the line. The new age has dawned. And the Sermon shows what human life is like after repentance and commitment to the King. In a word, life is very different. The injunction "Do not be like them" (6:8) encapsulates the tone of the whole Sermon. A sharp contrast is constantly being drawn between the standards of Jesus and all others. Here we meet a distinctive life-style, with radically different values and ambitions. Everything is at variance with life outside the kingdom.[25]

Thus, when implemented properly, a discipleship curriculum based on the Sermon on the Mount will keep pointing out the negative example of the Pharisees even as it helps disciples learn how to imitate Christ.[26] A recurring theme in such a discipleship curriculum will indeed be *"Do not be like them."*

Having endeavored to improve our understanding of Pharisaism in part one of this book, and having sought to deepen our understanding of the Sermon on the Mount in part two, in part three we will seek to better understand how Jesus' most famous sermon can be used as the foundation for a discipleship experience that can help evangelical churches defeat Pharisaism. What does it mean to make a disciple? How is this best accomplished? These are just a couple of the crucial disciple-making questions we will attempt to answer in the next chapter.

Notes

1. This view does not lack scholarly support. Many scholars see a connection between the various exhortations presented in 7:1–12 against the backdrop of Jesus' critique of the Pharisees. See J. Dwight Pentecost, *Design for Living: Lessons on Holiness from the Sermon on the Mount* (Grand Rapids: Kregel Publications, 1999), 177; John R. W. Stott, *Christian Counter-Culture: The Message of the Sermon on the Mount* (Downers Grove, IL: InterVarsity, 1978), 178; John Wick Bowman and Roland W. Tapp, *The Gospel from the Mount* (Philadelphia: Westminster Press, 1957), 148; and Georg Strecker, *The Sermon on the Mount: An Exegetical Commentary* (Nashville: Abingdon, 1988), 99.

2. See Craig L. Blomberg, *Matthew*, The New American Commentary, vol. 22 (Nashville: Broadman Press, 1992), 127; D. A. Carson, *The Sermon on the Mount: An Evangelical Exposition of Matthew 5–7* (Grand Rapids: Baker, 1978), 99; and Robert Guelich, *The Sermon on the Mount* (Dallas: Word, 1982), 349–50.

3. Philip Yancey, *What's So Amazing About Grace?* (Grand Rapids: Zondervan, 1997), 38.

4. Ibid.

5. For example, see Guelich, *The Sermon on the Mount*, 351–52, who cites Joachim Jeremias with approval.

6. William Barclay, *The Gospel of Matthew*, The Daily Bible Study Series (Philadelphia: Westminster Press, 1975), 1:267–68.

7. Blomberg, *Matthew*, 128–29.

8. With regard to Jesus' use of the word "evil" in 7:11, some commentators, such as Robert Guelich, do not see Jesus indicting his listeners (disciples) of being especially morally degenerate, but of being fallen and imperfect, particularly as compared with God. Thus, Jesus' point was that if fallen, imperfect fathers can be counted on to do right by their children's sincere requests, how much more can our heavenly Abba be counted on to give good things to his children in response to their sincere, persistent prayers. See Guelich, *The Sermon on the Mount*, 378.

9. Lewis Smedes, *My God and I: A Spiritual Memoir* (Grand Rapids: Eerdmans, 2003), 151.

10. Ibid., 151–52.

11. Pentecost, *Design for Living*, 177.

12. Ibid., 180–81. Pentecost writes: "The rabbis who interpreted the Old Testament stated this principle negatively. One of the precepts of the rabbis was: 'Do that to no man that thou hatest.' One could refrain from something injurious

to another man, but that would not fulfill the righteousness of the Law; it commanded that he do what was for his good. The negative interpretation of the rabbis fell short of the righteousness of the Law, for the Pharisees said if you do not pick up a stone and smite your brother, you have fulfilled the Law. If you do not gossip about your brother, you have fulfilled the Law. If you do not steal your brother's wife, you have fulfilled the Law. The brother might starve to death, but as long as you did not injure him, you fulfilled the Law.

"Our Lord by His interpretation, summary, and application (v. 12) showed that righteousness is not only to refrain from what is forbidden, but also to do what is righteous. 'Whatsoever ye would that men should do to you, do ye even so to them,' for this positive righteousness is a manifestation of the righteousness of the Law."

13. William Barclay writes (*The Gospel of Matthew*, 1:277): "It is perfectly possible for a man of the world to observe the negative form of the golden rule. He could without serious difficulty so discipline his life that he would not do to others what he did not wish them to do to him; but the only man who can begin to satisfy the positive form of the rule is the man who has the love of Christ within his heart. He will try to forgive as he would wish to be forgiven, to help as he would wish to be helped, to praise as he would wish to be praised, to understand as he would wish to be understood. He will never seek to avoid doing things; he will always look for things to do. Clearly this will make life much more complicated; clearly he will have much less time to spend on his own desires and his own activities, for time and time again he will have to stop what he is doing to help someone else. . . . If the world was composed of people who sought to obey this rule, it would be a new world."

14. F. D. Bruner, *The Christbook* (Waco: Word, 1987), 275–76; cited in Blomberg, *Matthew*, 129.

15. See Stott, *Christian Counter-Culture*, 205.

16. Ibid., 194.

17. Pentecost, *Design for Living*, 184.

18. Pentecost himself would probably agree. He writes, "Obedience is the sign of a true faith. . . . If one does not obey the One he calls Lord, his disobedience proves he does not own Him as his Lord. The test of whether Jesus Christ is Lord in a man's life is obedience to the command of the One he calls Lord." Pentecost, *Design for Living*, 199.

19. For example, see Donald Hagner, *Matthew 1–13*, Word Biblical Commentary, vol. 33A (Dallas: Word, 1993), lxiii. By "charismatic enthusiasts," Hagner seems to be referring to followers of Jesus who have become obsessed with spiritual gifts, especially the prophetic ones: e.g., prophecy, speaking in tongues, words of wisdom and knowledge.

20. Guelich, *The Sermon on the Mount*, 408.

21. Pentecost, *Design for Living*, 192–93.

22. Ibid., 206.
23. Ibid.
24. W. D. Davies, *The Sermon on the Mount* (Nashville: Abingdon, 1966), 86–90.
25. Green, *The Message of Matthew*, 89.
26. Sinclair Ferguson, *The Sermon on the Mount: Kingdom Life in a Fallen World* (Carlisle, PA: Banner of Truth Trust, 1997), 9. Ferguson explains that the Sermon on the Mount is filled with negatives due to the fact that Jesus' teaching (discipleship) methodology was to keep contrasting life in the kingdom of God with other ways of living.

Part 3

USING THE SERMON ON THE MOUNT TO DEFEAT PHARISAISM

9

THIS IS HOW BUSINESS GETS DONE: EFFECTIVE DISCIPLE-MAKING IN THE CONTEMPORARY CHURCH

During the heyday of the church growth movement, when churches were encouraged to imitate the structures and practices of successful secular corporations, we pastors were advised to continually ask ourselves two key questions: (1) What business are we in? and (2) How's business? Some excesses surely occurred; and it is appropriate, I believe, for pastors to rethink the goal of trying to run their churches as if they were just another enterprise dotting the commercial landscape. And yet it also seems to me that, aside from the "business" rhetoric utilized, these two questions—the questions of purpose and efficiency—remain valid. Surely Jesus endeavored to give his followers a sense of purpose (see Matthew 4:19), and his explanation of his parable about the four soils seems to indicate a certain interest in efficiency (see Matthew 13:23). So I put the questions to you: What business is your church in? And how's business?

Throughout this book I have been insisting that a careful reading of the first Gospel reveals that Jesus took the "business" of disciple-making very seriously and that leaders of contemporary evangelical churches should do likewise. Leaders of evangelical churches can and should develop a discipleship curriculum based on the Sermon on the Mount: a curriculum that will effectively draw disciples near to Jesus even as it directs them away from the traits and tendencies exhibited by his antagonists, the Pharisees. In the remaining two chapters of this book I want to stimulate some deep thinking about how this very important "business" really gets done. My goal in this chapter is to lay a foundation for the disciple-making endeavor, enabling the leaders and workers in evangelical churches to arrive at a shared understanding of such foundational issues as the importance of disciple-making, the four prerequisites for an effective disciple-making ministry, and the one ministry dynamic that nearly all truly effective contemporary disciple-making ministries seem to employ. While the statistical research recounted in this chapter is reflective of the state of disciple-making in American evangelical churches in particular, I am convinced that the principles presented here are applicable to evangelical congregations located anywhere in the world.

The Importance of Disciple-Making

In his book *The Disciple-Making Pastor*, Bill Hull ponders how one assesses the true strength of a local church. All too often the question that is asked is "How many people are present?" Hull contends, "The right question is 'what are these people like?' What kind of families do they have, are they honest in business, are they trained to witness, do they know their Bible, are they penetrating their workplaces, their neighborhoods, reaching friends and associates for Christ? Are they making the difference in the world for Christ that He expects? These are the right questions, the issues of the heart, and the criteria for greatness."[1]

According to this provocative quote, a truly great church is one that trains its members to be the kind of people who make a difference in the world for Jesus Christ. Another name for this type of difference-making church member is *disciple*. Hull argues that the evangelical church is presently experiencing a crisis precisely because it has lost sight of what it is supposed to be about: the making of disciples. Not mincing his words, this concerned pastor writes:

> The evangelical church has become weak, flabby, and too dependent on artificial means that can only simulate real spiritual power. Churches are too little like training centers to shape up the saints and too much like cardiopulmonary wards at the local hospital. We have proliferated self-indulgent consumer religion, the what-can-the-church-do-for-me syndrome. We are too easily satisfied with conventional success: bodies, bucks, and buildings. The average Christian resides in the comfort zone of "I pay the pastor to preach, administrate, and counsel. I pay him, he ministers to me. . . . I am the consumer, he is the retailer. . . . I have the needs, he meets them. . . . That's what I pay for."[2]

Hull's concern is that churches are catering to church members instead of discipling them. Church leaders are so concerned about merely keeping people coming to church that they have failed to challenge them to take up Christ's cross and follow him. The church has focused on attracting and maintaining pew-sitters when the real goal should be the training of difference-makers. The church's real mission should be to penetrate the world as spiritual salt and light, representing Christ's ministry of kingdom proclamation and demonstration and enabling lost men, women, boys, and girls to be reconciled to the reign of God.

In his book *The Divine Conspiracy*, Dallas Willard registers a similar concern. With respect to the state of discipleship taking place in contemporary churches, Willard writes:

Nondiscipleship is the elephant in the church. It is not the much discussed moral failures, financial abuses, or the amazing general similarity between Christians and non-Christians. These are only effects of the underlying problem. The fundamental negative reality among Christian believers now is their failure to be constantly learning how to live their lives in The Kingdom Among Us. And it is an *accepted* reality. The division of professing Christians into those for whom it is a matter of whole-life devotion to God and those who maintain a consumer, or client, relationship to the church has now been an accepted reality for over fifteen hundred years.[3]

Also sensing a lack of discipleship at work in the church, Christian pollster George Barna did some research on the topic. His findings were published in his *Growing True Disciples: New Strategies for Producing Genuine Followers of Christ*. In this very helpful book, Barna forthrightly states his concern that discipleship is simply not happening in our churches the way it should. After quoting Matthew 28:18–20 and commenting on its importance, Barna makes the following observation: "In one recent nationwide survey we asked people to describe their goals in life. Almost nine out of ten adults described themselves as 'Christian.' Four out of ten said they were personally committed to Jesus Christ, had confessed their sins, and believed they will go to heaven after they die because of God's grace provided through Jesus' death and resurrection. But not one of the adults we interviewed said that their goal in life was to be a committed follower of Jesus Christ or to make disciples."[4]

Sadly, it appears that those of us who are evangelical church leaders have not been as intentional about the making of disciples as we should have been. Perhaps this is the reason why New Testament Pharisaism seems to be so prevalent in our churches and why so many young adults are having trouble crossing the bridge from their youth group experience into full participation in the "adult" church. As someone who works every day with young adults in a university setting, I consider it crucial that the leaders of evangelical churches regain a sense of passion for the making of disciples.

Much has been said in recent days about the fact that the ministry context for churches in America and Western Europe is becoming increasingly post-Christian (i.e., growing numbers of people in Western countries consider themselves to be "over" Christianity and "done" with the church). My observation, from both an academic and pastoral perspective, is that we need to take the cultural changes we are presently experiencing seriously. Simply stated, the future of the evangelical movement hinges on this. An increasingly post-Christian ministry context will eventually "eat the lunch" of any evangelical church that is not very deliberate about the making of disciples, sincere followers of Christ equipped to be salt and light in a world that desperately needs both!

The Prerequisites for an Effective Disciple-Making Ministry

Jesus never implied that creating an effective disciple-making ministry would be easy. Indeed, a survey of the pertinent literature suggests that several dynamics have to be in place before a local church can succeed at doing more than simply inaugurating yet another program. For example, George Barna, author of the previously cited *Growing True Disciples*, conducted an in-depth study of a dozen American churches with a proven ability to make Christian disciples.[5] The churches studied ranged in size (from 150 to 4,500 adult attendees), came from a wide variety of theological positions (both sides of the Calvinist-Wesleyan divide), were located in various geographical locations (all four regions of the United States), and varied in age (churches ranging from seven years old to more than 150 years old).[6]

Barna reports that while each of these churches approached the disciple-making task a bit differently, there were some commonalities. On this basis, Barna is able to provide his readers with a succinct summary of the dynamics that must be in place before a church can succeed in making disciples. According to Barna, the prerequisites for an effective disciple-making ministry are: (1) a clear goal or idea of what discipleship involves and what a fully formed follower of Christ will be like; (2) a philosophy of ministry that prioritizes and supports the disciple-making endeavor; (3) an actual plan to form disciples; and (4) a process of evaluation whereby the success of the disciple-making ministry is continually being monitored so that needed adjustments can be made.[7]

The heart of this chapter's discussion of discipleship will be organized around these four prerequisites.[8] I truly believe that the concepts presented in these pages can both inspire and enable the leaders and workers of local churches everywhere to create communities of faith that are truly effective at helping congregation members experience genuine spiritual transformation.[9]

Prerequisite #1 – A Clear Goal for the Disciple-Making Endeavor

An effective disciple-making ministry begins with a lucid understanding of what the process of discipleship involves and what a fully formed disciple will look like. Thus, some definitions are in order.

"Disciple"

For his part, Barna speaks of disciples who are "committed to Jesus Christ as Savior and Lord and growing daily in their knowledge, love and service to Him."[10]

In *Following the Master: A Biblical Theology of Discipleship*, Michael Wilkins insists that the word *disciple* is the "primary term used in the Gospels to refer to Jesus' followers and therefore refers to the person who has come to Jesus for eternal life, has claimed Jesus as Savior and God, and has embarked upon the life of following Jesus."[11]

In *Discipleship Essentials*, Greg Ogden defines a disciple thusly: "A disciple is one who responds in faith and obedience to the gracious call of Jesus. Being a disciple is a lifelong process of dying to self while allowing Jesus Christ to come alive in us."[12]

Dallas Willard explains that to be a disciple of Jesus is to function as his apprentice, learning from him how to live life in the kingdom of God. In other words, Jesus' disciples are those who are engaged in a serious learning process, endeavoring to grow in their ability to live their lives the way Jesus would if he were they.[13]

Keeping all of these offerings in mind, the idea of being a Christian "disciple" may be defined like this: *Christian disciples are those who have committed themselves to a lifetime of following and imitating Jesus Christ, a lifetime of learning what it means to live their lives the way Jesus would if he were in their shoes.*

"Discipling"

If a disciple is a lifelong apprentice of Jesus, then what does it mean to "disciple" someone, or to engage in "discipling"? I want to suggest that "discipling," understood in a Christian context, is *the process of helping other people become genuine lifelong apprentices (imitators) of Jesus Christ.* George Barna seems to have the discipling process in mind when he writes, "It is about the intentional training of people who voluntarily submit to the lordship of Christ and who want to become imitators of Him in every thought, word, and deed. On the basis of teaching, training, experiences, relationships, and accountability, a disciple becomes transformed into the likeness of Jesus Christ."[14]

I concur with this understanding of what it means to disciple someone for several reasons. First, I like its reference to intentionality. I am convinced that genuine disciple-making does not just happen; we must engage in the process on purpose.

Second, I appreciate the way it speaks of submission to the lordship of Jesus. This definition gives the impression that the person in training has come to recognize that Jesus is special, that Jesus is worth following, that Jesus is Lord. The exclusivity with which the New Testament refers to Jesus is implicitly acknowledged in this definition of discipling (see Matthew 16:13–17; John 14:6; Acts 4:12; Romans 10:9; 1 John 5:1, 5, 10).

Third, this definition correctly refers to the fact that Christian disciples are those who are learning to imitate Jesus in *every* way (thought, word, and deed), with the result that they are experiencing a gradual spiritual transformation. This is a progressive, holistic, and supernaturalistic understanding of discipleship. To become a Christian disciple is not simply a matter of gaining certain knowledge (correct doctrine) or mastering certain skills (e.g., how to communicate the four spiritual laws). No, we must never forget that to become a Christian disciple is ultimately about becoming new people committed to handling *every* situation life throws at them the way Jesus would if he were they.

Finally, this definition understands that the process of spiritual transformation requires more than the stimulus of good biblical teaching, as important as this is. It is in the *combination* of teaching, training, experiences, relationships, and accountability that disciples are forged over time. (I will have more to say about the importance of a multifaceted disciple-making environment in a subsequent section.)

The Essential Earmarks of the Maturing Christian Disciple

If the "business" of the local church should be the making of disciples, we really must form a very clear picture of what a maturing Christian disciple will look like. Such a description will not only help us evaluate from time to time how our "business" is doing, it should also inform the disciple-making process we employ.

I have already suggested that disciples should be defined as persons who have committed themselves to a lifetime of following and imitating Jesus Christ. While Jesus exhibited many distinctive character traits, perhaps the most amazing capacity Jesus modeled for the world was a profound ability to love God with all of his heart, mind, soul, and strength and to love his neighbor as himself (see Mark 12:30–31). Thus, *there is a sense in which the ultimate earmark of maturing Christ-followers is a significant growth in their ability to demonstrate a profound love for God and their fellow human beings.* Though this may seem simplistic and naïve at first glance, my experience as a disciple-making pastor has been that if we set our sights on anything less than a Spirit-enabled transformation of consumerist-minded church members into loving agents of God's kingdom, the root of Pharisaism is given room to thrive.

Having made this important point, it is possible, of course, to press ahead and create a list of concomitant actions and attitudes present in the life of Jesus that his apprentices should strive to emulate. Of the many lists of this sort that I have run across,[15] one that strikes me as especially remarkable for its brevity, balance, and biblical support is contained in the following quote from Michael Wilkins:

Jesus declared that to be a disciple is to become like the Master (Matthew 10:24–25; Luke 6:40). Becoming like Jesus includes going out with the same message, ministry, and compassion (Matthew 10:5ff.); practicing the same religious and social traditions (Matthew 12:1–8; Mark 2:18–22); belonging to the same family of obedience (Matthew 12:46–50); exercising the same servanthood (Mark 10:42–45; Matthew 20:26–28; John 13:12–17); and experiencing the same suffering (Matthew 10:16–25; Mark 10:38–39). The true disciple was to know Jesus so well, was to have followed him so closely, that he or she would become like him. The ultimate goal was to be conformed to his image (cf. Luke 6:40; Romans 8:28–29).[16]

A willingness to "go"; to minister with compassion; to practice certain spiritual disciplines; to belong to a community that enables obedience to God; to lead through serving; and to serve though it involve suffering: Are these not the actions and attitudes that accompany those who love God supremely and their neighbors as themselves? I am convinced that these are the earmarks of the maturing Christian disciple and that, with God's help, we can create disciple-making ministries that enable church members to acquire these Christlike characteristics—defeating Pharisaism in the process.

Prerequisite #2 –
A Philosophy of Ministry That Emphasizes the Significance of Discipleship

If leadership is not everything when it comes to most things having to do with the local church, it is nearly so. In his attempt to encourage church leaders to develop a philosophy of ministry that will effectively support an ongoing ministry of disciple-making, Barna challenges pastoral leaders to reconsider the attributes of truly healthy, successful churches. Instead of focusing on the traditional criteria of success, Barna asks, "Suppose we were to de-emphasize attendance statistics, square footage, and income figures in favor of a commitment to depth and authenticity in discipleship?"[17] The point Barna is trying to make is that for a church to be truly effective at disciple-making, a whole new ministry mindset is required. *Churches need to shift from being congregations that possess discipleship programs to becoming disciple-making congregations.*

But as anyone who has led a local church can attest, effecting change in a congregation's culture is nearly always a delicate matter. The attempt to alter a traditional church's philosophy of ministry is especially tricky and not for the faint of heart! Perhaps this is why so many books devoted to disciple-making refer to the great need for the senior pastor of a local church to provide strong leadership for the disciple-making ministry. For example, Dallas Willard boldly attributes the discipleship deficit at work in many evangelical churches to the message being proclaimed from their pulpits:

> The situation we have just described—the disconnection of life from faith, the absence from our churches of Jesus the teacher— is not caused by the wicked world, by social oppression, or by the stubborn meanness of the people who come to our church services and carry on the work of our congregations. It is largely caused and sustained by the basic message that we constantly hear from Christian pulpits. We are flooded with what I have called "gospels of sin management," in one form or another, while Jesus' invitation to eternal life now—right in the midst of work, business, and profession—remains for the most part ignored and unspoken.
>
> Must not all who speak for Christ constantly ask themselves these crucial questions:
>
> Does the gospel I preach and teach have a natural tendency to cause people who hear it to become full-time students of Jesus?

Would those who believe it become his apprentices as a natural "next step"?

What can we reasonably expect would result from people actually believing the substance of my message?[18]

Likewise, Bill Hull, author of *The Disciple-Making Pastor*, argues persuasively that the senior pastor must be absolutely committed to placing disciple-making at the heart of the church. "Without this kind of commitment himself, he [the pastor] will not move his people toward disciple making, much less lead them to become reproducing believers. It all starts at the heart of the matter—where he places disciple making in relation to the church."[19]

Growing True Disciples also has something to say about the importance of a strong pastoral commitment to discipleship. In a subsection entitled "The Driving Force," Barna discusses the pivotal role the senior pastor plays in successful disciple-making congregations.

> In highly effective disciple-making churches, the senior pastor was acknowledged to be the catalyst behind the commitment to spiritual growth. In most cases the day to day management of the process has been handed over to someone on staff or to an elder or other lay leader. However, most of the people we interviewed suggested that it is the passion of the senior pastor that prevents the church from becoming lazy in this dimension of ministry. . . .
>
> For context, we also interviewed pastors and leaders in many churches that are not doing well in discipleship. In almost every case, we learned that either the senior is silent about discipleship or merely gives lip service to its importance.[20]

Based on the observations put forward by Willard, Hull, and Barna, we may conclude that if the aim of becoming a disciple-making congregation is to be achieved with any degree of excellence, it is absolutely imperative for a church to possess a philosophy of ministry that is radically committed to the making of disciples and that the congregation be led by a senior pastor who is likewise committed to this endeavor.

Prerequisite #3 –
An Actual Plan for Forming
Christian Disciples

Talking about making disciples is one thing; actually doing it is another. What is needed is a well-conceived approach to making disciples that a local church can employ with persistent intentionality. Such a plan will not only involve a discrete, *initiatory* disciple-making event, but a ministry structure that provides ongoing discipleship training. The focus in this chapter is on the erection of an *ongoing* disciple-making ministry structure.

Furthermore, since we will also touch on this topic later on in this chapter, in this section I simply want us to focus our attention on what I consider to be the biblical foundation for any successful disciple-making plan, understanding that this foundation should inform the shape of whatever ministry structure we erect upon it. I also want to underscore here the truth that any plan for forming disciples has to include a method by which church leaders can succeed at motivating their members to participate in it.

The Biblical Foundation for a Successful Disciple-Making Plan

A careful reading of the Book of Acts indicates that in the first few weeks and months after Pentecost the leaders of the earliest church did not simply evangelize; they discipled as well. In particular, Acts 2:42–47 seems to suggest that the early church ordered its life around five ministry dynamics in particular: *worship, nurture, community, mission,* and *stewardship.*[21] I believe it can be argued that these five dynamics function as the developmental means by which Christian disciples are made; that is, while it is true that Christian disciples do more than engage in certain practices, it is also true that it is by means of these five foundational practices that church members develop into fully formed followers of Christ.[22]

What this means is that, in order for a church's disciple-making plan to be truly biblically grounded, such a plan will need to do its best to steer church members toward an *ongoing* engagement in (1) transformative *worship* encounters with a God who is both holy and merciful (see Isaiah 6:1–8); (2) those devotional disciplines necessary to *nurture* a trust relationship with Christ (see 1 Timothy 4:7); (3) the experience of genuine Christian *community*—involvement in a small group that provides a significant amount of both acceptance and accountability (see Hebrews 10:24–25); (4) Christian *mission* (or praxis)—the re-presentation of Jesus and his message of the kingdom to the world through both words and works (see Matthew 5:14–16)[23]; and (5) a faithful, enthusiastic *stewardship* of the resources entrusted to them by God (see 2 Corinthians 9:6–15).

My experience has been that the overall success of any disciple-making ministry depends on the degree to which it succeeds at steering congregants toward a consistent, ongoing engagement in all five of these developmental practices. Such a well-balanced disciple-making ministry really can succeed at forming Christ-followers who are committed to doing their best to imitate Jesus' capacity to love God supremely and his neighbor as himself. Therefore, I would contend that whatever ongoing disciple-making ministry structure we erect needs to be built upon the biblical foundation provided for us in Acts 2:42–47.

Motivating Spiritual Maturity among Church Members

Contrary to what any movie catch-phrase might suggest, there is no guarantee that if we will but build a disciple-making ministry structure, church members will flock to it.[24] Indeed, according to George Barna's research, one of the main reasons why disciple-making is so rare among evangelical churches today is that many of the members of these churches lack the motivation necessary to become seriously involved in it.

Between January 1999 and June 2000, Barna's research team conducted a nationwide telephone survey of 1,337 adults who professed to be "born again" (i.e., they indicated they had made a personal commitment to Jesus Christ that is important in their lives and they believed they would have eternal life because they had confessed their sins and accepted Jesus Christ as their Savior). One of the survey questions administered by the research group sought to measure the intensity of the respondents' commitment to spiritual growth. The interviews produced the following data: "Not quite 18 percent (one out of every five) said that their effort to grow spiritually is the single most intense commitment in their life today. Half of the believers said that even though they work at spiritual growth consistently, they have not reached the level of maturity or commitment to maturity that they would like. One out of every five said they occasionally delve into spiritual development, but they are not consistent about those efforts. The remaining one out of ten believers admitted they are neither involved nor interested in spiritual development."[25]

Barna states that his overall assessment of the data is that "most believers say their faith matters, but few are investing much energy in the pursuit of spiritual growth."[26] But rather than simply bemoan the lack of commitment to spiritual growth that exists in the minds and hearts of many church members, Barna suggests that more church leaders follow the example of those who lead the "most effective" churches and proactively assume the responsibility to motivate their members toward an enthusiastic engagement in becoming and making disciples.

One of the most basic things a church can do to increase the motivation of its members toward discipleship is to publicize the fact that it views disciple-making as a key ministry priority. Barna indicates that only half of the believers interviewed by his team felt that discipleship is one of the two or three highest ministry priorities of their church and that the other half said it was just one of many ministries or programs offered by their church.[27] Furthermore, says Barna, only small numbers of the born-again adults interviewed reported that their church had offered to help them "develop specific paths to follow to foster spiritual growth."[28] The implication of these observations is that many evangelical church members do not feel that the leaders of their church take discipleship very seriously!

Something else a church can do to motivate its members toward spiritual growth is to provide them with an instrument by which they can measure the present level of spiritual maturity (or immaturity). According to Barna, "Only one out of every five believers stated that their church has some means of facilitating an evaluation of the spiritual maturity or commitment to maturity of the congregants."[29]

Though many churches choose to develop elaborate, complex self-assessment instruments for their congregants to use, my sense is that the ultimate goal of causing church members to become aware of their need for discipleship training can also be accomplished in a less formal, technical manner by simply describing from the pulpit what a transformed life might look like. For example, in *The Divine Conspiracy* Dallas Willard poses a series of rhetorical questions designed to help his readers better understand the truly profound effect that the imitation of Christ will have upon their lives.

Wouldn't you like to be one of those intelligent people who know how to live a rich and unshakable life? One free from loneliness, fear, and anxiety and filled with constant peace and joy? Would you like to love your neighbors as you do yourself and be free of anger, envy, lust, and covetousness? Would you like to have no need for others to praise you, and would you like to not be paralyzed and humiliated by their dislike and condemnation? Would you like to have the inspiration and strength to lead a constant life of creative goodness? It sounds pretty good thus far, doesn't it?

Wouldn't you also like to have a strength and understanding that enables you genuinely and naturally to bless those who are cursing you—or cheating you, beating you out on the job, spitting on you in a confrontation, laughing at your religion or culture, even *killing* you? Or the strength and understanding merely to give further needed assistance to someone who has forced you to drop what you are doing and help out? To offer the other cheek to someone who has slapped you? Clearly, our entire inner reality of thought and feeling would have to be transformed to bring us to such a place.[30]

Willard's contention is that the key to motivating church members to respond to the arduous call to discipleship is to "ravish" them with the kingdom of God. By this he means that church leaders should be careful to teach "what Jesus himself taught in the manner he taught it."[31] In other words, pastors and church leaders should boldly proclaim the availability of God's kingdom through Jesus Christ, intelligently teach church members what it means to live their lives in the power of God's kingdom, and then prayerfully, passionately, and humbly model this kind of lifestyle before them. Should this kind of proclamation, teaching, and modeling occur, says Willard, most sincere church members will "quite certainly respond well" to it.[32] My own experience as a pastor has proved that Willard's counsel is spot-on.

Prerequisite #4 – A Process of Evaluation

The last prerequisite for an effective disciple-making ministry is a formal process by which church leaders and workers can accurately assess the progress they are making. Such an evaluation process is necessary if the ministry is to amount to more than just another program that begins well and then stalls due to a lack of ongoing effectiveness and, hence, support.

In a section of *Growing True Disciples* entitled "Measuring Progress," Barna reports that the most effective disciple-making churches are careful to monitor how well people are doing in their "efforts to emulate Christ." Furthermore, says Barna, these effective churches "go beyond collecting and reciting affirming anecdotes." Instead, the churches with truly successful discipling ministries have developed specific tools that help leaders gain a sense of "what is happening spiritually in people's lives." These assessment tools include such things as "knowledge measurements, behavioral assessments, gift inventories, attitudinal and behavioral surveys, and goal statements and measurements."[33]

Furthermore, the pastors and leaders of highly effective churches seem to understand that if motivation is to be maintained it is important for church members to sense progress in their journey toward spiritual maturity. For this reason, the most successful discipleship ministries provide congregants with tools by which they can measure their spiritual growth. According to Barna's research, these measuring devices include:

- self-evaluations of how they are doing in reaching their predetermined spiritual goals
- discussions with family and small group members regarding progress

- filling out church-developed or standardized assessment tools
- regular advisory sessions with more mature Christians to discuss growth patterns and experiences
- encouraging people to journal and to review previous journal entries to sense progress or barriers
- challenging people to identify ways in which they apply the lessons from recent sermons
- reflective prayer, seeking direct revelation from God as to what is and is not working in their discipleship efforts.[34]

The leaders of highly effective churches also employ assessments designed to reflect the degree to which the congregation as a whole seems to be growing toward Christian maturity. These leadership-driven assessments scrutinize such things as the number of volunteers in any given evaluation period; the ease with which congregation members are recruited for ministry responsibilities; the number of congregants who turn in a personal growth plan; the number of visitors attending the church due to invitations by church members; the number of divorces among congregants; the quality of the church's experience of community as indicated by the number of serious friendships being developed among congregants; congregant involvement in short-term missions projects; and the level of spiritual growth among church members observed by small group overseers.[35]

I cannot imagine any evangelical pastor not being very eager to see his or her congregation evidence increasing maturity in the ways just described. According to Barna, however, it is not enough to simply inaugurate a disciple-making ministry. Such a ministry must be carefully monitored so as to ensure its effectiveness. The only discipleship ministries that endure are the ones that produce obvious spiritual growth among congregation members. Perhaps this explains why Barna can report, "Worthy of note is the fact that the pastors we talked to had a very solid understanding of the percentage of adults who were involved in a discipleship process. When we quizzed them as to the basis of the figures they were using, each offered solid, substantive reasons for the figures they were suggesting. The implication: *Successful pastors care about the discipleship commitment of their people, they monitor it closely, and they respond when the numbers suggest a waffling of dedication to spiritual advancement.*[36]

The One Ministry Dynamic Common to Nearly All Successful Contemporary Disciple-Making Ministries

Experience indicates that becoming a disciple-making congregation will usually require that church leaders do more than simply adopt in toto an approach to disciple-making utilized by some other church, regardless of that church's size or renown. This does not mean, however, that we cannot learn from what other churches are doing to see life transformation occur in the lives of their members.

In *Growing True Disciples*, Barna provides his readers with an overview of five approaches to disciple-making that are currently being employed by the highly effective churches examined in his study. Barna refers to these five approaches as the *Competencies* Model,[37] the *Missional* Model,[38] the *Neighborhood* Model,[39] the *Worldview* Model,[40] and the *Lecture-Lab* Model.[41] Following Barna's thorough analysis of each of these successful contemporary models, he proffers his own model that includes what he considers to be the best of each approach.

While I encourage you, if you have not already done so, to consult *Growing True Disciples* for yourself in order to glean all that you can from what each of these disciple-making models (including Barna's) has to offer, I want to focus here on the very interesting fact that in one way or another each of these successful contemporary disciple-making ministry models utilizes a combination of large, small, and mid-sized group experiences to help disciples gain the knowledge, skills, and motivation necessary to become more Christlike. *The one ministry dynamic that nearly all successful contemporary disciple-making ministries employ is a smaller interactive group experience that encourages and enables congregants/disciples to process and apply to their lives the teachings they are receiving in plenary worship services.* Wisdom would seem to dictate that any church wanting to become an effective disciple-making congregation will need to do whatever is necessary to implement this particular ministry dynamic.

All of the models presented in *Growing True Disciples* are examples of successful disciple-making structures. It seems to me that a church might learn from any of these models (especially Barna's "best of" model) in order to create a disciple-making ministry that will help life transformation take place in the lives of its members. However, this does not mean that these disciple-making structures can or will, by themselves, defeat Pharisaism. What is still needed is a discussion of how we might use the Sermon on the Mount as a curriculum for a distinct, initial disciple-making event, so powerful in its impact that it will exercise a dramatic effect on the church's corporate culture. Can this really happen? I believe it can.

But before we turn that corner, I need to acknowledge that not a few church leaders and workers may be tempted to respond with dismay to the observation that truly effective disciple-making seems to require that church members not only attend weekend worship services but also regularly participate in at least one small group meeting each week. Is this a reasonable expectation? Is it realistic to think that a significant number of contemporary evangelical church members will be willing to participate in a weekly small group meeting given the busyness of their lives and their tendency toward an individualist mindset?

As counterintuitive as it may seem, this expectation may be more reasonable than we think. Obviously, the highly effective churches included in Barna's study have somehow found a way to motivate their congregants to invest the time and energy required by their respective disciple-making ministries. This is supported by Barna's overall research findings, which seem to suggest that *if the congregants of an evangelical church are adequately convinced that their church's approach to disciple-making is likely to actually produce results, odds are that many of them will eagerly participate.*[42]

In concert with these findings, Dallas Willard offers these words of encouragement:

> Although I have not been a pastor for many years, I have always continued to teach quite regularly in churches and churchlike settings. The appeal and power of Jesus' call to the kingdom and discipleship is great, and people generally, of every type and background, will respond favorably if that call is only presented with directness, generosity of spirit, intelligence, and love, trusting God alone for the outcome.
>
> We may not soon have bigger crowds around us—and in fact they may for a while even get smaller—but we will soon have bigger Christians for sure. This is what I call "church growth for those who hate it." And bigger crowds are sure to follow, for the simple reason that human beings desperately need what we bring to them, the word and reality of The Kingdom Among Us.[43]

So, how is business? I sincerely hope that reading this chapter has inspired you to believe that it really is possible to create disciple-making ministries that can effect genuine life transformation in evangelical church members. According to Willard there is a sense in which the making of disciples can, ultimately, be good for "business" even from a church growth perspective: that is, while the focus is first and foremost on building bigger Christians, he offers that bigger crowds are likely to follow.

Even more to the point being made in this book, however, is the fact that disciple-making is the key to defeating Pharisaism in our evangelical congregations. We have seen that Jesus went to great lengths to disciple the tendency toward Pharisaism out of the lives of his first followers. I am convinced that we need to follow his lead. In the final chapter of this book I will show how the Sermon on the Mount can be used as the foundation for a disciple-making ministry that will allow this vitally important "business" to *really* get done.

Notes

1. Bill Hull, *The Disciple-Making Pastor* (Grand Rapids: Revell, 1988), 12–13.
2. Ibid., 12.
3. Dallas Willard, *The Divine Conspiracy: Rediscovering Our Hidden Life in God* (San Francisco: HarperSanFrancisco, 1998), 301, italics in original.
4. George Barna, *Growing True Disciples: New Strategies for Producing Genuine Followers of Christ* (Colorado Springs: WaterBrook Press, 2001), 7–8.
5. Ibid., 106. Barna notes that the study initially began with a list of two dozen churches, each of which was reputed by their peers to possess a special expertise in the area of disciple-making. After conducting extensive on-site interviews, however, the study narrowed to a dozen churches. Barna writes, "The bottom line was that we had firsthand evidence that people's lives were being consistently transformed so that they became more Christlike. Effective discipleship is about life transformation, and these were churches that facilitated such life change."
6. Ibid., 106–7.
7. Ibid., 32.
8. As a result, this chapter will lean heavily on Barna's work in *Growing True Disciples*.
9. In a subsequent work entitled *Revolution: Finding Vibrant Faith Beyond the Walls of the Sanctuary*, Barna predicts that local churches will continue to lose large numbers of people, not because these disaffected folks have succumbed to spiritual lethargy but because their hunger for genuine spiritual transformation is not being met by their participation in traditional churches. As a result, these revolutionary disciples are opting for a churchless Christianity, finding ways, as the book's subtitle indicates, to develop a vibrant faith beyond the walls of the sanctuary. Barna's prediction should serve to motivate evangelical church leaders and workers to redouble their efforts to see their congregations become adept at making authentic Christian

disciples! George Barna, *Revolution: Finding Vibrant Faith Beyond the Walls of the Sanctuary* (Carol Stream, IL: Tyndale, 2005).

10. Barna, *Growing True Disciples*, 6.

11. Michael J. Wilkins, *Following the Master: A Biblical Theology of Discipleship* (Grand Rapids: Zondervan, 1992), 40–41.

12. Greg Ogden, *Discipleship Essentials: A Guide to Building Your Life in Christ* (Downers Grove, IL: InterVarsity, 1998), 24.

13. Willard, *The Divine Conspiracy*, 282–83.

14. Barna, *Growing True Disciples*, 17–18.

15. For example, Bill Hull, *Jesus Christ: Disciple-Maker* (Colorado Springs: NavPress, 1984), 11–12; Hull, *The Disciple-Making Pastor*, 14; David Watson, *Called and Committed* (Wheaton: Harold Shaw Publishers, 1982), 49–51; Barna, *Growing True Disciples*, 20–21, 165–66.

16. Wilkins, *Following the Master*, 357.

17. Barna, *Growing True Disciples*, 4–5.

18. Willard, *The Divine Conspiracy*, 57–58.

19. Hull, *The Disciple-Making Pastor*, 117.

20. Barna, *Growing True Disciples*, 116–17.

21. I am indebted to Steve Barker and Ron Nicholas, *Good Things Come in Small Groups: The Dynamics of Good Group Life* (Downers Grove, IL: InterVarsity, 1985) for the idea that worship, nurture, community, and mission form the heart of the Christian experience.

22. The reciprocal relationship between *being* and *doing* in discipleship is a theme taken up by New Testament scholar William Klein, who writes: "While spiritual formation is not primarily about 'doing,' *doing is still crucial.* Those who become spiritually formed as Jesus intends do all kinds of behaviors that please God and that profit themselves and others." *Become What You Are: Spiritual Formation According to the Sermon on the Mount* (Tyrone, GA: Authentic Publishing, 2006), xii (italics in original).

23. I think it is important to emphasize that, at its best, evangelicalism does a good job of engaging in both personal evangelism and social action. For an excellent treatment of this dynamic see Ronald J. Sider, *Good News and Good Works: A Theology for the Whole Gospel* (Grand Rapids: Baker, 1993).

24. I am alluding here to the phrase "If you build it, he will come," repeated several times in the film *Field of Dreams*.

25. Barna, *Growing True Disciples*, 42.

26. Ibid., 34.

27. Ibid., 46.

28. Ibid.

29. Ibid., 47.

30. Willard, *The Divine Conspiracy*, 312, italics in original.

31. Ibid.

32. Ibid., 312, 372.
33. Barna, *Growing True Disciples*, 110–11.
34. Ibid., 113–14.
35. Ibid., 112.
36. Ibid., 115, italics in original.
37. Ibid., 137.
38. Ibid., 140–41.
39. Ibid., 146.
40. Ibid., 149.
41. Ibid., 153.
42. Ibid., 35–36.
43. Willard, *The Divine Conspiracy*, 372–73.

10

BRASS TACKS:
HOW TO DEFEAT PHARISAISM IN
YOUR CHURCH

A popular version of an observation famously made by G. K. Chesterton goes like this: "Five times in the last 2,000 years the Church has to all appearances gone to the dogs. In each case it was the dogs that died."[1] Chesterton's point was that we should never count the church (i.e., the Christian faith) down and out, no matter how dire the circumstances might seem.

Fully mindful of the truth of this observation, I have argued in this book that the ongoing presence of Pharisaism within evangelical churches poses a serious problem for the evangelical movement. Without apology, I have also insisted that contemporary evangelical pastors and church leaders should develop a disciple-making curriculum based on the Sermon on the Mount in order to defeat the Pharisaism at work in their churches. In this final chapter, I will demonstrate how such a Pharisee-defeating curriculum might be structured.

A Crucial Caveat: A Discipleship Experience Versus a Disciple-Making Environment

Because Jesus' disciple-making strategy was to use the Pharisees as an anti-model, and because the Sermon on the Mount is filled with so much anti-Pharisee rhetoric, a curricular discipleship experience that is properly reflective of the teachings presented in Jesus' most famous sermon cannot help but steer contemporary disciples away from the traits and tendencies of the Pharisees. Still, since genuine disciple-making is a lifelong process, what is ultimately needed is not simply a specific disciple-making *experience* (no matter how powerful) but a disciple-making *environment*—an ethos that makes it easy for authentic Christianity to thrive while choking the life out of any Christian Pharisaism present in the congregation. Before going on to describe how the Sermon on the Mount can serve as the foundation for a highly impactful disciple-making experience, I want to explain what is involved in the creation of a highly effective disciple-making environment.

Such a ministry environment is created when local churches do two things. First, as I suggested in the previous chapter, the effective disciple-making church will take each of the five ministry dynamics alluded to in Acts 2:42–47 very seriously. These churches are careful to steer church members toward an ongoing engagement in (1) transformative *worship* experiences; (2) spiritual disciplines that *nurture* their ability to trust in God's love regardless of circumstances[2]; (3) the empowering experience of genuine Christian *community*; (4) Christian *mission* (praxis) involving both personal evangelism and social action; and (5) a faithful, enthusiastic *stewardship* of their stuff. We cannot pick and choose here. This is how the wheels come off of many disciple-making ministries: well-intentioned church leaders focus on one or two or three of these five ministry dynamics and neglect the others. This will not do. Again, no one ever said making disciples would be easy. But we have every reason to assume that God's

Spirit will help us fashion a well-balanced, biblically grounded ministry environment if we humbly ask him to (see James 4:6).

The second thing that a congregation must do in order to create a supremely effective disciple-making environment is to create an integrated ministry structure—a structure in which the various ministries of the church are so intertwined that the congregant cannot help but be exposed to more than one ministry dynamic, in more than one kind of setting, in more than one kind of manner. Such an integrated structure will work against the modern consumerist/individualist mentality that is present in the lives of so many contemporary churchgoers. Rather than catering to the congregants' desire to "pick and choose" which ministry dynamics they will or will not participate in, it is possible to structure the ministry of the church in such a way that an ethos of growth and commitment is created—a church culture wherein there exists a certain expectation that members in good standing do more than attend the weekly plenary worship service. Instead, the congregants feel a loving pressure to take their apprenticeship to Jesus seriously and cooperate with the church's attempts to help them become mature followers of Christ.

This sort of disciple-making environment is created when the local church takes deliberate steps to develop a strong connection between the main teaching service and other ministry events taking place during the week. Sooner or later it becomes obvious to congregation members that the clear expectation at work in this church is that its congregants do more than sit through a weekly sermon. They are expected to take this teaching to the next level and actually put it to work in their day-to-day lives (Matthew 7:21,24–27).

This is what must happen if the discipleship deficit in the American evangelical church is to be reduced. Local churches must strive to create well-balanced, biblically grounded, integrated disciple-making environments. And to the degree that the local church will consistently maintain the same kind of anti-Pharisee emphasis that Jesus employed in his own disciple-making ministry, I am convinced that the disciple-making experience described in the next several pages has what it takes to create an overall ministry environment that will prove to be quite successful at defeating Pharisaism.

John Wesley's Discipleship Method: Interlocking Groups

Of particular value when it comes to creating a balanced, integrated ministry structure is the disciple-making methodology utilized by John Wesley in eighteenth-century England. Interestingly, all of the contemporary disciple-making models presented in George Barna's book *Growing True Disciples* have much in common with Wesley's method of having disciples participate in several "interlocking groups."

John Wesley was an Anglican priest who, after experiencing an evangelical awakening, became a prolific evangelist. Not welcome in many Anglican churches, Wesley's evangelistic zeal led him to begin preaching to men and women in the open air. Converts were made by the dozens.

Wesley was rightfully concerned about follow-up. The system he devised proved to be extremely effective. His converts experienced a radical moral and spiritual transformation. So numerous were Wesley's converts, and so profound was the change toward Christlikeness that took place in their lives, that the tenor of the nation as a whole was affected. Some historians have gone so far as to say that it was largely due to the Wesleyan revival that England managed to avoid the kind of bloody revolution that took place in France.[3]

The genius of Wesley's approach to disciple-making was that it emulated the multiple-meeting pattern evident in the New Testament. Acts 2:42–47 indicates that the Jerusalem church utilized a multipronged approach to the *nurture* of its congregants: the church members met frequently as a large congregation in the temple; they also met in smaller groups in various homes throughout the city. In like manner, Wesley created a disciple-making structure that called for its participants to meet in two, possibly three, groups of varying size each week.

In his book *John Wesley's Class Meeting: A Model for Making Disciples*, D. Michael Henderson describes the "method" behind the discipling movement that came to be known as "Methodism." "Wesley's unique 'method' combined several interlocking group techniques to construct a ladder of personal spiritual improvement. All sincere Christians, whatever their intelligence or background, could work up that ladder by faithful participation, from one level of spiritual maturity to the next. The 'rungs' on Wesley's ladder of Christian discipleship were small interactive groups—the class meeting, the band, the select band, the penitent band, and the society. Each group within the system was designed to accomplish a specific developmental purpose, and each group had its own carefully defined roles and procedures to ensure that the central objectives were accomplished."[4]

In other words, Wesley rediscovered the value of having Christian disciples meet in different groups each week in order to accomplish different purposes. In doing so he avoided a mistake that many modern churches are guilty of making: *he did not try to accomplish all the goals of discipleship in just one kind of group meeting.*

Though Henderson's description makes reference to five different groups, Wesley's writings make it clear that the three main groups in his disciple-making system were the society, the class, and the band.

The Society: The Cognitive Mode

While Wesley himself never broke with the Anglican Church, he did organize his converts into Methodist societies. Henderson explains that each Methodist society was "the group which included all the

Methodists in a given area or locality."[5] Therefore, the term "society" is nearly synonymous with the term "congregation."[6]

The main goal of the society meeting was to teach sound doctrine. This Sunday evening meeting was essentially a worship service that included "lecture, preaching, public reading, hymn singing, and 'exhorting.'"[7] Since this was a larger group meeting (fifty or more people), there was little or no opportunity for personal response or feedback. The major aim of the society meeting was to "present scriptural truth and have it clearly understood."[8]

The Class Meeting: The Behavioral Mode

At first, the Methodist "class" was simply a small group of members who lived in a particular geographical area. Class leaders were to visit each member in the class once a week to inquire "how their souls prosper." It did not take long for the early Methodists to decide that it would make more sense to have the class members meet together once a week to provide each other with mutual support and accountability.[9] Henderson writes:

> The class meeting was the most influential instructional unit in Methodism and probably Wesley's greatest contribution to the technology of group experience. Although amazingly simple, it has elicited the praise of educators and religious leaders as a profoundly effective educational tool. Henry Ward Beecher said, "The greatest thing John Wesley ever gave to the world is the Methodist class-meeting." Dwight L. Moody, nineteenth-century revivalist, offered this commendation: "The Methodist class-meetings are the best institutions for training converts the world ever saw." To the class meeting must go much of the credit which many historians have attributed to Methodism for the radical transformation of England's working masses. It was a

triumph not of any human personality, but of an ingenious set of instruments designed for behavioral change.[10]

The Methodist class meeting was a dynamic small group experience. But unlike the small group ministries that function in most contemporary churches, the Methodist class meeting was not an option for Methodist society members. In order to be a member-in-good-standing of the society, the believer had to be a member-in-good-standing of a class.[11] The mandatory nature of the class meetings indicates that Wesley was convinced that in order to grow in their ability to obey the teachings of Scripture believers needed to experience more than good teaching; they also needed the reinforcing, motivating support and accountability that could best be experienced in "an intimate group of ten to twelve people who met weekly for personal supervision of their spiritual growth."[12]

Little or no teaching occurred in Wesley's class meetings. The focus here was almost entirely on the application of scriptural truth to the members' lives. After singing a brief hymn, the leader of the class meeting would be the first to "check in" with the rest of the group. The leader would candidly share regarding the condition of his or her spiritual life.[13] Henderson explains, "The leader would then give a short testimonial concerning the previous week's experience, thanking God for progress and honestly sharing any failures, sins, temptations, griefs, or inner battles. In this sense, the leader was 'modeling the role' for the others to follow."[14]

As each class member followed the leader's example in turn, an affirming, supportive environment was created that served to raise the members' level of spiritual motivation. As previously indicated, the purpose of the class meeting was not to introduce new information (teaching) to the members, but simply to encourage a consistent and thoughtful day-to-day practice that ultimately produced new behavioral patterns.[15]

Several group dynamics made the class meeting a very successful structure for the cultivation of Christian character. First, since the members of the class tended to stay together for years at a time, a deep level of interpersonal trust and sensitivity was created. The small group could tell if one of its members was being less than truthful, if he or she seemed to be struggling in some area, or if his or her spiritual zeal seemed to be waning.[16] Second, it appears that the sheer consistency with which the class members met together for mutual support and accountability had a powerful, awareness-raising, behavior-modifying effect upon them. Third, Wesley himself made it very clear (in his own way) that the dynamic of having the content of what had been preached in the society meetings repeated, explained, and enforced coincided with the overarching goal of producing fully devoted followers of Christ (see James 1:22–25).[17]

The Band: The Affective Mode

In Wesley's disciple-making approach, each of the three interlocking groups addressed a different dynamic involved in life transformation. The focus of the society meeting was cognitive instruction. The class meeting created an environment of accountability that encouraged behavioral change. The third group experience, meeting with one's "band," facilitated affective redirection.[18] In other words, the goal of the band meeting was to help its members grow in their ability to actually experience love for God and neighbor.

The Methodist band was the smallest of the three groups. This was a "homogeneous grouping, not only by sex, but also by age and marital status."[19] Unlike the class meeting, the band meeting was optional. This small group experience had to be voluntary since the purpose of the band was to stimulate growth in "love, holiness, and purity of intention."[20] Speaking of the band, Henderson notes, "The group environment was one of ruthless honesty and frank openness, in which its members sought to improve their attitudes, emotions, feelings, intentions, and affections.

It could be said metaphorically that the society aimed for the head, the class meeting for the hands, and the band for the heart."[21]

There were some similarities between the class meetings and those of the band, perhaps even a bit of planned redundancy. As in the class meeting, there was no new information or teaching offered. Instead, the members simply took turns quizzing one another and speaking to one another about the condition of their souls and their respective levels of passion for the things of God. The big difference between the two meetings was that the leader's role in the band meeting was much less conspicuous and there tended to be a greater level of maturity on the part of the members, as indicated by the "depth of their openness, and the readiness with which they spoke of their feelings."[22]

In order to provide a bit of structure and consistency to these weekly meetings that were designed to focus so greatly on subjective, affective realities, the bands used a set of prescribed questions provided by Wesley himself. In a document entitled "The Rules of the Band Societies," Wesley indicated that the main purpose of the band meeting was to make it possible for Christian believers to obey the biblical command found in James 5:16 to "Confess your faults one to another, and pray one for another, that ye may be healed."[23] Wesley went on to stipulate that the following five questions be responded to, in turn, by each member of the band:

1. What known sins have you committed since our last meeting?
2. What temptations have you met with?
3. How were you delivered?
4. What have you thought, said or done, of which you doubt whether it be sin or not?
5. Have you nothing you desire to keep secret?[24]

While the class meetings allowed for visitors to attend every other meeting,[25] no visitors were allowed at any of the band meetings.[26] It was crucial for the band to develop a radical degree of trust and openness if the sharing of its members was to be of sufficient depth and honesty to genuinely affect the condition of their hearts. The content of the self-examination and sharing in the band meeting was not so much about the members' practices or behaviors but their "motives and heartfelt impressions."[27] It cannot be overstated that Wesley saw the interlocking groups complementing one another, working together to produce a spiritual and moral transformation of the believer into the image of Christ. The society affected the head; the class affected the hands; the band affected the heart.

Though some aspects of Wesley's system of interlocking groups might seem odd or perhaps intimidating to modern believers, its value as a disciple-making model is incontrovertible. In its day it was very effective in helping all kinds of people experience spiritual growth toward Christlikeness. Furthermore, the fact is that many contemporary disciple-making models seem to have been influenced by it. Perhaps the key to the success of Wesley's method was that it created a balanced, integrated disciple-making environment, a church culture that made it virtually impossible for spiritual formation not to happen in the lives of its regular adherents.

A Disciple-Making Curriculum That Proactively Addresses Christian Pharisaism

Having identified the value of Wesley's system of interlocking groups as a disciple-making methodology, and having established the utility of Jesus' Sermon on the Mount as the foundation for a disciple-making curriculum, the goal now is to demonstrate how these two ministry dynamics can be combined to create a disciple-making event so powerful that it contributes to an environment that is capable of defeating Christian Pharisaism. What follows is a very brief overview of a simple disciple-making strategy based on the Sermon on the Mount and that follows the basic contours of the Wesleyan method of making disciples.

This proposed strategy consists of three main activities: first, a sermon or teaching series based on the Sermon on the Mount that is delivered in either a large or mid-sized group setting (reminiscent of Wesley's society meeting); second, a small to mid-sized group "Application" meeting, wherein six to sixty disciples engage in an application-oriented discussion of the most recent sermon (reminiscent of Wesley's class meeting); third, a very small group "Accountability" meeting, during which two to four disciples hold each other accountable for their respective efforts to live out the teaching presented in the most recent sermon and to speak frankly to one another regarding the present level of their spiritual passion (reminiscent of Wesley's band meeting).

Please note, however, that the three-pronged strategy presented here is designed to serve as an initiatory, *short-term* disciple-making experience that focuses on the goal of exposing congregants to the Sermon on the Mount. I want to suggest that for the *long term* a two-pronged strategy involving a plenary teaching session (focusing on any biblical text) followed up by just one small group meeting each week, in which congregants discuss and apply the teaching to their lives (holding each other accountable for commitments made in the process), can serve a church well as an ongoing disciple-making structure.[28]

Helping Disciples Understand the Sermon on the Mount (the Cognitive Aspect)

The disciple-making strategy proposed here calls for each member of the congregation to be exposed to a teaching series based on the Sermon on the Mount. Obviously, for this sermon series to aid in the battle against Christian Pharisaism it is incumbent upon the pastor/teacher to approach the texts found in Mathew 5–7 keeping Matthew's apologetic aim in mind. It is possible to construct a teaching series based on the Sermon on the Mount wherein each and every teaching serves to remind congregants that they have a choice to make: Will they choose to pursue the path of authentic Christian discipleship that is laid out by Jesus in his sermon, or will they succumb to the temptation to approach their religious faith in the same ways that the Pharisees approached theirs?

Sitting through a sermon or teaching series that seeks to explain what Jesus was saying in the Sermon on the Mount, keeping the polemical tension between Jesus and the Pharisees continually in mind, cannot help but steer congregants away from the traits and tendencies of New Testament Pharisaism and toward an authentic, kingdom-centered Christian discipleship.

Helping Disciples Apply the Sermon on the Mount (the Behavioral Aspect)

Merely hearing a sermon or teaching delivered each week is not sufficient for life transformation. The ultimate goal of the "Application" meeting, as the name suggests, is to challenge disciples to practically apply the teachings of the Sermon on the Mount to their lives. In the course of this weekly meeting the disciples are encouraged to prayerfully discern the unique way in which Christ is speaking to them through the portion of the Sermon on the Mount most recently presented to them and to specify before the other members what practical things they believe Christ is calling them to do in response.

Just as Wesley prescribed a set of questions to be utilized in his small groups, the leadership of the local church might choose to create a standardized set of application-oriented questions for each "Application" group to use in the course of their meetings. Such a set of questions might contain the following inquiries: 1) What, in your view, were the main themes presented in last Sunday's sermon? 2) Which of these main themes do you consider to be especially important and applicable to your life? 3) With regard to the specific issue(s) dealt with in last Sunday's sermon, where would you honestly place yourself at this stage in your spiritual journey on a continuum between authentic Christian discipleship on the one hand and a Pharisaical approach to the Christian faith on the other? 4) What specific thing(s) is Jesus calling you to do between now and next Sunday in order to respond obediently to the message that has come to you through last Sunday's sermon? 5) In what specific ways should the rest of us be praying for you as you attempt to live out this portion of the Sermon on the Mount?

A nonjudgmental atmosphere must be created and maintained, of course, in order for a sufficient degree of honesty to be exhibited in these small group meetings. Whatever other training the leaders of these "Application" meetings receive, they must be prepared to model continually Christ's acceptance and to lovingly confront any Pharisaical judgmentalism that might emanate from members of the group.

Helping Disciples Become Accountable for the Sermon on the Mount (the Affective Aspect)

Profound life change would undoubtedly occur simply by having contemporary evangelical congregants experience this strategy's version of Wesley's society and class meetings. Still, even more profound effects might be achieved if a way is found to encourage disciples to participate also in this strategy's version of Wesley's band meetings, the "Accountability" meeting.

Since there are only two to four members in attendance, the weekly "Accountability" meeting need not take longer than an hour. The goal of this gathering is to raise the disciples' level of awareness to an even greater degree. The presumption here is that an essential element in Christian spirituality is an increased awareness on the part of the disciple: a heightened, ongoing sensitivity to the things of God in general and to the empowering presence of Christ in particular (see Colossians 3:1–17).

Another presumption at work here is that one of the keys to seeing a disciple's awareness of spiritual realities raised is a consistent experience of genuine Christian community, a community where the mutual confession and support alluded to in James 5:16 can occur on a regular basis.

These are the ultimate goals of the weekly "Accountability" meeting. In this intimate setting the following six questions can be asked and answered in an environment that allows for mutual mentoring: (1) What specific commitments did you make in your "Application" group meeting? (2) Have you followed through on these commitments? If not, why? (3) How strong, honestly, is your passion at present to keep growing toward an authentic Christian discipleship? (4) What changes need to occur in your heart for you to be able to succeed at living out the section of the Sermon on the Mount we have been focusing on this week? (5) What could you do in the next twenty-four hours to remind yourself of how much God loves you and how blessed you are "in Christ"? (6) Will you do this?

After a short season of serious prayer for one another, this meeting may conclude with all of the disciples involved having experienced an intense awareness-raising dynamic. If the results of Wesley's disciple-making ministry are any indication, the simple strategy presented here will be extremely effective in helping evangelical church members mature toward a genuine Christian maturity.

The Core Component: A Teaching Series Based on The Sermon on the Mount

As indicated above, the core component of the disciple-making strategy being presented here is a sermon or teaching series delivered on a weekly basis to either a large or mid-sized group of disciples. The goal of the final section of this final chapter is not to dictate how the Sermon on the Mount must be taught, nor even to provide thorough teaching outlines, but only to suggest how a teaching series that directly addresses the perennial problem of Christian Pharisaism might be derived from it. As you look over this suggested list of Pharisee-busting teachings, I encourage you to keep referring to my analysis of the Sermon on the Mount (chapters six to eight of this book) to help you get some idea of how each teaching might be structured.[29]

The overall theme for such a teaching series might focus on the idea that in his Sermon on the Mount Jesus was calling for his disciples to experience life in the kingdom of God (see Matthew 4:17). Accordingly, an overview of the main discipleship topics treated would look like this:

- *Welcome to Life in the Kingdom* (an introduction to what authentic Christian discipleship involves)

- *The Core Values of the Kingdom* (the attitudes and actions of authentic Christian disciples that set them apart from the Pharisees)

- *The Cost of the Kingdom* (the treatment authentic Christian disciples can expect from the world in general and the Pharisees in particular)

- *The Ethics of the Kingdom* (the call for authentic Christian disciples to—unlike the Pharisees—truly discern the heart of God and do his will)

- *The Spirituality of the Kingdom* (the call for authentic Christian disciples to avoid the hypocritical piety of the Pharisees and to commune with God in the depth of their souls)

- *The Priority of the Kingdom* (the call for authentic Christian disciples to—unlike the Pharisees—make the choice to trust in and serve God rather than money and things)

- *The Ministry of the Kingdom* (how authentic Christian disciples can—unlike the Pharisees—succeed in influencing other people for God)

- *The Challenges of the Kingdom* (why authentic Christian disciples must stay on guard against all forms of spiritual deception, especially those provided by the Pharisees)

Now, let us see how some specific teachings might help fill out this broad discipleship curriculum.

Welcome to Life in the Kingdom

In order to maximize the effect this teaching series has on the listeners, it is necessary to spend several sessions laying the groundwork, introducing the topic, and easing the congregation into an anticipatory, receptive posture. Therefore, no less than three teachings might be devoted to the task of introducing the series.

The first introductory teaching might be entitled "Investigating the Invitation." While it is possible to use John 3:16 and Mark 1:14–15 as biblical texts, this teaching is not really a biblical exposition as much as it is a thoughtful analysis of chapters one and two of Dallas Willard's excellent book, *The Divine Conspiracy*. The ultimate goal of this initial teaching is to produce a degree of healthy tension in the hearts and minds of the congregation. Is it possible that most evangelical believers have not completely understood the full implications of Jesus' invitation to experience the kingdom of God? Could it be that very few evangelical church members are actually living their lives in the power of God's kingdom that is available to them?

Since the Sermon on the Mount contains Jesus' teaching regarding life in the kingdom of God, a second introductory teaching (also based on chapters one and two of Dallas Willard's *The Divine Conspiracy*), possibly entitled "Coming Kingdom-Correct," might be devoted to an exploration of the nature of the kingdom and a discussion of how one enters it. The goal of this teaching would in fact be to evangelize those congregants who have yet to make a personal commitment to become one of Christ's apprentices.

A third introductory teaching, one intended to establish the rhetorical setting of the Sermon in Matthew's Gospel, would be loosely based on the material in Matthew 1:1 to 5:2 (that is, from the beginning of the Gospel to Jesus taking his place on the mount). Possibly entitled "The Irony of It All," this teaching might highlight Matthew's use of irony in the material leading up to the Sermon and would prepare the congregants for the presence of irony in Jesus' sermon.

The Core Values of the Kingdom

"The Beatitudes: A Shocking Sermon Introduction" (Matthew 5:3–12) is a possible title for what might be a multi-installment teaching contrasting the earmarks (virtues) of the Christian disciple with the characteristics (vices) of the typical Pharisee as depicted in Matthew's Gospel. It is perhaps true that no utterance of Jesus has earned more commentary than his Beatitudes. Unfortunately, most commentaries largely ignore the fact that Jesus' understanding of the eight virtues he listed at the beginning of his sermon would have been grounded in the teaching of the Old Testament. Much insight can be gained by carefully evaluating what the Old Testament has to say about each of these eight virtues, and how the Synoptic Gospels seem to portray the Pharisees as lacking the same.

The Cost of the Kingdom

"Who the Real Heroes Are" (5:11–16)[30] would be a teaching that makes the point that despite the reputation the Pharisees had in Jesus' day as spiritual exemplars, it is those who embrace and exhibit the core values of God's kingdom (the Beatitudes) who are the true spiritual heroes. These are the ones who, following in the footsteps of the Old

Testament prophets, will be persecuted (ironically, by the Pharisees) for the sake of righteousness. Nevertheless, authentic disciples of Jesus will make their contemporaries thirsty for God and will enlighten them as to the true nature of the kingdom. Helping lost people be reconciled to God—the stuff of kingdom heroes indeed!

The Ethics of the Kingdom

The next teaching in this series, possibly entitled "A Crucial Clarification" (5:17–20), would explain why Jesus had to defend himself against the Pharisees' charge that his habit of associating with obviously impious people proved that he possessed a low view of God's moral law and that he was therefore soft on sin. The upshot of this message would be that, on the contrary, Jesus had a very high view of God's law, properly interpreted. The implication for contemporary evangelicals is that (a) to be sensitive to spiritual seekers does not mean that one is soft on sin; (b) despite the moral relativism of the modern/postmodern era, contemporary Christians should, like Jesus, take sin very seriously; and (c) it will take more than the ritualistic, self-serving piety of the Pharisees to enter into God's kingdom; God is looking for people who will strive to discern his heart and do his will.

Now, since Matthew 5:21–48 is a lengthy pericope within the Sermon on the Mount that has Jesus illustrating for his followers how they, unlike the Pharisees, can live their lives in such a way as to genuinely please the God of heaven, it will likely require six teachings to do justice to this very important section of the Sermon. "There's More Than One Way to Commit Murder" (5:21–26) would strive to make the point that Christ's followers are not to follow the Pharisaical practices of nursing grudges, writing people off, and assassinating people's characters.

In "Adultery Begins in the Head, Not in the Bed" (5:27–30), the disciple would be challenged and empowered to deal with the phenomenon of "heart adultery." Christ's followers must not succumb to the Pharisaical argument that as long as the physical act of adultery does not occur, what happens in one's mind and heart is not, strictly speaking, a violation of the law of Moses.

The teaching possibly entitled "Jesus: On Divorce" (5:31–32) would encourage the congregant to interpret what Jesus says about divorce in the Sermon on the Mount not as a new law but as a corrective against the Pharisaical practice of serial monogamy. According to Jesus, the Pharisaical practice of legally divorcing one wife *in order to marry another* constituted adultery in the eyes of God. On the one hand, this teaching promotes a high view of marriage, arguing against the loophole hermeneutic employed by the Pharisees of Jesus' day. On the other hand, it strives to subvert the Pharisaical tendency present in many modern evangelical churches to treat divorced and remarried people as second-class citizens in God's kingdom.

"Kingdom People Don't Twist the Truth" (5:33–37) would be a teaching that makes it clear that Jesus' followers, unlike the Pharisees of the first century, are to be straight shooters who don't use slippery speech in order to deceive and manipulate people.

"Don't Worry, Show Mercy" (5:38–42) would make the important point that because Christ's followers can trust God to do right by them in terms of their reputation and resources, they possess a profound, supernatural freedom to—unlike the Pharisees—respond with an amazing generosity of spirit to people who do not deserve it.

"What God's Kids Can Do" (5:43–48) would seek to help disciples recognize that, because they are so radically loved by God, they have been called and empowered to radically love other people, even their enemies. In the process, this teaching would point out that the Pharisees would have thought and taught that while the Old Testament law calls for the children of Israel to love their neighbors, not even God expects his covenant partners to love their enemies. The contrast between Jesus' understanding of the heart of God and that of the Pharisees could not be presented in a more explicit manner.

The Spirituality of the Kingdom

A teaching based on Matthew 6:1–4, "Jesus: On Giving," would encourage congregants to be genuinely generous givers without following the Pharisaical practice of giving so as to garner attention.

"Jesus: On Praying" (6:5–15) would teach Christ-followers how they *should* pray (secretly, simply, sincerely, and submissively) and how they *should not* pray (like the Pharisees, in order to impress other people). It also makes the point that it is possible to structure our prayers in such a way as to be reminded on a daily basis of the reality and availability of God's kingdom.

Via "Jesus: On Fasting" (6:16–18), the disciple would be enabled to understand why Jesus said "when you fast" in verses 16 and 17 rather than "if you fast." The legitimacy and value of this spiritual discipline would be underscored even as the Pharisaical abuse of it is pointed out.

The Priority of the Kingdom

The teaching entitled "The Bottom Line" (6:19–34)[31] would focus on money matters. Against the backdrop provided by the statement in Luke 16:14 that the Pharisees loved money, this teaching might provide disciples with five self-examination questions designed to help them evaluate the degree to which their lives are inappropriately focused more on money than on God: (1) Am I investing enough of my resources in God's kingdom cause? (2) What does my checkbook say about what's really important to me? (3) What does my datebook say about what my life is really focused on? (4) Do I need to make a fresh decision about who or what I'm going to serve? (5) What does the fact that I spend so much time worrying about material concerns indicate about the real state of my faith?

The Ministry of the Kingdom

"Becoming the Kind of Person People Will Listen To" (7:1–12) would likely be another multi-installment teaching. In such a miniseries of teachings, congregants would be made aware of the five things Jesus said we must do if we are going to affect the hearts and lives of other people effectively: (a) we, unlike the Pharisees, must not be in the habit of writing people off in a critical, judgmental manner; (b) we, unlike the Pharisees, must not set out to "fix" others while denying the dysfunction in our own lives; (c) we, unlike the Pharisees, should not try to force our help on people who are not yet in a position to really understand and appreciate the ministry that is being offered to them; (d) we, unlike the Pharisees, must always remain persistent in our practice of prayer, realizing that through sincere prayer the hardest of hearts can be broken, including our own; and (e) we, unlike the Pharisees, must learn to treat other people with the love, respect, dignity, and sensitivity that we ourselves would hope to receive.

The Challenges of the Kingdom

The final teaching, based on Matthew 7:13–29, might be entitled "How to Become a Spiritual Survivor." In this very important teaching the disciple would be warned to beware of the three things that can cause him or her to "crash and burn" spiritually: (a) like the Pharisees, not taking the road less traveled (7:13–14); (b) not staying on guard against false prophets in general and the Pharisees in particular (7:15–23; cf. Matthew 3:7–10; 12:22–37; 21:43–45); and (c) not recognizing how foolish it would be, having acknowledged Jesus' spiritual authority, to fail nevertheless to put his teachings into practice (7:24–29). The upshot of this final teaching is that to become spiritual survivors we have to go all the way to the end, rendering to Christ what Eugene Peterson eloquently refers to as "a long obedience in the same direction."[32] Thus, the teaching series as a whole would conclude with a powerful admonition for congregation members to be careful to follow the path of authentic Christian discipleship rather than the one tread by the Pharisees and all other faux followers of Christ.

Please note how, from start to finish, this proposed teaching series based on the Sermon on the Mount is careful to keep the polemical tension between Jesus and the Pharisees in view. Rather than doing injury to the text, I believe this hermeneutical method yields important insights into what the Matthean Jesus might have been endeavoring to accomplish as he explicated for his followers what life in the kingdom of God could and should be like.

Whether you choose to employ any part of the model teaching series put forward here or to develop your own, it is important to remember that Jesus was *proactive* about steering his followers away from the beliefs and practices, the traits and tendencies, of the Pharisees. By basing a disciple-making curriculum on Jesus' Sermon on the Mount, the leaders of contemporary evangelical churches can do likewise. We can do this! We can succeed at creating a disciple-making environment that points people to Christ, even as it directs them away from New Testament Pharisaism.

A Personal Pastoral Reflection

Perhaps this is a good time to discuss, if only briefly, the effect that the disciple-making strategy I am describing in this book had upon the church I served as senior pastor from 1996 to 2007. Having founded the church with the goal of becoming a no-nonsense, modern, postmodern, post-postmodern disciple-making community of believers, the congregation's awareness of the need to avoid the fundamentalism so often present in many traditional evangelical/Pentecostal churches was already raised. Still, I am convinced that an observation of my personal commitment to overcome Pharisaism in my own walk with Christ, along with their having been exposed in a modified, gradual manner to the disciple-making strategy proposed in these pages, had the effect of mitigating the harmful effects of Pharisaism within this church family. [33]

While not perfect, this community of Christians was amazingly healthy and Pharisaism-resistant. These folks were accepting of each other and wonderfully welcoming toward newcomers. Differing personalities, politics, and ministry philosophies did not result in the formation of cliques, much less divisions, in the congregation. Instead of suffering from a tendency toward spiritual myopia, these believers stayed focused on the big picture, which for us involved a commitment to function as a missional re-presentation of Christ to our community.

Worship wars? While various church members did express their personal preferences regarding the kind of music utilized and the form of liturgy employed in our worship services, and though some congregants did voice a measure of concern over the casual attire adopted by members of the worship team—along with my unwillingness to post a sign at the entrance of the worship space banning food and drink from that space—still, the health of this congregation was evidenced in the fact that we were able to talk through these issues without coming to blows, figuratively speaking. The members understood that the goal of worship is the glory of God and the experience of his life-transforming presence. Due to our having worked through the Sermon on the Mount, the kind of music and liturgy we used was never considered to be the main thing, certainly not something over which to quarrel.

When a member stumbled into sin, his or her comrades were quick to restore rather than reject. Amazingly, even when adherents would occasionally feel the need to move on and become a part of another church family, those left behind did not feel the need to demonize their departing friends in order to keep feeling good about themselves.

Finally, when it became apparent to this congregation that it was God's surprising will for it to disband so that its pastor could focus full-time on teaching, writing, and mentoring future church leaders, and so that commuting members would be forced to find communities of faith closer to home, these folks continued to love God, one another, and their too-busy pastor. Despite some understandable feelings of sadness and disappointment, the final celebration service was earmarked by expressions of peace, hope, joy, and a legitimate feeling of pride. My sense is that everyone in this congregation is not only attending a church closer to home but that nearly all of them are involved in small groups, continuing their journey toward authentic Christian discipleship.

If the antithesis of Pharisaism is an ability to handle some ambiguity without capitulating to the craving for certainty, this church family demonstrated an amazing degree of non-Pharisaism. I could not be more proud to have been a part of such a ministry experiment/experience.

Thanks for bearing with a bit of boasting on my part regarding a community of believers I still dearly love and the disciple-making strategy to which I am so very committed. Once again, we can do this! We can create communities of faith that are essentially Pharisaism-free. In the conclusion that follows, I want to share a few final thoughts about the key role that pastors and other church leaders and workers must play in this ministry project—and why the endeavor is well worth the undertaking.

Notes

1. Actually, the quote runs, "At least five times, therefore, with the Arian and the Albigensian, with the Humanist sceptic [sic], after Voltaire and after Darwin, the Faith has to all appearance gone to the dogs. In each of these five cases it was the dog that died." G. K. Chesterton, The Everlasting Man (San Francisco: Ignatius Press, 1993), 255.

2. One of these spiritual disciplines will be a consistent study of God's Word in both public and private settings.

3. D. Michael Henderson, *John Wesley's Class Meeting: A Model for Making Disciples* (Nappanee, IN: Evangel Publishing House, 1997), 12.

4. Ibid., 11.

5. Ibid., 83.

6. Ibid.

7. Ibid., 84. It should be noted that Wesley's society meetings were never intended to replace attendance at Anglican church services conducted on Sunday mornings.

8. Ibid.

9. Rupert Davies, ed., *The Works of John Wesley* (Nashville: Abingdon, 1989), 261–62.

10. Henderson, *John Wesley's Class Meeting*, 93.

11. Ibid., 95.

12. Ibid., 96.

13. Since the classes were coeducational, class leaders could be men or women.

14. Henderson, *John Wesley's Class Meeting*, 99.

15. Ibid., 102.

16. Ibid.

17. Ibid., 110–12. See also p. 132, where Henderson makes the interesting observation that "Wesley anchored his behavior-shaping ministry in the Sermon on the Mount, in which Christ presented the behavioral norms for his disciples to follow. The capstone of that sermon is the parable of the wise man who built his house on the rock and the fool who built on the sand. The wise man, Jesus said, was the one who heard his words *and did them*, while the fool was only a hearer. Saint James added the injunction, 'Be doers of the Word; not hearers only.' And Wesley follows in the same tradition with a central focus on *doing*. Methodism was not just a message to be proclaimed, it was a lifestyle to be embodied." [italics in original]

18. Ibid., 112.

19. Ibid.

20. Ibid.

21. Ibid.

22. Ibid., 118.

23. Albert Outler, ed., *John Wesley* (New York: Oxford University Press, 1964), 180.

24. Ibid., 181.

25. Henderson, *John Wesley's Class Meeting*, 107. Not allowing visitors to attend every meeting provided the classes with a certain amount of privacy which, in turn, helped them create an atmosphere of trust in which significant personal sharing could occur.

26. Ibid., 119–21.

27. Ibid., 113.

28. Due to the fact that my own congregation was made up of many adherents who commuted significant distances to attend the main worship service, we actually made it possible for these members to engage in a small group sermon-processing meeting on Sunday mornings immediately following the worship gathering. This strategy proved to be very effective in enabling busy Southern California church members to have a powerful small group discipleship experience.

29. It is with no little trepidation that I suggest here some possible titles for each teaching. If these titles prove not to be helpful, please disregard them and focus instead on the intended theme of each teaching.

30. Notice that my suggested teaching series calls for 5:11–12 to be treated in both "The Beatitudes: A Shocking Sermon Introduction" (Matthew 5:3–12) and "Who the Real Heroes Are" (5:11–16).

31. Due to the fact that this teaching ambitiously aims to treat a large segment of Matthew 6, it may be necessary to divide this teaching into two parts. My personal preference is to keep the big picture of what the author of a biblical text had in mind, even if this necessitates what may be thought of as a "series within a series."

32. Eugene Peterson, *A Long Obedience in the Same Direction: Discipleship in an Instant Society* (Downers Grove, IL: InterVarsity, 1980).

33. The strategy presented in these pages represents an improvement over what the members of my own congregation experienced, because this book's thesis developed over time and in several stages. Between January and August 2000, I took my small start-up church through a study of the Sermon on the Mount, presenting to them the interpretive insights included in chapters six to eight of this book. Though at this time we did not process each teaching in a small group setting, still the effect of this sermon series was great. A very healthy biblically informed atmosphere was created: one that evoked a raised awareness of both the perils of Pharisaism and the promise of life in the kingdom. In March 2001, I presented an academic paper entitled "The Sermon on the Mount as a Polemic against the Pharisees: Implications for Pentecostalism" at a meeting of the Lewis P. Wilson Institute for Pentecostal Studies held at Vanguard University of Southern California. During this same period, I completed a Fuller Seminary Doctor of Ministry seminar entitled "Growing Disciple-Making Congregations." It was at this point that two important ideas coalesced for me: first, that a curriculum based on the Sermon on the Mount was ideal for making disciples committed to avoiding Pharisaism; second, that John Wesley's system of interlocking groups was a biblically informed and historically proven delivery method that had great potential in our contemporary era, earmarked as it is by much sociological and psychological fragmentation. While our church had always conducted a small group ministry, it was several years later that the elders of my church agreed to a rather bold ministry experiment. In addition to the other small groups (based on gender) that met mid-week and that eventually came to function for us as our version of Wesley's band meetings, we restructured our Sunday morning worship service so as to provide the opportunity

for a small group experience for *all* our members, even those whose commute to church each Sunday from some distance away made it very difficult for them to attend our mid-week small group offerings. Thus, our reformatted Sunday morning worship service that met from 10:30 to 11:20 a.m. began to function as our version of Wesley's society meeting. A ten-minute break from 11:20 to 11:30 a.m. allowed for guests to be greeted and for departing church members to make their exit in a non-embarrassing manner. Then, from 11:30 to 12:00 (often 12:15), we conducted our version of Wesley's class meeting. Small groups of church members met throughout the church's worship space (a rented facility) to discuss and prayerfully apply to their lives the teaching delivered that very morning. They did this knowing full well that next Sunday the other members of their small group would hold them accountable (in a gentle, loving manner) for any commitments to application they would make! The sermon-processing questions we utilized in these "class" meetings were essentially the same as the ones presented earlier in this chapter. The results of this four-month ministry experiment were nothing less than amazing: a ministry structure that succeeded at involving at least two-thirds of our church's members (even the commuters) in a small group experience that radically improved their ability to become not merely hearers of God's Word, but doers also (James 1:22–25)!

Though my decision to leave the pastorate to become a full-time educator hindered a second study of the Sermon on the Mount, it was on the heels of this successful field-testing of a modified version of Wesley's interlocking groups that I made the decision to reformat my doctoral dissertation, entitled "Pharisaism in the Evangelical Church: Its Cause and Cure," into a more accessible work called "Defeating Pharisaism: Recovering Jesus' Disciple-Making Method." Thus, my personal pastoral experience is such that I feel very comfortable recommending the disciple-making strategy presented in this book to any evangelical church desiring to create a dynamic disciple-making environment that can succeed in steering church members away from Pharisaism toward authentic life in the kingdom.

CONCLUSION

The purpose of this book has been to encourage church leaders and workers to recognize that something can be done about the problem of Pharisaism in evangelical churches. Pastors and other church leaders can employ the disciple-making strategy of Jesus and proactively steer their congregants away from Christian Pharisaism toward an authentic, biblically informed Christian discipleship instead. In the process of accomplishing this purpose, an attempt has been made to better understand the origin and essence of Pharisaism, as well as its presence in evangelical churches (part one); the role Pharisaism played in Jesus' approach to disciple-making (part two); and how a disciple-making strategy based on Jesus' Sermon on the Mount (Matthew 5–7) can succeed at defeating the phenomenon of Christian Pharisaism in contemporary evangelical churches (part three).

A final word needs to be addressed to those pastors and church leaders who make the decision to address proactively the problem of Christian Pharisaism by discipling it out of their congregants. The crucial role the pastor plays in the process of initiating and maintaining a disciple-making ministry in general was underscored in chapter nine of this book. What is needed at this point is a vital reminder of the key role that pastors and other church leaders play in the process of defeating Pharisaism in particular.

Since the core component of the disciple-making strategy presented here is a sermon or teaching series based on the Sermon on the Mount, it should be obvious that the first responsibility of the pastor/teacher who would defeat Pharisaism in his or her church is to make sure that as many congregants as possible are exposed to this biblical teaching. This would probably mean that, in addition to being presented during the main services of the church every few years, arrangements would need to be made for additional presentations of this foundational teaching series via other venues (e.g., classes for new believers, classes for new members, Sunday School classes, spiritual growth seminars, podcasts downloaded from the church's website, etc.). Furthermore, it is crucial that this preaching/teaching series does justice to the apologetic aim of the Gospel of Matthew in general, as well as the anti-Pharisee rhetoric observable in Jesus' sermon in particular. The key to the Sermon on the Mount's ability to contribute to a Pharisee-defeating church culture is to constantly keep the polemical tension between Jesus and the Pharisees in view while presenting it.

And yet it goes without saying that pastors and church leaders must do more than preach and teach the Sermon on the Mount. Once again, allow me to speak out of my own personal pastoral experience. My experience as a church leader determined to nurture an ecclesial culture antagonistic to Pharisaism indicates that we must do five things in order to accomplish this goal. The key words are *model, imitate, steer, confront,* and *ravish.*

First, we pastors must strive to *model* for our congregants what the Sermon has to say about being an authentic Christian disciple versus a faux follower of Christ. This book must not conclude without the point being made once again that it is possible for us church leaders to become Pharisaical in the very process of attempting to defeat the Pharisaism at work in our evangelical churches. If we aren't careful, we can become harsh, judgmental, and pugilistic toward those we consider to be harsh, judgmental, and pugilistic. A continual battle must be waged against spiritual pride, arrogance, and blindness, lest we church leaders become guilty of the same hypocrisy Jesus condemned in the lives of the religious leaders of his day.

Second, we must never miss an opportunity, even when preaching or teaching from biblical texts other than those that make up the Sermon on the Mount, to *imitate* Jesus' method of pointing to the Pharisees as anti-models of what authentic Christian disciples are to be and do. The trick is to do this without appearing redundant. But because the rest of the New Testament contains so many passages that warn against the Pharisaical attitudes and actions described in this book,[1] it is actually possible for the alert pastor to raise the issue of the ongoing struggle against Pharisaism quite often without appearing to be riding a personal hobbyhorse. Furthermore, pertinent stories from church history and contemporary life can serve as poignant illustrations of what it means to be judgmental, separatist, super-spiritual, doctrinaire, legalistic, etc. in our spiritual lives. These kinds of stories can often be shared without the anti-Pharisee application being underscored from the pulpit: simply allow church members to reflect on the implications of these illustrative narratives for themselves. To the degree we have been careful in our teaching to point out the anti-Pharisaical message of Scripture, the difference between these historical and contemporary anti-models of discipleship and what we know Jesus and his apostles had to say about genuine life in the kingdom will become powerfully evident.

Third, we must proactively *steer* our congregations away from Christian fundamentalism toward a chastened evangelicalism and a humble orthodoxy. The trick is to do this without appearing Pharisaical ourselves. In light of that, I am loath to actually name names when it comes to Pharisaical people and organizations. I believe the better course is simply to make our congregants aware of the history of the fundamentalist-modernist controversy, pointing out that while the fundamentalist movement meant well it ended up becoming a fear-based overreaction to liberalism that has done as much harm as good. Over time, church members will begin to associate a fighting fundamentalism (whether on the right or left side of any ideological divide) with the dynamic of Pharisaism.

Furthermore, I believe it is important to help church members recognize and avoid the false antithesis between theological fundamentalism and liberalism; there is a middle ground between these two very different responses to modernity. Endorsing the concepts of a chastened evangelicalism and a humble orthodoxy, while also emphasizing the need for evangelical churches to function as radically welcoming communities, will, I am convinced, enable most evangelical church members, on their own, to discern and then steer clear of this or that teaching, philosophy of ministry, or ministry personality that seems to bear the earmarks of Christian fundamentalism/Pharisaism.

Fourth, we must be courageous and constantly vigilant in order to lovingly, yet resolutely, *confront* any exhibition of Pharisaism that occurs within our communities of faith. This will not be easy, but it is necessary if we are to create in our churches a culture inhospitable to the spirit of Pharisaism. Speaking softly and humbly, we should nevertheless be brave enough to come alongside church members who are manifesting Pharisaical attitudes and actions and bring this to their attention.

Once again, the trick is to do this without appearing (or actually being) Pharisaical ourselves. Toward this end, I have found that it is helpful for us church leaders to keep pointing out to ourselves and our congregants the significant reality that since the heart of Pharisaism is a craving for certainty, something all of us human beings possess in varying degrees, we are all capable of it. Thus, it really should not surprise any of us all that much when we see some Pharisaism in ourselves and others. Keeping this reality in mind, and before our congregations, can enable us to conceive of any pastoral confrontations that need to occur over a manifestation of a Pharisaical spirit as a form of peer mentoring—one imperfect Christ-follower endeavoring to help another imperfect Christ-follower overcome the very strong temptation to live our Christian lives out of fear rather than faith and trust in God's love for us.

We can then go on to announce the good news that Pharisaism need never be final. God's grace is greater than our susceptibility to Pharisiaism! Thus, our message as pastoral counselors should be that whenever we find ourselves behaving in a Pharisaical manner, or have such behaviors pointed out to us in a loving way by others, we can and should humbly repent and receive fresh empowerment to do otherwise. We church leaders can model such humility before our congregants, honestly admitting our own battles with Pharisaism. We can keep trumpeting the slogan *Semper Reformanda*—"always reforming"—along with the conviction that this dynamic should characterize not only the church but the lifestyle of individual Christ-followers as well.

If we will do these things, we really can effectively confront outbreaks of Pharisaism in our churches before they become "pockets" of Pharisaism, and then malignant cliques. Yes, it is true that such confrontation will occasionally result in the loss of adherents. But perhaps that is the price we church leaders must be willing to pay in order to lead our churches toward becoming truly effective, genuinely healthy disciple-making communities.

Finally, recognizing that at the heart of Pharisaism is a fear-based search for spiritual certainty exacerbated by a flawed understanding of the grace and love of God, the Pharisaism-defeating pastor/church leader will be careful to continually—as Dallas Willard puts it—"ravish" his or her congregants with the kingdom of God. That is, these church leaders must recurrently proclaim, celebrate, and model what it means to embrace the good news that through Jesus Christ it is possible to possess an intimate, interactive relationship with God as one's heavenly Abba.

Despite the natural inclination toward legalism, ritualism, traditionalism, formalism, etc. that exists within the hearts of most people of piety, once an evangelical church member *truly* experiences the power of

God's loving reign in her heart, she will become amazingly resistant to the poison that is Pharisaism. In fact, not only will the church member who is an authentic Christ-follower be enabled to eschew Pharisaism for herself, she will also possess the ability to infect other church members with the life of the kingdom.

It is possible for evangelical church members to function authentically as sources of spiritual salt and light, making people thirsty for a real relationship with God and then showing them the way to him through Jesus Christ. It is possible for evangelical congregations to become genuine Christian communities that energize rather than burn out their pastoral leaders and workers. It is possible for evangelical churches to worship and serve Christ in such a way as to not alienate an emerging generation of young people. We can give the lie to the false antithesis which says that young adult Christians must choose between a rigid, pugilistic fundamentalism, on the one hand, or a new form of theological liberalism on the other. A restored, renewed, recentered evangelicalism can function as that balanced, biblically informed, Spirit-empowered via media—that middle way—which leads sincere seekers to an authentic experience of God's kingdom both now and in the age to come.

This is wonderfully good news for those of us who are evangelical church leaders. Though Pharisaism may be alive and well in our churches, there is a cure for what ails us. It is possible to create a church culture that does not allow Christian Pharisaism to survive, much less flourish, in its midst. Disciple-making and Jesus' Sermon on the Mount are the keys to creating such a Pharisee-defeating environment. All of us who are evangelical pastors, church leaders, and workers would do well to develop a disciple-making curriculum that centers on the Sermon on the Mount. May God bless your attempt to do just that.

Note

1. See note #3 in my introduction to this book.

WORKS CITED

Alter, Margaret G. *Resurrection Psychology: An Understanding of Human Personality Based on the Life and Teachings of Jesus.* Chicago: Loyola University Press, 1994.

Anderson, Ray S. *An Emergent Theology for Emerging Churches.* Downers Grove, IL: InterVarsity, 2006.

———. *The Soul of Ministry: Forming Leaders for God's People.* Louisville: Westminster John Knox Press, 1997.

Argyle, A. W. *The Gospel According to Matthew.* London: Cambridge University Press, 1963.

Augustine, Saint. *Confessions.* New York: Oxford University Press, USA, 1998.

Baeck, Leo. *The Pharisees and Other Essays.* New York: Schocken Books Inc., 1947.

Barclay, William. *The Gospel of Matthew*, The Daily Bible Study Series. Philadelphia: Westminster Press, 1975.

Barker, Glenn W., William Lane, and J. Ramsey Michaels. *The New Testament Speaks.* New York: Harper & Row, Publishers, 1969.

Barker, Steve, and Ron Nicholas. *Good Things Come in Small Groups: The Dynamics of Good Group Life.* Downers Grove, IL: InterVarsity, 1985.

Barna, George. *Growing True Disciples.* Colorado Springs: WaterBrook Press, 2001.

————. *Revolution: Finding Faith Beyond the Walls of the Sanctuary.* Carol Stream, IL: Tyndale, 2005.

Barrett, C. K., ed. *The New Testament Background.* San Francisco: HarperSanFrancisco, 1987.

Bauman, Clarence. *The Sermon on the Mount: The Modern Quest for Its Meaning.* Macon, GA: Mercer University Press, 1985.

Beare, Francis W. *The Gospel According to Matthew.* Oxford: Basil Blackwell Publisher, 1981.

Bloesch, Donald. *The Evangelical Renaissance.* Grand Rapids: Eerdmans, 1973.

————. *The Future of Evangelical Christianity.* Colorado Springs: Helmers & Howard Publishers, 1988.

Blomberg, Craig L. *Matthew*, The New American Commentary. Vol. 22. Nashville: Broadman Press, 1992.

Bowman, John Wick, and Roland W. Tapp. *The Gospel from the Mount.* Philadelphia: Westminster Press, 1957.

Bruner, F. D. *The Christbook* (Waco: Word, 1987).

Cairns, Earle E. *Christianity Through the Centuries.* 3rd ed. Grand Rapids: Zondervan, 1954.

Camery-Hoggatt, Jerry. *Speaking of God: Rhetoric of Text, Rhetoric of Sermon.* Peabody, MA: Hendrickson, 1995.

Carpenter, Joel. *Revive Us Again: The Reawakening of American Fundamentalism.* New York: Oxford University Press, 1997.

Carson, D. A. *The Sermon on the Mount: An Evangelical Exposition of Matthew 5–7.* Grand Rapids: Baker, 1978.

Chesterton, G. K. *The Everlasting Man.* San Francisco: Ignatius Press, 1993.

Clarke, Howard. *The Gospel of Matthew and Its Readers.* Bloomington, IN: Indiana University Press, 2003.

Coleman, William L. *Those Pharisees.* New York: Hawthorn Books, Inc., 1977.

Crosby, Michael H. *Spirituality of the Beatitudes: Matthew's Challenge for First World Christians.* Maryknoll, NY: Orbis Books, 1981.

Davies, M. D. *Matthew.* Sheffield, England: JSOT Press, 1993.

Davies, Rupert, ed. *The Works of John Wesley.* Nashville: Abingdon, 1989.

Davies, W. D. *Introduction to Pharisaism.* Philadelphia: Fortress Press, 1967.

————. *The Sermon on the Mount.* Nashville: Abingdon, 1966.

————. *The Setting of the Sermon on the Mount.* Cambridge: The Cambridge University Press, 1964.

Dayton, Donald L. *Discovering an Evangelical Heritage.* Peabody, MA: Hendrickson Publishers, 1976.

Dobschütz, Ernst von. "Matthew as Rabbi and Catechist." In *The Interpretation of Matthew.* Graham Stanton, ed. Philadelphia: Fortress Press, 1983.

Drane, John. *Introducing the New Testament.* San Francisco: Harper & Row Publishers, 1986.

Ferguson, Sinclair B. *The Sermon on the Mount: Kingdom Life in a Fallen World.* Carlisle, PA: Banner of Truth Trust, 1997.

Findlay, J. Alexander. *The Realism of Jesus.* London: Hodder and Stoughton, n.d.

Finkel, Asher. *The Pharisees and the Teacher of Nazareth.* Leiden, Holland: E. J. Brill, 1964.

Fischer, John. *12 Steps for the Recovering Pharisee (like me).* Minneapolis: Bethany, 2000.

France, R. T. *Matthew.* The New International Commentary on the New Testament. Grand Rapids: Eerdmans, 2007.

———. *Matthew.* The Tyndale New Testament Commentaries. Grand Rapids: Eerdmans, 1985.

———. *Matthew: Evangelist and Teacher.* Exeter, England: Paternoster Press, 1989.

Gibbs, Eddie, and Ryan K. Bolger. *Emerging Churches: Creating Christian Community in Postmodern Cultures.* Grand Rapids: Baker, 2005.

Greenfield, Guy. "The Ethics of the Sermon on the Mount." *Southwestern Journal of Theology* 35 (1992): 13–19.

Grenz, Stanley. *Revisioning Evangelical Theology.* Carol Stream, IL: InterVarsity, 1993.

———. *Renewing the Center.* Grand Rapids: Baker, 2000.

Guder, Darrell, ed. *Missional Church: A Vision for the Sending of the Church in North America.* Grand Rapids: Eerdmans, 1998.

Guelich, Robert. *The Sermon on the Mount: A Foundation for Understanding.* Dallas: Word, 1982.

Gundry, Robert Horton. *Matthew: A Commentary on His Handbook for a Mixed Church Under Persecution.* Grand Rapids: Eerdmans, 1994.

———. *Matthew: A Commentary on His Literary and Theological Art.* Grand Rapids: Eerdmans, 1982.

Guthrie, Donald. *New Testament Introduction.* Downers Grove, IL: InterVarsity, 1970.

Hagner, Donald. *Matthew 1–13*, Word Biblical Commentary. Vol. 33A. Dallas: Word, 1993.

Harrison, Everett F. *Introduction to the New Testament*. Grand Rapids: Eerdmans, 1971.

Henderson, Michael D. *John Wesley's Class Meeting: A Model for Making Disciples*. Nappanee, IN: Evangelical Publishing House, 1997.

Herford, R. Travers. *Pharisaism: Its Aim and Its Method*. New York: G. P. Putnam's Sons, 1912.

———. *The Pharisees*. London: Unwin Brothers, Limited, 1924.

Hill, David. *The Gospel of Matthew*, The New Century Bible Commentary. Grand Rapids: Eerdmans, 1972.

Hitchens, Christopher. *The Missionary Position: Mother Teresa in Theory and Practice*. London: Verso, 1988.

Hovestol, Tom. *Extreme Righteousness*. Chicago: Moody, 1997.

Howell, David B. *Matthew's Inclusive Story: A Study in the Narrative Rhetoric of the First Gospel*. Sheffield, England: JSOT, 1990.

Hull, Bill. *The Disciple-Making Pastor*. Grand Rapids: Revell, 1988.

———. *Jesus Christ: Disciple-Maker*. Colorado Springs: NavPress, 1984.

Hunter, Archibald M. *A Pattern for Life: An Exposition of the Sermon on the Mount*. Philadelphia: Westminster Press, 1965.

Keller, Timothy. *The Reason for God: Belief in an Age of Skepticism*. New York: Dutton, 2008.

Kern, Kathleen. *We Are the Pharisees*. Scottdale, PA: Herald Press, 1995.

Kimball, Dan. *They Like Jesus But Not the Church: Insights from Emerging Generations*. Grand Rapids: Zondervan, 2007.

Kinnaman, David. *unChristian: What a New Generation Really Thinks About Christianity*. Grand Rapids: Baker, 2007.

Kingsbury, Jack Dean. *Matthew*. Philadelphia: Fortress Press, 1986.

———. *Matthew as Story*. Philadelphia: Fortress Press, 1988.

Klein, William. *Become What You Are: Spiritual Formation According to the Sermon on the Mount*. Tyrone, GA: Authentic Publishing, 2006.

Kümmel, Werner Georg. *Introduction to the New Testament*. Nashville: Abingdon, 1973.

Ladd, George Eldon. *A Theology of the New Testament*. Grand Rapids: Eerdmans, 1974.

———. *The Gospel of the Kingdom*. Carlisle, England: Paternoster Press, 1959.

L'Engle, Madeleine. *Walking on Water: Reflections on Faith and Art.* Colorado Springs: Shaw Books, 2001.

Lloyd-Jones, D. Martyn. *Studies in the Sermon on the Mount.* Vol. 1. Grand Rapids: Eerdmans, 1969.

Malina, Bruce J. *The New Testament World: Insights from Cultural Anthropology.* Louisville: Westminster John Knox Press, 2001.

Marsden, George M. *Fundamentalism and American Culture: The Shaping of Twentieth-Century Evangelicalism, 1870–1925.* New York: Oxford University Press, 1980.

———. *Reforming Fundamentalism: Fuller Seminary and the New Evangelicalism.* Grand Rapids: Eerdmans, 1987.

———. *Understanding Fundamentalism and Evangelicalism.* Grand Rapids: Eerdmans, 1991.

Martin, Ralph P. *New Testament Foundations: A Guide for Students.* Vol. 1. Grand Rapids: Eerdmans, 1975.

McLaren, Brian. *A Generous Orthodoxy.* Grand Rapids: Zondervan, 2004.

Mouw, Richard. *The Smell of Sawdust.* Grand Rapids: Zondervan, 2000.

Neusner, Jacob. *From Politics to Piety.* Englewood Cliffs, NJ: Prentice-Hall, Inc., 1973.

Noll, Mark. *American Evangelical Christianity: An Introduction.* Malden, MA: Blackwell Publishers Inc., 2001.

———. *The Scandal of the Evangelical Mind.* Grand Rapids: Eerdmans, 1994.

Ogden, Greg. *Discipleship Essentials: A Guide to Building Your Life in Christ.* Downers Grove, IL: InterVarsity, 1998.

Olson, Roger. *Reformed and Always Reforming: The Postconservative Approach to Evangelical Theology.* Grand Rapids: Baker, 2007.

Outler, Albert C., ed. *John Wesley.* New York: Oxford University Press, 1964.

Patte, Daniel. *The Challenge of Discipleship.* Harrisburg, PA: Trinity Press International, 1999.

———. *Discipleship According to the Sermon on the Mount.* Valley Forge, PA: Trinity Press International, 1996.

Pentecost, J. Dwight. *Design for Living: Lessons on Holiness from the Sermon on the Mount.* Grand Rapids: Kregel Publications, 1999.

Petersen, L. M. "Matthew, Gospel of." In *The Zondervan Pictorial Encyclopedia of the Bible.* Vol. 4. Merrill C. Tenney, ed. Grand Rapids: Zondervan, 1976.

Peterson, Eugene. *A Long Obedience in the Same Direction: Discipleship in an Instant Society.* Downers Grove, IL: InterVarsity, 1980.

Riddle, Donald Wayne. *Jesus and the Pharisees.* Chicago: The University of Chicago Press, 1928.

Rivkin, Ellis. *A Hidden Revolution.* Nashville: Abingdon, 1978.

Robertson, Archibald Thomas. *The Pharisees and Jesus.* London: Duckworth and Company, 1920.

Saldarini, Anthony. *Pharisees, Scribes and Sadducees in Palestinian Society.* Wilmington, DE: Michael Glazier, Inc., 1988.

Sanders, E. P. *Jesus and Judaism.* London: SCM Press, Ltd., 1985.

———. *Paul and Palestinian Judaism.* Minneapolis: Fortress Press, 1977.

Senior, Donald. *Matthew*, Abingdon New Testament Commentaries. Nashville: Abingdon, 1998.

Shelley, Bruce. *Church History in Plain Language.* Dallas: Word, 1982.

Sider, Ronald J. *Good News and Good Works: A Theology for the Whole Gospel.* Grand Rapids: Baker, 1993.

Simon, Marcel. *Jewish Sects at the Time of Jesus.* Philadelphia: Fortress Press, 1967.

Smith, Christian. *American Evangelicalism: Embattled and Thriving.* Chicago: The University of Chicago Press, 1998.

Smith, Robert H. *Matthew.* Minneapolis: Augsburg Publishing House, 1988.

Stemberger, Günter. *Jewish Contemporaries of Jesus.* Minneapolis: Fortress Press, 1995.

Stott, John R. W. *Christian Counter-Culture: The Message of the Sermon on the Mount.* Downers Grove, IL: InterVarsity, 1978.

Strecker, Georg. *The Sermon on the Mount: An Exegetical Commentary.* Nashville: Abingdon, 1988.

Tasker, R. V. G. *The Gospel According to St. Matthew: An Introduction and Commentary.* Tyndale New Testament Commentaries. Vol. 1. London: Tyndale Press, 1964.

Tenney, Merrill C. *New Testament Survey.* Grand Rapids: Eerdmans, 1985.

Tholuck, A. *Commentary on the Sermon on the Mount.* Philadelphia: Smith English and Co., 1860.

Tolar, William B. "The Sermon on the Mount from an Exegetical Perspective." *Southwestern Journal of Theology* 35 (1992): 4–12.

Torrance, James. "The Vicarious Humanity of Christ." In *The Incarnation-Ecumenical Studies in the Nicene-Constantinopolitan Creed A. D. 381.* Thomas F. Torrance, ed. Edinburgh: Handsel Press, 1981.

Umen, Samuel. *Pharisaism and Jesus.* New York: Philosophical Library, Inc., 1963.

Van Engen, Charles. *God's Missionary People: Rethinking the Purpose of the Local Church.* Grand Rapids: Baker, 1991.

Vardey, Lucinda. *Mother Teresa: A Simple Path.* New York: Ballantine Books, 1995.

Vaught, Carl. *The Sermon on the Mount: A Theological Interpretation.* Albany, NY: State University of New York Press, 1986.

Webber, Robert. *Common Roots: A Call to Evangelical Maturity.* Grand Rapids: Zondervan, 1978.

———. *The Younger Evangelicals: Facing the Challenges of the New World.* Grand Rapids: Baker, 2002.

Wilkins, Michael J. "The Concept of Disciple in Matthew's Gospel as Reflected in the Use of the Term *Mathetes*." PhD diss., Fuller Theological Seminary, 1986.

———. *Following the Master: A Biblical Theology of Discipleship.* Grand Rapids: Zondervan, 1992.

Willard, Dallas. *The Divine Conspiracy.* San Francisco: HarperSanFrancisco, 1998.

———. Lecture presented in Fuller Seminary Doctor of Ministry seminar, "Spirituality and Ministry." Sierra Madre, CA. June 20, 2002.

Windisch, Hans. *The Meaning of the Sermon on the Mount.* Philadelphia: Westminster Press, 1951.

Yancey, Philip. *What's So Amazing About Grace?* Grand Rapids: Zondervan, 1997.

Young, William P. *The Shack.* Los Angeles: Windblown Media, 2007.